Tell Me
It's Only a Phase!
A Guide for Parents of Teenagers

FAMILY · DATING · SCHOOLWORK · DIVORCE · VALUES
ACNE · ALLOWANCES · SEX · CURFEWS · AIDS · CONTRA-
CEPTION · SHYNESS · ADOPTION · BOYS · FRIENDSHIP
DRUGS · CAREERS · HOMOSEXUALITY · SUICIDE
WEIGHT · RELATIONSHIPS · PUNKS · HERPES · JEALOUSY
PORNOGRAPHY · EXERCISE · GIRLS · SIBLINGS

Tell Me
It's Only a Phase!
A Guide for Parents of Teenagers

DATING · SCHOOLWORK · DIVORCE · VALUES · ACNE
ALLOWANCES · SEX · CURFEWS · AIDS · CONTRACEPTION
SHYNESS · ADOPTION · BOYS · FRIENDSHIP · DRUGS
CAREERS · HOMOSEXUALITY · SUICIDE · WEIGHT · RELA-
TIONSHIPS · PUNKS · HERPES · JEALOUSY · PORNOGRA-
PHY · EXERCISE · GIRLS · SIBLINGS · ALCOHOL · GUILT
HICKEYS · PSYCHOTHERAPY · RACISM · HEALTH FOOD

Dr. Saul Levine
Introduction by June Callwood

ANXIETY · LOVE · INDEPENDENCE · MARRIAGE · PRIVACY
REBELLION · SEXISM · YUPPIES · FAMILY · DATING
SCHOOLWORK · DIVORCE · VALUES · ACNE
ALLOWANCES · SEX · CURFEWS · AIDS · CONTRACEPTION
SHYNESS · ADOPTION · BOYS · FRIENDSHIP · DRUGS
CAREERS · HOMOSEXUALITY · SUICIDE · WEIGHT · RELA-
TIONSHIPS · PUNKS · HERPES · JEALOUSY · PORNOGRA-
PHY · EXERCISE · GIRLS · SIBLINGS · ALCOHOL · GUILT

Prentice-Hall Canada Inc., Scarborough, Ontario

MASTURBATION · CAREERS · ABORTION · MUSIC · EMO-
TIONS · CIGARETTES · NUCLEAR WAR · SELF-ESTEEM
LONELINESS · VIRGINITY · HEIGHT · PUBERTY · MORALS
FLIRTING · SEPARATION · ANGER · DISCIPLINE · DIETS

Canadian Cataloguing in Publication Data

Levine, Saul V., 1938-
  Tell me it's only a phase

Includes index.
ISBN 0-13-903147-2

1. Parenting.   2. Youth.   3. Parent and child.
I. Title.

HQ796.L48 1987   649'.125   C87-094060-0

Prentice-Hall Inc., Englewood Cliffs, *New Jersey*
Prentice-Hall International, Inc., *London*
Prentice-Hall of Australia, Pty., *Sydney*
Prentice-Hall of India Pvt., Ltd., *New Delhi*
Prentice-Hall of Japan, Inc., *Tokyo*
Prentice-Hall of Southeast Asia (Pte.) Ltd., *Singapore*
Editora Prentice-Hall do Brasil Ltda., *Rio de Janeiro*
Prentice-Hall Hispanoamericana, S.A., *Mexico*

Production Editor: Sharyn Rosart
Design: Marcela Poblete-Gougain
Manufacturing Buyer: Don Blair
Composition: ISIS Communications Limited

ISBN: 0-13-903147-2

Printed and bound in Canada by Webcom

1 2 3 4 5 W 91 90 89 88 87

To Mike and Bess,
Wonderful Parents and
Grandparents

Table of Contents

Acknowledgements

First of all, I owe a special thank-you to all the teenagers and their parents who have communicated with me in some way over the years. Much of what I know about that age group is from studying, working with, talking to, and listening to them. But there is a certain type of knowledge one can only glean from personal experience: living with my three teenagers, Jaime, Mischa and Zachary, has been an unequivocally pleasurable and uplifting experience. In addition to general inspiration and evidence that adolescence can be a wonderful stage of life, they provided me with excellent suggestions for inclusion in this book.

I thank my wife, Eleanor, who was remarkably patient during the writing of this book, as she has been on so many other occasions.

Grace Deutsch provided the spark that started me writing this work initially; it was she who hooked me up with Prentice-Hall. Editors Iris Skeoch and Sharyn Rosart were always supportive and encouraging.

Kathleen Wilcox, my co-columnist on Youth Clinic, and collaborator on another book (*Dear Doctor*), was a constant source of encouragement and creativity.

Valerie Wine was always available for typing, word processing, collating, organizing, suggestions and stabilizing, as she has been on so many other projects, particularly these past few months.

To all of these I express gratitude and deep appreciation.

Preface

Not another how-to-book for the parents of teenagers! That's my own reaction when I look at the child-rearing shelves in bookstores and libraries. Why is this one so different? Well, I haven't read them all, but my views tend to differ somewhat from the ones I've read.

I base my opinions of parenting adolescents on many years of living and working with them — in my home, in my office, in hundreds of schools, camps, group homes, treatment centers, hospitals, jails, and institutions. I have lived with them, led them, spoken to them, played with them, sang with them, danced with them, taught them, corresponded with thousands of them, treated them, and learned from them. I have met and/or worked with almost as many of their parents. I have done research on them, written and published about them.

What all this has taught me is to be an optimist regarding our young people. Not only is this borne out by research on adolescents in different countries around the world, but just knowing them reaffirms my excitement about their potential. There is so much mythology about young people, much of it perpetrated by mental health professionals.

For example, it is not true that:
- the adolescent years are inevitably marked by storminess and turbulence;
- adolescence is the worst time of someone's life;
- teenagers have it rougher today than ever before;
- teenagers are worse today than ever before;
- the generation gap is ever-widening between teens and their parents;
- one's identity is wrestled with and resolved only during adolescence;
- there is an epidemic of adolescent suicide;
- adolescence is marked by rampaging, ravaging, rapacious sexuality;
- adolescence is marked by an epidemic of drug abuse;

- television is destroying our young people;
- youth unemployment is the scourge of our time;
- society is oppressing and victimizing our youth;
- our adolescents are wracked with woe, malaise, pessimism and despair.

I could give you more, but you get the picture. To be sure, living with teenagers can be tricky, even difficult at times, but so can living with me, and even you! Sharing a home with them can also be stimulating, fun, exciting, warm, educational, and enriching. They need love, compassion, support, opportunities, space — but they also need restrictions, limits, constraints, accountability, and consequences. We must give them all of it. They are in the space between childhood and adulthood, and as such, are alternatingly dependent and autonomous, needy and independent, weak and strong, tentative and assertive, meek and confident, conforming and provocative, obedient and testing, traditional and experimental. In short, parents of soon-to-be teenagers are embarking on an exciting and enriching journey, too short-lived, too transient, too excruciatingly brief. It is to be experienced, enjoyed and savored.

Introduction

The exquisite anguish of being a teenager, a state of mind and body fraught with unsettling change, is a source of huge amusement to most adults in the vicinity excepting those who happen to be the resident parents. As Saul Levine impressively documents, the despair that parents experience when confronting the aberrations and disdain of their adolescents is as old as the human tribe itself. Youth, it appears, has *always* alarmed and annoyed the elders.

Nothing new in that, but today's parent of a teenager with a safety pin in her nose is unlikely to draw any major comfort from knowing that Socrates was equally appalled by the youngsters of his day.

Dr. Saul Levine to the rescue. This man has knowledge (always useful in an emergency), and wit, and the pure-gold capacity to apply the poultice of common sense and sweet reason.

All I know of raising teenagers (four) is that when parents are loving and fair-minded, the errors of panic are tolerable. Both sides keep the faith, as best as can be accommodated in a situation in which the goal of the younger person is nest-leaving but not nest-destruction, and the goal of the older person is protection but not crippling. In a few years the relationship settles into adult friendship — lifelong, with an occasional regression into parenting, and even the switching of roles, which can be tender and deeply reinforcing of the bond.

Youth is not wasted on the young. It is invested. The unfolding of that investment occupies the rest of a lifetime and bears dividends that enrich the young person, the family and the community ever after.

June Callwood

The Lifestyles of Teenagers

Aside from the clue that they look younger than their parental generation, you can always identify an adolescent by his or her general demeanor. The truth is that adolescents *do* act differently. Their clothes are, well, different from ours, but just as conformist in terms of their own peers and perhaps even more trendy. Their hair styles, both male and female, might be conservative or outrageous. (Certainly there is a lot more of the stuff on the heads of young males than on ours.) Their cosmetics are experimental, with new and occasionally bizarre effects. The music they listen to is phenomenally popular, but most adults have some difficulty listening to it, let alone understanding or liking it. And their language always features new words and phrases, or often, old ones used in entirely novel ways.

There is a wide spectrum of "acceptable" or normal teenage behavior, ranging all the way from the conservative and stodgy to the outer reaches of punkdom. Adolescence is a time of dramatic change. In addition to physical (anatomical, physiological and hormonal) changes, adolescents are also undergoing psychological, cognitive, emotional and ideological ferment. They test out their new feelings, attitudes and ideas. They are wrestling with their senses of identity, who they are, and where they are going — a quest which is never completely resolved (as we grow older and circumstances change in our lives). And part of that quest for self-definition involves searching for the outer limits of their own autonomy. Essentially their question is "How am I different from my parents and my friends?" Adolescence is marked by a gradual progression towards independence — economic as well as psychological — and to that end, experimentation and flirting with what to parents seems like unusual or strange behavior is, in fact, de rigeur. Most adolescents will keep this dabbling in novelty to within easily tolerable limits. Some others will be more adventurous, and delve more deeply into the accoutrements of the youth culture, while still retaining a firm foothold on their families' and the community's traditions and supports. A relatively small percentage will go the whole way, seemingly abandoning and rejecting the values and behavior which they grew up with and which predominate in society. As time goes on, and these young people grow older, the need to assert their uniqueness becomes less a matter of how they look than of how they feel inside and how they behave. Except for a relatively small group, maturation will make these kids comfortable enough with their identities that they won't need to act out their differences so insistently.

This is a never-ending cycle, which has transcended the ages. Think back to your own adolescence, and your styles vis-à-vis your parents. To futher make the point that "the more things change, the more they remain the same" (*plus que ça change, plus c'est la même chose*) let me illustrate with three quotations.

In the third century B.C., Socrates said:

> I see no hope for the future of our people if they are dependent on the frivolous youth of today, for certainly all youth are reckless beyond words. When I was a boy, we were taught to be discreet and respectful of elders, but the present youth are exceedingly wise and impatient of restraint.

In the eighth century B.C., Hesiod stated that:

> Our adolescents now seem to love luxury. They have bad manners and contempt for authority. They show disrespect for adults and spend their time hanging around places gossiping with one another... they are ready to contradict their parents, monopolize the conversation in company, eat gluttonously, and tyrannize their teachers.

In the second act of *A Winter's Tale,* one of William Shakespeare's characters says:

> I would there were no age between ten and three-and-twenty, or that youth would sleep out the rest. For there is nothing in the between but getting wenches with child, wronging the ancientry, stealing and fighting.

The lyrics may change, but the melody lingers on and on....

1 **My son is 13, not quite pubertal. I'm waiting for the axe to fall. When should I expect the terrible teenage years to begin?**

Such a common question; such a common misconception; so potentially destructive. I'm not blaming you; I'm blaming us, the mental health professionals who have foisted on the public this myth of the inevitability of adolescent turmoil. We perpetrated the idea of "Sturm and Drang", the storminess and turbulence of youth, and in so doing, have done a disservice to thousands of parents and adolescents.

In study after study in different cultures, we learn that adolescence can be one of the most exciting, rewarding and enlightening phases of a human being's development. It is by no means inevitable that teenagers will have problems. The majority, in fact, go through their teen years quite smoothly. Sure, there are some pressures and problems inherent in this stage: the rapidity of bodily, emotional, social, and intellectual changes in a fast-moving society is a major cause of stress. But adolescents are not worse than ever before, they are not oppressed by society, and they are decidedly not in the blackest period of their lives. They may be passing through their best time, which many may look back on with longing and nostalgia.

Furthermore, by saying that turmoil is part and parcel of adolescence, we are agreeing that it is "just a stage." If we have this attitude, we can end up not taking real problems seriously. I am not saying that adolescence is an easy period for all young people. For some it can be dreadfully difficult. Those with serious problems don't grow out of them. Problem adolescents usually become problem adults, unless some beneficial change occurs. But we should be wary of helping to set the stage for problems by loudly proclaiming to our kids (and to ourselves) just how tough the ensuing years are going to be. Why don't you substitute for your fears an enjoyment and excitement about being a part of a new era in your son's life? At the very least, try to keep an open mind. You'll be doing both him and yourself a big favor.

2 **I was sitting on a bus filled with busy shoppers and others, and I heard a noise coming from the back that sounded like an uprising of a militia. I looked back to see three boys and two girls about 15 years of age at most, making the most horrific racket you could possibly imagine. The squeaks, raucous laughter and yelling were offensive, gross, and totally insensitive to all the other people around them, and they couldn't care less. Who are the parents of these animals? Is this what our youth is coming to?**

I don't want to act as an apologist for those boorish kids, but you are not exactly describing a new phenomenon. You have seen quotations from hundreds of years ago when adults decried the loud-mouthed louts of the younger generation. It is not even necessarily true that they come from bad families; many young adolescents feed into each other, egg each other on, and become emboldened by their mutual support. You can bet your bottom dollar that not one of these kids would be anything other than quiet and well-mannered if they were alone, or even as part of two instead of five. On a more mundane level, I have often noticed that young teenagers have trouble assessing the recently changed loudness of their voices; they only gradually learn to modulate their decibel level, after a fair share of "sh-h-h-h's!" are hurled their way. There is also the element of quite consciously disturbing the adult generation, as a silly and ineffective way of rebelling and defining themselves as independent beings. Rather, they give evidence of their immaturity and ineptitude.

You can rest assured that the noise will be short-lived, at least from these five. The bad news is that tomorrow there will be another five who might make even more of a disturbance. By the way, there is nothing wrong with a polite but authoritative statement to them to the effect that they are disturbing many other people. The bus driver can be requested to intervene along those lines, too. If they are truly obnoxious and uncontrollable, he can enlist the aid of police to throw them off the bus.

3   **Because of my position in the United Way, I work with many agencies and families, and see such discord. We hear so much about the "generation gap". What can be done to overcome this tremendous abyss between the parental generations and their teenagers? Surely if we can bridge that gap, we will go a long way toward bringing harmony to families and even to society, which is wracked by mutual suspicion between the generations.**

That term "generation gap" was coined in the sixties by famed anthropologist Margaret Mead, who likened parents living with teenagers in the latter part of that decade of social upheaval as immigrants to a new land. It was the era of drugs, hippies, Yippies, flower children, drop-outs, and so on. Mead said that the music, the clothing, the language and the values were so new and different then, that the parental generation had to learn anew what was expected of them, in order to understand their youth.

Well, Margaret Mead was a brilliant anthropologist, but as a psychologist/sociologist, she struck out. Even at that time, studies showed disconcerting similarities between parents and their adolescents, so much so that those of us (at that time) caught up in the Utopian ideals were either chagrined or plainly didn't believe what we read. We wanted (as did Mead) to imbue the youth with personality characteristics and values which were somehow more lofty, more humanitarian. What studies then and subsequently showed was a strong confluence of values between adults and teens, even in areas where you'd expect gross discrepancies — attitudes to money, politics, drugs, sex, religion and marriage, for example, were and are remarkably similar. In some areas, the young people were more conservative than their parents.

The stereotypes of adolescents as bad or going down the tube are just as ill-founded as is depicting them as flower children. To illustrate how these views of youth haven't changed throughout the millenia, we have another timely reminder of the horror some adults have always felt about contemporary youth. The following quotation was inscribed on a stone tablet unearthed during the excavations of the Biblical city of Ur (2000 BC): "Our civilization is doomed if the unheard-of actions of our younger generations are allowed to continue."

Such ancient comments should convince us that adults have always felt some degree of estrangement from adolescents. But it has as much to do with their views of themselves as entrenched and fixed as it has with their perceptions of the changing adolescent. There *are* clear differences; they are what this book is all about, but we shouldn't overstate the case and by so doing, create a monster — which just isn't there.

4 **My 15-year old daughter Sandy and her friends have become punks. Shaven heads, Mohawk haircuts, leather and buckles, pins and hooks. They are weird and frightening. She refuses to speak to us and I am worried sick.**

In my experience, most kids who have gone the punk route have done so as relatively young teenagers and usually during a period of anger, unhappiness and some confusion. There is certainly no doubt in my mind that punkers use their dress and demeanor to give the rest of us a loud-and-clear, non-verbal, nasty message, otherwise known as "Fuck You!".

Punkers gravitate to each other, and give each other strength, perpetuating their cultish mode, and thereby prolonging the act. Left to their own devices, young people into punk soon peter out. As a matter of fact, you can at least rest assured that it is very likely a temporary aberration and that Sandy will give up this grotesquerie.

But that still begs the question: What to do about her anger and sadness? (that is, if my theory applies to her). Most ex-punkers return to traditional values, dress and behavior, and she may well do so. Others give up the punk style, but continue to rebel in other antisocial ways. If Sandy reveals a lingering negative attitude to school, activities, chores, her parents and her life in general, or if she is heavily involved in drugs or other dangerous behavior, she should speak to a counsellor at a teen clinic, or some other adolescent resource.

There is a relatively small group of long-term punkers who are heavily engaged in antisocial behavior. They take the weird effects far enough to become destructive and even dangerous. These misfits are usually older, are clearly estranged from society and are often involved with the police. Sandy is probably not swept up in this extreme kind of group, but her progress should be followed.

5   **Our 15-year-old daughter, Elise, worked as an *au pair* in England this past summer for a family we knew. There she got caught up with an unsavory group of kids in the neighborhood. When she returned seven weeks later, we couldn't recognize her, although we had been forewarned to expect a difference. Her hair was in spikes and dyed purple and pink, her lips were crimson red on a face with whitener on it, and there was a safety pin through the front of the left side of her nose. When we spoke to our friends in England, they weren't too concerned. We are shocked! Her interests are now only in rock music and in her appearance, although I'm not sure that she had any different interests before she left. Is this punk thing dangerous?**

This "punk thing" refers to teenagers dressing, acting and making themselves up in the most outrageous manner in order to a) attract attention, b) conform to each other (in a small band of outcasts), c) tell us (adults, society, authority), to "shove it!", and d) feel better about themselves. Of all of these, the last one is really the crux of this (or almost any other) behavior.

The punk phenomenon is usually short-lived, running its course in a few months, after which the kids tire of it. Frankly, most punks that I have known were more like sad waifs — when

I've seen them alone — than their tough facade would suggest. And a good number of them were social and psychological "losers", acting like outcasts because they felt like outcasts. There are also others who use the experience almost as a constructive game, in the process of defining a self-identity.

I obviously don't know where Elise fits in. I must say that I, too, would be upset if my daughter came home looking like a bizarre creature. Most parents have handled it successfully by waiting it out, and stomaching the appearance for a while. Others I know have been very authoritarian, and have forbidden their teenager any privileges unless and until the pins and spikes disappeared. My own approach might be similar to the latter, since I'd have trouble eating while seated across from her at the table each night. But the crucial point of strategy in both types of approaches is to ferret out what is behind the disguise. Is it fun? Is it fury? Is it a feeble attempt at achieving self-esteem? Is it sadness? In these answers will lie the crux of your concerns. Elise may be healthy, or Elise may be in trouble, but *not because of* her grotesque appearance.

6 **Graham is 15 and really quite a delightful son. You can imagine our shock and horror when he came home sporting an earring dangling from his left ear. Doesn't this mean he's gay?**

If all the guys wearing earrings in one ear were gay, we would have to totally reassess and multiply the estimated incidence of homosexuality in our society. It may well be that a decade or so ago unilateral earrings on males were a sign of a same-sex orientation, but that certainly is not the case now. Earrings are no longer seen more frequently on homosexual than on heterosexual males.

Your shock and horror are both unnecessary and ill-advised. If Graham is as delightful as you say, there is no reason whatsoever to be perturbed. As Peggy Lee sings, "Is that all there is?" That is, if wearing an earring is his sole aberration or symptom — or the only concern that you have of Graham — then there is no problem. The bauble is a mild form of individualism and re-bellion. It is a quite typical adolescent statement of uniqueness (from adults); a form of mockery, conformity (to peers), style and attractiveness. It is only if wearing an earring is seen in conjunction with other behavior that bothers you, such as poor school performance, antisocial activity, drugs, destructive friends, antagonism, or personal unhappiness, that you need be con-cerned. And in that case, you would not need the earring to tell you that there is trouble in your son's life. As it is, I would curb your panic, express some surprise and even aesthetic criticism, but leave it at that.

7   **Our 14-year-old daughter Suzanne is absolutely obsessed with her appearance. Every hair has to be in place, her lipstick, eye make-up, blush, colors and what-have-you have to be applied with painstaking care. Her clothes all have to be au courant, trendy and "in". She spends literally hours (would you believe three to four a day?) grooming herself, and making us see red. Is this typical?**

Well, it certainly is within the outer range of normal. I have known many teenage girls, and boys, too, for that matter, who are preoccupied with their appearances. Suzanne seems to take it to a ridiculous extreme, but I know some kids that have out-done even her. This is most commonly seen among young teen-agers, whose sense of self depends upon how attractive and acceptable they are to other people their age, both boys and girls.

Invariably they outgrow this phase. While there are many older adolescents and adults who spend far too much time in-dulging in their appearance, their *degree* of preoccupation is much less than with your daughter.

She too will pass through this stage fairly soon (another year at most), at least at this level. I trust, however, that there are other things in her life (school, friends, sports, music) which will pick up the slack when she begins to cut back on her cosmetic compulsion. Also, I assume that her parents are good role models in that respect, not overly concerned and focussed on their own outward appearances (or on hers, for that matter).

8 **If memory serves me right, when I was a teenager, there was more to life than dating. I am the mother of two girls, and there is nothing on their minds except boys, or things which may attract them (body, clothes, make-up, jewelry, and so on). I hate to say it, but they are air-heads, and they are boring. I can't talk to them about anything. Where will they end up?**

I do happen to know many teenagers who are interested in sports, school, music and other non-sex-related pursuits. But I must say that your daughters are in good company; many teenagers are preoccupied with the opposite gender, attractiveness, competition and dating, almost to the exclusion of anything else. Rest assured that this is a time-limited phase, that the chances are excellent that they'll give up this overwhelming fervor within a few months to a year or two. Even if attracting boys remains a cause célèbre, it is usually toned down to manageable limits, and put in proper perspective as these young people grow and mature.

You can treat their obsession with humor and some mild digs, but not with support, and not with dismissal. They should know that there is a certain amount of foolishness associated with their behavior, and that you are awaiting the time when they will broaden their horizons. If you notice them manifesting some signs of embarrassment or sheepishness, you should feel gratified: it is then just a matter of time.

9 **Our 14-year-old daughter, Allison, is a naturally gifted pianist, who could have made a career as a concert soloist. That's how good she is. I am a professor of music, and my wife gives private**

lessons, and we are appalled that she not only won't practice, but has given up all interest in the piano. She is doing well at school, and has good friends, but all she talks about is boys and make-up.

I don't have to tell you, I'm sure, that your daughter's preoccupations are not at all uncommon for girls her age. Appearance, attraction, competition and sexual titillation are often central issues for teenagers. Many parents who have developed serious interests and values are chagrined and shocked at the frivolous nature of their teenagers' new activities. This has always been and will continue to be the case. We can take comfort in the fact that our own parents bemoaned the ridiculous ideas of some of us as teenagers. And look how we turned out! Uh, maybe that's a mistake....

But your situation is more complicated, although as you know better than I, also not uncommon. I know of many budding ballerinas, musicians, gymnasts, swimmers and other very talented youth who have given up the rigor and demands of an arduous, dedicated, daily practice routine to opt for the more normal lifestyle of their friends, who are extremely important to them at that age — even more important than their family — at times. Some of these young people give up their disciplines for a while and then go back, having tasted the fruits they felt they were missing. Others wait too long, and discover when they return to their schedules that they have lost the momentum necessary for success at the highest level. They might have to settle for a lesser career in their chosen field. Finally, many do not go back, some with, some without, regrets.

There is little more to be done than discuss, urge, cajole — and then lay off! Allison will hear you loud and clear, but she may not listen. Equally important is the fact that she is happy, has friends, and is doing well at school. If these ingredients were lacking, I would be concerned. But as it is, you may have to swallow your pride along with your own ambitions for her.

10 **I am afraid that my 16-year-old daughter, Sara, is just like me — painfully shy. Can I do anything to help her?**

Shyness is one of the most common and painful of social experiences. It's best described as a lack of self-confidence with people. I frankly do not know of a single person who has never experienced shyness at some point in life, and that uncomfortable anxiety about being rejected, embarrassed, ridiculed or humiliated is most poignant during adolescence. If, in addition, your daughter has used her mother as a model, well, she could be excused if shyness afflicts her, too.

You can help, even if you are shy. You can tell Sara about your social successes, about the times that you overcame your own shyness and enjoyed yourself. You could regale her with stories about her mother's assertiveness (surprise, surprise!) in certain situations. You could convey to her the importance of pursuing interests, group sports, school activities, hobbies, and joining groups where socializing is secondary to a shared common interest.

You should let her know just how prevalent this feeling is, that even kids who seem to have it all wallow in self-doubt, given the right (wrong) circumstances. You can point out to her some previous instances in her own life, with friends, activities, school, or athletics, when Sara was able to overcome her shyness. Finally, you can reassure her that in the vast majority of cases, shyness dissipates as one grows older and feels more sure of oneself. None of us ever shakes shyness completely: we're always confronting new faces, new challenges, new cliques. Remind her that it takes a while to break down social barriers. If all of this reassurance is of no avail, Sara might benefit from a teen group-therapy experience. In most cities, there are social assertiveness training groups, or specialized clinics and groups (e.g., Freedom from Fear), who work with the most troublesome, overwhelmingly restrictive cases of shyness. She can go to an adolescent clinic in your area. Perhaps individual counselling might be helpful. Your family doctor can refer you to the proper resource, if necessary.

11 **Jesse is our only son (aged 18) and for the life of us we can't fathom his low opinion of himself. He's good looking, bright, popular and athletic — everything a boy could possibly want, right? Wrong! Jesse is always criticising himself, putting himself down, comparing himself unfavorably to others. We try to reassure him, but it has no effect.**

Jesse has a problem with self-esteem. Low self-esteem is actually an extremely common concern for many people. I would even go so far as to venture a guess that most people feel somewhat inferior to the standards that they themselves set. And the utter crux of fear of most people who go for psychological help is that they will be exposed, found out, humiliated. They will finally be seen for the frauds that they fear they are. The truth will come out! Strong words, right? But in the cold light of dawn, during periods of demoralization, these are the ultimate fears, felt even by titans of industry, leaders, lovers and laborers. Fear is a great equalizer.

Why should it be different in adolescence, when the core of identity is being developed, honed and shaped? It is difficult for me to evaluate Jesse's low self-esteem, given that it is quite normal for adolescents to harbor self-doubts. It then becomes a question of *degree* of low self-esteem. Jesse may be self-critical, but I don't know if he is more so than most of his peers. Furthermore, the discrepancy between your report of his low opinion of himself and the way you describe his positive attributes is quite remarkable. Is he being honest with you? Or does he know how to get a rise out of you? You'd think that a teenager with the degree of low self-esteem and frequent self-flagellation that you describe would be despondent and morose. But Jesse is popular and active.

If you're still concerned about Jesse, why don't you ask him to speak to your family doctor or to a counsellor at an adolescent clinic? If he follows through, this will be a measure of his own concern and motivation.

12 **Our 15-year-old daughter, Carol, is really a sweet kid, but sometimes I wonder if she has a mind of her own anymore. Whatever she does, she has to check to see if that's what's "in", what the other kids are doing, if it's acceptable or has their stamp of approval. It's as if she's afraid to make the wrong move, wear the wrong clothes, say the wrong thing, lest they (the leaders of the pack) don't accept her. How can we get her to trust her own judgment?**

What you are talking about, is of course, conformity, one of the catchwords of the fifties. It was fashionable among pop sociologists in those days to decry the needs of young people to be carbon copies (clones in the 1980s) of each other. Nor should this surprise you, because if you think back to your own adolescence, you will likely recall your insistence at that time on certain clothes as acceptable, and others definitely impossible. And money wasn't the only criterion, was it? Furthermore, while conformity may well be a particular issue for teenagers, are we really that different? Don't we flock to trendy places, wear "in" clothes, aspire to acceptable levels of performance? Isn't style entirely about manipulation of the collective taste of the masses?

So it should come as no surprise to us that young people, who are in a state of particular flux, in the midst of defining their own unique identities, should want some acceptance and affirmation from the group. Adolescents will certainly dress differently from the parental generation, as one way of defining themselves. You will also see subgroups of teenagers, each with their own style of dress and demeanor (you may identify punks, folksong types, rock and rollers, junior executives, jocks, studs, artists, and so on.)

Carol will gradually evolve the style of life that she is most comfortable with, and which will make the statement *she* wants to make about who she is. In the meantime, bear with her.

$\underline{13}$ **Our 15-year-old daughter, Lynn, is lonely, and usually angry. She is not particularly shy, but can't seem to make or hang on to friends. We are a gregarious, warm family, always surrounded by close relatives and friends. But Lynn keeps to herself, or says things which are followed by abject silence. She keeps telling us that she desperately wants a boyfriend, but her morose, cynical demeanor only seems to turn people off. She gets furious if I make any comments.**

Lynn is obviously the cause of her own problems. Her abrasive or withdrawn manner only alienates her further from people. The problem is that this becomes a classical vicious circle: the more she feels repudiated and rejected, the worse she feels; the worse her mood, the more bitter she becomes; the more her bitterness increases, the more acute her sarcastic and cynical nature, and the greater the ostracism. It is a circuit which she cannot break; her tension rises, and only perpetuates her feelings of isolation. Living in a family with socially comfortable siblings and parents only points up her own social ineptness. She berates herself, and is probably resentful and envious of you all. Furthermore, this cynicism may be a cover for more anxiety-provoking internal questions about her self-worth, and other conflict-ridden situations.

Luckily, Lynn is quite young and can still turn her attitudes around. But it is going to require some humility, and the recognition that she indeed has a problem. The difficulty with people who regularly alienate others is that their degree of insight into their effect on people is minimal. Lynn is going to have to stop blaming others for her loneliness, and confront her own role in setting up rejecting situations. She *is* being rejected; it is not a figment of her imagination, but she has to realize that she is the architect of her own destruction.

What can she do? Ideally, Lynn would realize what is happening, involve herself in interests and activities that turn her on, and stop her angry cycle. More practically, Lynn should be in a situation where she can get gentle, helpful feedback about the way she is coming across to others. Such help would not come through brutal confrontation, which could only further depress her, and help her to justify her self-hate and anger toward the world. In a supportive group, Lynn could also ventilate her own fears and insecurities. It is often remarkable to me how some significant improvement in one or two areas generalizes to an adolescent's general view about him-or-herself. My suggestion is that you show Lynn your letter and this answer. I recommend that she see a counsellor at an adolescent (teen) clinic in your area. Or perhaps your family physician can refer you to an adolescent psychotherapist who runs groups. While individual counselling and psychotherapy might be in order, I think that group therapy would prove to be most useful to Lynn.

14 My daughter's loneliness has us very concerned. Cindy is 20 years old and fairly attractive and yet she has never dated. She had one close girlfriend who moved away last year, and since then she stays at home, watching TV or listening to music, moping around, miserable to herself and us. What can we do?

You have presented a very complex situation in a few short lines. I am wary about jumping to conclusions before I know a lot about a situation. But here is a young woman who has had a relatively unhappy adolescence, a period when friends and social activities are usually prominent. I do not feel that all kids have to be gregarious and social. Many are not, and do well with a couple of friends and quiet activities. But the more important issue is *her* degree of dissatisfaction with her life, and the resultant effect on others.

It is likely that your daughter plays a role in her difficulties in acquiring friends. This may have to do with shyness, but for many people, shyness is a conditioned response to lack of social success. We lose our self-confidence, and don't put our best foot forward when we are with people. But it may also have to do with some other "vibes" which she is giving off, perhaps turning people off, or giving them a message of disinterest. She may also be somewhat depressed. Nevertheless, no matter which of these problems pertains, her situation is correctible. She should see a mental health professional (psychiatrist, psychologist or social worker) to evaluate her problem, and set about doing something constructive to change the direction in which she is heading. It is likely that, if she is left to her own devices, Cindy's present situation will worsen, and it will be more difficult to resolve in the future. She may be reluctant, but her parents' role here is to be caring — as you obviously are — yet also insistent that she get help. Deep down she knows that she needs it.

15   **Joan used to be the closest possible child that one would imagine or wish for; we shared everything until she reached her teen years. She is 15 now and won't tell me anything! She seems to think it is an intrusion if I ask her the slightest thing about her friends, activities or whereabouts. Am I right to be concerned?**

Given Joan's age, I would say, "Yes, you are quite right!" You certainly have a legitimate right to know more than Joan is willing to share. As adolescents get older, they develop more of a sense of identity, of being separate and independent of parents. But fifteen isn't eighteen. (How's that for a profound statement?) With teens of that age, parents are entitled to — no, have to — know about their teenagers' close friends, their activities and their whereabouts. Even if Joan is not involved in blatantly destructive behavior such as drug use or premature or promiscuous sex, you should nevertheless be kept aware of her activities.

Now, how do you convey this to her? The question is, why has she removed herself so insistently? Why the dramatic change? She obviously is wrestling with her sense of autonomy. She may also be protecting herself from what she may expect to be inevitable criticism for some misdeeds. It is important for you to examine your own approach to Joan. Sometimes we parents have difficulty loosening our ties to our kids. It could be that your questioning of her is perceived as the third degree, a kind of antagonistic, suspicious, adversarial confrontation. Is there any validity to this? I am assuming that there is not — even though Joan perceives it as such.

Joan needs to hear that you understand that she is entitled to her privacy in her personal life. But you have to draw up some rules of communication, so that you are assured that she is safe. If all else is well with Joan, she will probably agree to a modification in her stance of a wall of silence. But if this extreme privacy is a cover for other problems — poor school performance, antisocial behavior, destructive relationships — an evaluation of her relationship with you may be in order.

16 **My kids' rooms are pigsties! They are both in their teens, but I think their rooms are worse now that when they were young children. How do I get them to clean up their act?**

This is probably the most common complaint parents have of their teenagers. In a worst case scenario, the dishevelled state of a kid's room is reflective of psychological problems. In most instances, however, the pigsty (and it often *is*) indicates an attitude of "I don't care," and/or "Mom will fix it". Some parents ignore the offending room; others close the door and pretend it doesn't exist. Many make demands, backed up by loss of allowance or privileges.

I don't think there is a single right approach. What you do about the problem will depend on how tolerant you are as parents, and the extent to which the mess pervades your teenagers' whole existences and affects your own lives.

I usually advise (and institute with my own teenagers) a kind of compromise in which their rooms have to be neat and tidy at least once a week, at which time allowances will be forthcoming, or not.

In a nutshell, if a messy room is the only problem, then it's not usually a problem. If there are other concerns, then the pigsty is a symptom, and must be considered in that light.

17 **My 15-year-old son, Julian, watches about six hours of television a day. Will this harm him?**

This is actually a complicated and controversial issue. I'm sure that you've heard that television will only provide your son with a propensity towards violence, victimization and the wrong values. It's been estimated that the average child will have seen the equivalent of 13,000 murders on TV by the time he or she reaches adulthood (including cartoons, news, mysteries, movies, and so on). One could then conclude that the violence in our society is a direct result of TV and that TV is to blame for the U.S.A. being an armed camp, a society under siege. My own opinion is that TV reflects rather than imposes social values. The violent crime rate in Canada, the U.K. and most of the Western World is miniscule compared to that of the United States, yet TV is watched equally often and is equally violent in most western countries.

It is easy to condemn TV as the cause of our ills, but comparing lab experiments to real behavior is fraught with difficulties. A young man or woman who performs a kind of violent act "as a result of" watching a show which demonstrated that act, is not only not typical, but obviously had a propensity to violence which could have been kindled by anything.

Having said all that, however, I do have a concern about your son watching the tube so much. But it has more to do with what he is *not* doing while fixated on the screen. He is *not* reading, doing chores, studying, playing sports, socializing with guys or girls, earning money, pursuing hobbies, listening to music, learning, discussing, thinking, or dreaming. He is the passive recipient of pap and pablum; unthinking, immobile, fixed in position and perception. In short, he is in a vegetative state. What can you do? Show him your letter and this answer; turn off the TV, or if that fails, disconnect it; too much TV means too little allowance; make sure that his vegetating in front of the TV is not a symptom of general depression or withdrawal from life. If one of the latter is the cause, he needs help.

18 **My kids are into the likes of Platinum Blond, Prince, Motley Crue, and similar groups. Weird, sinister sounds blast out of their rooms, shaking the whole house. We've taught them about Mozart, Bach and Beethoven, but they're not interested. We'd even settle for Sinatra and the Beatles.**

You gotta be kidding! Mothers and fathers in the 1940s hated the sound of skinny Sinatra, and in the early 60s, the Beatles were vilified by "proper" parents. The "weird and sinister" sounds you hear are called the music of the 80s. They'll give this music up soon enough. By the way, what was *your* favorite music when you were their age? (Don't tell me it was Presley!).

19 **How do we tell our 16-year-old daughter, Barbara, that we don't like her friends? We find them disrespectful, self-centered and shallow. They hang around gossiping, smoking cigarettes and criticising serious students or anyone who is not like them. We feel that they are a bad influence on her and she has become more rude to us since she met them a year ago. Before that she was a really good kid. How can we get her to see the light, and find a better group?**

This is actually a very tough question. On the surface it looks simple and straightforward enough: just explain to Barbara why you don't like her friends, and then forbid her to see them. You know as well as I that the chances of that approach being successful are slim indeed.

Barbara is now an integral part of that group of girls (and boys?). You may feel that she is being led astray by this gang, but it may well be that some parents of others in the group feel that it is your daughter who is the negative influence. The fact is that the group is viable and cohesive precisely because they fulfill emotional needs for each other. They share common values, attitudes and pleasures. It is because of this cohesiveness that criticizing her friends will be construed by Barbara as a frontal attack on her. I am sure that she will react to your critical remarks with self-righteous indignation. Suggesting to her some "better" friends would be like applying the kiss of death to these individuals. Barbara is in the process of defining her identity or sense of self and she is sensitive to her deficiencies. She is also defensive.

When you say you dislike her friends, does this mean every last one of them? Are they all to be written off as lost causes? Can you not find exceptions in the group? Or, better still, can you not see positive characteristics in just about every one of them?

By all means, gently raise with your daughter your concerns about the negative aspects of her friends' behavior. Forbidding her access to these kids will be draconian to her, and may even backfire. Consciousness raising is very important. By pointing out the behaviors which you find unpleasant or unacceptable, without rejecting the total personality, you will have more credibility with Barbara. As far as her own rudeness is concerned, this is clearly unacceptable, and it is this behavior (if it is unprovoked) which must be forbidden in non-negotiable terms. If Barbara is as good a kid as you say she was, you should see positive changes in her behavior soon.

20   **Our 14-year-old daughter, Maggie, is one of those kids who can do no wrong. I know that sounds pompous, but everything she has touched has been remarkably successful. She is a top student, athlete and musician, and she is seen (by others, too) as beautiful. She is also a warm, charming person, with a number of good friends. Why is it then that a girl in her school has seen fit to not only tease and torment her, but to organize many of the other kids against her. Maggie has become more fearful each day of this organized hate campaign in school by someone who hasn't got as much going for her in her whole**

body as Maggie has in her little finger. What do you suggest we do?

I have certainly heard this story before, and there are some things to be done. But more information is needed before a strategy is implemented. If Maggie has had this problem before, if she has been victimized by individuals or groups of kids in the past, then I would be more inclined to wonder about her role in this terrible behavior. From what you say, Maggie does not seem to be the type of kid who invites this hateful attack. Even in this particular instance, however, I would want to know more about the specifics of the relationship between Maggie and her tormentor. Does she do it to other kids? Is it only "fun" that all the kids indulge in? It certainly doesn't sound like it. Is it envy, jealousy or maliciousness? How is it that the other kids are so easily led against Maggie? Whatever the cause, the girl's nasty behavior is unconscionable and not permissible. Even if there is an explanation, and it is relatively benign — which seems unlikely — Maggie is suffering unnecessarily, and a stop has to be put to it.

Sometimes the parents of the aggressive child are called, and the matter is discussed. This works at times, if they are reasonable and sensitive people. But I have been astounded to hear of venomous and abusive responses from parents who blindly defend their own children, even when there is a blatantly guilty individual. This reaction is often accompanied by a mean-spirited and cruel attack on the victim for bringing it on him-or-herself. I have found a more useful, or at least predictably positive response, from speaking to the home-room teacher, or to the vice-principal. They could gingerly assess the situation and get all the facts. If someone has to speak to the nasty girl, or her parents, it would much better be an official rather than an informal contact. As difficult as it might be, the good news is that the intervention is almost always effective. Go for it.

21   **Our 14-year-old grandson, Ivan, was at a dance at his high school when some thugs with chains and bats from a rival school from across town**

arrived unannounced (and uninvited). They savagely beat up Ivan and a couple of other kids at random, it seems, and then took off. Ivan sustained a concussion and was hospitalized. He's usually a very enthusiastic kid, but seems depressed lately. Should he see a psychiatrist? Also, should I encourage my daughter (Ivan's mother) to press charges? Everyone seems to know who the attackers are.

This must have been a terrible experience for Ivan to have endured. Unfortunately, these things happen occasionally, and innocent bystanders are often harmed (remember *West Side Story?*) I assume that the attack was random and that Ivan had no previous dealings with these cretins. Usually, victims are wary for a while, and gradually understand the incident as a rare chance, an unfortunate happenstance. Occasionally, longer-term consequences result, such as fear, anxiety or depression. If the latter persists for a few weeks or even months, I would suggest an evaluation interview with a psychiatrist, so that Ivan can discuss any thoughts and feelings which he has not been able to share with his parents.

As far as pressing charges is concerned, I am all for it. The difficulty comes about in finding witnesses willing to testify. They often vanish into thin air because they fear reprisals from these dangerous dolts. But if your daughter can mobilize support, then I would recommend going after those miserable thugs, and make them rue the day they ever considered violence a viable way of resolving disputes or of getting their cheap thrills. I hope that your daughter calls the police, and they throw the book at those hoods.

22 **Our 17-year-old son, Alan, is a talented musician. I mean, he is no Vladimir Ashkenazy, but he has played the piano well enough to have entered and done well in Kiwanis competitions. He's also been a very good student, until last year, that is,**

**when he and three others formed a high school
rock band and his marks dropped sharply. The
band is a huge success, at least in our town. So
when they're not practicing, they have all kinds
of gigs — school dances, sponsored concerts,
and bars. He seems to think that nothing else
matters in life — he doesn't crack a book, he
hasn't been seeing his old friends, and he's seldom home. What can we do?**

In a strange way, there may be little that you can do. I'm sure that
you've discussed your concerns, that you've advised, encouraged, cajoled, threatened and demanded. Perhaps you have even
attempted to bribe ("you can practise, but only three times a
week, or only if your grades are up"), because this is a sequence
which many parents go through when their children have chosen
a somewhat dubious path. I say dubious, because this description obviously reflects your feelings. The thing that is of utmost
importance to Alan right now, you look upon as frivolous, and
perhaps even dangerous. There is no doubt, if he is intent on
embarking on a career in rock music, that it will be a rough road
and few make it big. This story of Alan's behavior is typical of
many rock musicians and other artists whose parents felt that
they should have a back-up position — such as a college degree.

There is no mention of drugs, debauchery, depression or
other unpleasantries of life — Alan is happy. If you've gone
through that sequence and explained your fears, but Alan continues to be totally committed to this way of life, and nothing
has worked to change his course, for now you would be wise to
let him be. I'll bet, however, that a compromise between you can
be found.

23 **Cheryl is our 15-year-old daughter, the youngest
of our three children. We don't have any problems with any of them, but I am worried about
her, not because of what she is or isn't doing, but
rather because of her unrealistic dreams. She**

has been taking piano lessons, practising and playing avidly since the age of five. She has received considerable recognition and even acclaim on a small scale (Kiwanis Club second prize). But she ain't no Rubinstein, Horowitz, Gould, or Hewitt. And that's the problem: she thinks she is. She talks about her career as a concert pianist, the fame, the fortune, the glory, and she wants nothing else. Her past teachers have encouraged her aspiration, but my own feeling is that she has been misled (with all good intentions). I am a musician, but I would feel less confident in my assessment if Cheryl's present teacher disagreed with me. But she, too, feels that Cheryl is building herself up for a big disappointment. She's just not that good.

Luckily, Cheryl is young enough that time, experience and motivation will likely take care of her unrealistic ambitions. If she were a few years older, her overwhelming commitment to personal stardom would be bordering on the delusional. As it is, it is very likely that she'll learn that she is just one of thousands of excellent pianists around. This doesn't mean that she won't be able to perform in a professional or amateur orchestra, depending on her level of ability, or change instruments, or broaden into pop music, or teach piano to others. After high school she may want to take a degree in music in university, and as she grows older, the possibilities will actually broaden, so that her unfulfilled quest for stardom may not be as painful as it might be otherwise.

If, on the other hand, she is less interested in furthering her piano technique than being in the limelight, she may seek other means of achieving the gratification of that elusive — and usually unrewarding — goal. Being a star carries with it its own burdens, and seldom makes the bestowed individual any intrinsically happier. Moreover, if that is the object of the quest, the chances of its being fulfilled are infinitesimally small. It is hopeful that she will see that light, too.

It is your role as her mother (father, teacher, and so on) to convey to her the reality of her talents, and the ephemeral nature of being numero uno. She may not like to hear the messages, but it is time to start — gently — conveying them to her now.

24 **I think that we've created a monster. Michelle, our 14-year-old daughter, has had the benefit of all kinds of lessons — dance, figure skating, swimming, piano, gymnastics, skiing — you name it. Actually, all her friends were doing the same things, so we were quite comfortable with all the activity. Well, Michelle has now taken matters into her own hands. She is in grade nine (first year of high school) and in addition to her school work, she is doing drama, choir, swim team, band, orchestra, tennis, jogging, horseback riding, student council, newspaper and debating. I get breathless just thinking about it. I am concerned about her school performance, although she is maintaining a B average, but I am most upset by this frenetic activity. Am I wrong?**

Well, let's say that you are not necessarily wrong. We judge that our teenagers are in trouble when they show "symptoms", or engage in behavior which gives us cause for concern. The major sign of trouble would be a significant change in Michelle's demeanor, which could raise a red flag. Some examples of these symptoms are insomnia, withdrawal, crying, decreased concentration or school performance, somatic complaints and fears. I don't "hear" any of this from you regarding Michelle. If there are no changes in her apparent good mood, or in her relationships with family or friends, and her productivity is good, what are your worried about?

The number and variety of Michelle's activities are impressive. I do feel that we push too many lessons and preparations at our kids, but when everyone is doing the same thing, it is a difficult trend to break. I have actually more faith in the common sense of kids to know their levels and limits of involvement, than I do in some parents that I have met. It's true that developing adolescents can be enriched by exposure to a wide variety of new experiences, but it can easily be abused. Some mothers and fathers push their kids in order to vicariously fulfill their own desires, and to make their children more impressive or marketable. Michelle, however, appears to be one of the kids who can handle it all, and then some. She sounds terrific.

25 **Karen is our 15-year-old daughter who is giving us some unexpected trouble. She met some kids at summer camp who are having a reunion in Detroit in December, and she'd like to join them. She wants to go down there unchaperoned, a distance of five hundred miles from here, and we have absolutely refused. Well, we didn't expect the blood letting — tears, rages, melancholy, threats and begging — all almost within the same breath. She won't face the fact that there's a lot of danger out there, but as her parents, we have a responsibility to protect her. She thinks that we are ogres. Are we?**

No, I do not think that you are ogres. You are exercising your parental responsibility. You have assessed the situation completely, and in your maturity and wisdom have deemed that Karen's safety would be sufficiently at risk if you allowed her to go on this trip. Who am I to second-guess your decision? Not only might I do exactly the same thing if I were in your shoes, but the same kinds of thoughts and concerns would cross my mind. Even if I disagreed, and felt that Karen could safely make the reunion, I would have to be reassured that the parents of the host girl or boy were going to always be present; that nothing dangerous was being planned, or rather, that all the planned activities were wholesome and chaperoned or supervised; that she would be greeted and escorted when she got off the plane, train or bus; that the travel officials were well aware of her solitary travelling state at a young age, and had taken steps to help and protect her; and that frequent communication would be planned. You could probably think of other caveats, but you get the gist.

I actually find it amazing that for all your concerns about her security, there is nary a word about the costs involved. Such an affluent culture! Kids hop planes today with more ease than when we took buses in our own youth. I must admit to a feeling of unease about our remarkable mobility and nonchalant jet-setting. On the one hand it shows technological progress; on the other, I am left with a feeling of seeing unbridled self-indulgence unleashed. I guess I'm just an old fogey....

26 **How do we get our teenagers to pull their weight at home? We have three of them (ages 14, 16, 17), all good kids who are popular, and not in any trouble. Yet dishes, cleaning up, garbage, errands, and so on are curiously left for their parents or the hired cleaner. We remind, cajole, demand and threaten and have done so for years, but to no avail.**

Your kids obviously have a good deal at home: loving, caring parents who oblige them by picking up after them and making sure that all the household chores get done. At this rate, they'd be fools to move out when college days loom; who else will cater to their needs and whims as well as you do? There are two questions, one the developmental and historical one, which is "Why is this still going on after all these years?"; and the second, "What can you do about it?"

As for the first, I'm sure that I don't have to tell you that these expectations of children should not begin in adolescence. Age-appropriate chores, sharing of duties, and divisions of labor can be initiated in early childhood. It can be done by assignment as well as by modelling and demonstration. The family team should pull together; everyone will have something to do, not just the child, who will otherwise feel burdened unfairly. Also, if there are "perqs" and privileges, like allowance, favors or treats, these can in part be tied to what has been earned by the child. There have to be consequences for not following through on clear and realistic expectations. This principle is applicable in all families, from the most impoverished to the most affluent. As the years progress, the pulling of weight becomes part and parcel of living in the family, in their house. Doing one's part is not an added painful imposition, but a responsibility which goes with sharing and love.

The second question is how to deal with the problem right now. A family conference is in order, with your demands now translated into both rationale (explanation) and consequences. If your teenagers are as good as you describe, then they will both understand and pitch in. If it doesn't work, either they are not so good, or you are having inordinate difficulties conveying your feelings. I would then suggest sitting down with a family therapist or counsellor, either in private practice or with the Family Service Agency, and see what else is going on that is preventing a seemingly straightforward resolution of your difficulties.

27   **Should I give my 17-year-old son, Sheldon, an allowance or should he get a part-time job? We are comfortable but not wealthy, and we are trying to teach him the value of money.**

I have known plenty of kids who have had part-time jobs and no allowance, and who never learned the value of money. I know others who have never worked a day in their youthful lives, and are careful with their savings and spending. Knowing the value of money usually means the ability to operate within a budget, and there are many determinants of that talent. For example, how good as models are you and your husband? What are your son's friends like?

The point I'm making is that you should do what feels right for you. There are no specific rules. There is a general feeling in some families that a 17-year-old young man should earn money, learn about the real world, and pay for some of his own expenses. I tend to agree with this general sentiment. But there are exceptions. Some 17-year-olds are extraordinarily involved in extracurricular activities, or carry an extremely heavy academic load; others have enormous amounts of time on their hands. Obviously, parents will have different expectations of young people in each of these categories.

As with all other human endeavors, no one learns a lesson from a single experience. Complicated behavior has complex causes underlying it, and Sheldon's care with cash will depend on his relationship with you, his self-esteem, his acceptance by his peers, the nature of his friends and his own personality.

28 **My sister's daughter, Kayla, is a sweet girl (aged 16), but her parents are really upsetting her. They are quite comfortable, yet they make her pay for absolutely everything! She has received some modest gifts of money over the years and she has earned money from part-time jobs, but she has no savings left. Not because Kayla is a spendthrift (she is in fact quite frugal), but rather because she is required to pay for *all* her clothes, books, entertainments, snacks, gifts, toiletries, you name it. She receives no allowance. She has complained, but her parents think that this is as it should be. I don't think that it's fair, do you?**

No, I don't, but I'm not sure what anyone can do about it. If Kayla's parents are united in their approach to her spending of her own money, then there is little to be done. Certainly, there is no way that one can construe this lack of allowance as deprivation or abuse, so that the help of external authorities cannot be enlisted. Parents are entitled to set their own rules, as long as abuse is not perpetrated. Kayla's complaints are met with firmness, so I'm not sure how far an aunt will get, even if she is particularly close with her sister.

It is important that we inculcate appropriate values in our youth, which obviously includes learning the significance of money — how to earn it, handle it, take responsibility for it and save it. I do feel that Kayla's parents are unduly demanding of their daughter and I can't second-guess their motives from this distance. They obviously have convinced themselves that Kayla will benefit from this rather oppressive approach. I find it hard to believe, however, that there are not other areas of her life at home which they do not also attempt to stringently control (although you don't mention anything else).

You could, of course, speak to your sister, but you'd be taking a chance on a reaction of resentment. People are remarkably sensitive to being criticized by others for their child-rearing practices. It depends on how strongly you feel about Kayla's predicament, and on your relationship with your sister. The worst part of this is that they are inadvertently alienating their daughter. If her resentment continues to grow, she is going to withhold more and more from her parents (not only money, but also emotions), and impatiently wait for her break to freedom.

29 **My teenagers are a joy. I wish I could say the same about myself (their father). Jessica (15) and Jamie (17) are both tolerant of me, but I know that I can be very trying, even impossible. At times I am pleasant and loving, but more often than not, I am morose, irritable, critical and sarcastic. Outside you'd never know this, since I am seen as easy-going, effective and warm. I am a successful lawyer. My wife and kids steer clear of me when I go into one of my nasty moods, and I am always regretful and apologetic later. They seem to be doing well, but I am concerned that I am doing them irreparable damage.**

It's hard for me to say what harm, if any, you are inflicting on your teenage children. I gather that your castigating them remains in the verbal sphere; that is, you don't inflict physical abuse on them (not that we can't hurt people with our rapier comments). Kids are remarkably resilient, but obviously there are vulnerabilities and limits to self-protection. I find it hard to believe that you've been married for about twenty years and your wife has never suggested that you seek marital or individual counselling. Either she sees her role to be an adoring, dutiful, obedient and subservient wife, or you have her so bamboozled and intimidated that she is afraid to confront you. Is this what Jessica and Jamie are learning from their mother about handling a difficult family member? You seem to imply that the modus operandi at home is to "tolerate" and "steer clear" of the great man, lest he indulge his destructive tendencies.

If I sound hard on you, it is because you have allowed yourself and have been allowed by others, the luxury of "letting it all hang out" at home, hurting the ones you love, but never showing that side of you to people with whom you are not at all close. I will soften my remarks, because interspersed among the negative adjectives you use (nasty, irritable, critical, sarcastic, impossible), are some potentially redeeming features. You also say that you are morose and regretful. Now, I don't believe in making excuses for people's destructive behavior, especially when that's all there is. But you obviously are in pain; you are ashamed and despondent.

It is obvious that you need professional help. Your mood swings suggest a biological underpinning, but the fact that you restrict your sadness and anger to your family is suggestive of unhappiness and frustration on the home front, perhaps in your marriage. Whatever the cause, you should see a psychiatrist. At some point, a marital or family counsellor may well be in order. As far as Jessica and Jamie are concerned, level with them. Tell them exactly what you've told me, and that you are finally going to do something about it.

Body

Except for infancy, the human body changes most dramatically and quickly during the years of adolescence. Teenagers can grow three inches over a summer! We can well imagine the threats to our self-image when we are almost suddenly a quarter of a foot taller in two short months. On the average, teenage boys double their strength between the ages of 13 and 16; an immature 13-year-old swinging at his mother in a temper tantrum is bad enough, but manageable. An immature 16-year-old doing the same thing puts his victim in real jeopardy. There are additions and newly enlarged appendages — breasts, penises, pubic hair. There are new and intensely perceived experiences — menstruation, ejaculation. There are annoying new bodily developments — facial hair, acne (zits) and body odor.

Nothing is static; little is entirely predictable. And these constant physical and psychological changes are occurring in a context of major flux in a whole host of dimensions; hormonal, emotional and cognitive. The sex drive raises its head, bringing excitement and insecurity, and to a certain degree, a constant state of arousal.

In fact, sexual concerns permeate the teenager's bodily preoccupations. The extent to which a young person perceives him or herself as comparatively attractive to the opposite sex (if heterosexual) is a topic of thought bordering on obsession. Hence the preening and posturing, combing and curling, covering blemishes and zits, and agonizing over clothing. So much for the overt behavior which is the tip of the iceberg; private thoughts, worries and fantasies really comprise the bulk of that 'berg.

It takes adolescents a while to come to grips with their physical "deficiencies". Very few of us are perfect "10"s. We all have blemishes, bulges, or bony prominences; too many or too few pounds or inches. At first, such imperfections are upsetting; some people, and especially teens, are even obsessed by them. These feelings generally give way to chagrin, and finally we become accustomed to our physical quirks. Ultimately we realize that "it ain't all bad" and that there are more important issues in our lives.

Rather than nuclear war, the generation gap, crime in the streets, unemployment and poverty — all important issues — it is the body and its changes which dominate the thinking of young adolescents. Just as it was in our day, remember?

30   **Andrea is our 15-year-old daughter who is con-**
─────   **vinced that she is ugly. No matter what we or**
      anybody else says, she believes that her appear-
      ance turns everybody off. The truth is that she is
      not beautiful, but nobody could call her ugly, or
      even unattractive. (She has even been called
      pretty by numerous people). But we can't con-
      vince her of her attractiveness.

Andrea is an exaggerated example of the preoccupation many
young (and old) people have with their appearances. It is no
accident that the cosmetics industry is a multibillion dollar enter-
prise around the world. Concerns about appearance affect both
sexes, all socioeconomic classes, most cultures and all ages.

We can't all be paragons of beauty and Andrea will have to
learn that. It is particularly during adolescence that we come to
grips with the physical imperfections and deficiencies that we all
have. Her obsession with this belief of her ugliness may have a
number of possible derivations. At worst, she may be harboring a
delusion (a false belief) which is indicative of a psychotic illness,
but I mention this extreme only for completeness — she is not
psychotic. Does she have an obsessional personality — does she
develop unshakeable preoccupations over other matters, too? It
doesn't sound like it. Is she emulating her parents, or others close
to her, who may also be overly involved with how they look? Is
her facial skin breaking out in pimples or acne? Is there a
correctible defect such as a large nose? You don't mention either
as a possibility. Has she been teased because of her appearance?
Are the other girls beginning to date, and is she feeling left out?

You can surmise by my line of questions that a seemingly
single concern can actually be a complex problem. And yet this
kind of worry usually fades in relative importance as the young
person gets older. Ideally, Andrea would develop other interests
and preoccupations, and begin dating and her unhappy belief
would dissipate. It is the degree and the immutability of her belief
in her ugliness which give me cause for somewhat more concern.

I would reassure her, as you have been doing, show her
your letter and this response. Speak to a dermatologist or
even a cosmetician about maximizing the good qualities of her

appearance, so that she feels better. Encourage her to take part in other activities in which appearance is of secondary or lesser importance. But monitor the overwhelming nature of her belief. If it doesn't change in a year or so, Andrea should speak to a staff member of an adolescent clinic.

31 **Our son, Lawrence, is 14 years of age and only 5 feet tall. He is by far the shortest child in his junior high school class. He has not yet reached puberty; is now the time we should try to get him growth hormones?**

Whoa, slow down. Newly discovered synthetic growth hormone is very hard to get, tricky to use, expensive, and is used only for cases of pathological and extreme shortness. There is an extraordinarily wide range of normal, both during puberty, and when individuals reach their full height. Just look around you.

Before an endocrinologist would deem your son's shortness as necessitating hormonal intervention, he would take a history of pubertal growth and height in your entire extended family, check the height of (you) his parents and siblings, and take a "bone age" x-ray of your son (his wrist) to make an educated estimate of his expected ultimate height.

Until these things are done, nobody is going to prescribe or give natural or synthetic growth hormone. The chances are excellent that Lawrence will soon undergo pubertal changes (including a growth spurt), and will achieve a normal range of height (although possibly on the short side), and not need hormone injections.

Consult your pediatrician now, he (she) is used to this dilemma.

32 **My daughter, Phyllis, has a largish nose. But she's actually quite an attractive girl. She has a lot of friends, is beginning to date, and is doing well at school. But she's convinced that she's**

ugly, and the sole cause of that state, according to her, is the "immense" size of her proboscis. It's not that big, by any means, although she won't listen to reason. Should we consult a plastic surgeon? Or a shrink?

My plastic surgeon colleagues will want to lynch me, but I feel that they've gone much too far in their cosmetic work. They've convinced the public (especially the well-heeled public) that they can — for a hefty price — change noses, smooth wrinkles, lift sags, reduce and lift breasts, and so on, and in so doing bring on an enhanced self-image and personal happiness. Well, I have yet to be convinced. I have seen some people absolutely delighted with their post-surgical results, but a year or so later, I have found that there is really no change in their outlook on life or themselves. We are too preoccupied with our appearances, and certainly have misguided ideas that smooth youthful skin is equivalent to personal fulfillment. It just ain't so.

Phyllis is not about to believe that she is attractive. She has a singularly narrow view of herself, and it is entirely in negative terms, focussing especially on her nose. Most reputable plastic surgeons will take a careful history from the applicant for cosmetic nasal surgery. In addition, they often work with a mental health professional who will look for signs of immaturity or instability. They ask about the patient's expectations of the operation, especially in terms of how realistic they are. Those who are responsible practitioners will try to ascertain specifically if Phyllis is expecting a dramatic change in her life (even if it's already good!), and or in her self-esteem and happiness. If there is any doubt, she will be referred for a more detailed and sensitive interview.

You haven't refused her request, which means that the door is still open, and her hopes are high. Why don't you ask around — your family doctor is a good place to start — and find a plastic surgeon who is not only a master craftsman (if it's going to happen, let it at least be done right!), but in addition is a caring, realistic, open and humane individual. Arrange an interview. Without that experience, Phyllis may well feel cheated.

33 **My daughter, Margaret, has dark hair on her face and it embarrasses her to no end. She is very unhappy because it is so visible. What can we do about it?**

A very short question, and it could just as well have been written about your daughter's thin hair on her head, or your son's absence of body hair, or some other bothersome pattern of hair growth. Too little hair, too much hair, hair in the wrong place, the wrong kind of hair; that's the sum total. None of these problems is (usually) pathological. They tend to be genetic in origin, inherited from parents and other ancestral suppliers of genes and chromosomes. Occasionally, as in Margaret's case, there should be a good medical examination in order to rule out, for example, a hormone-producing tumor, or other disease process, which can produce changes in male or female pattern hair distribution.

Most of the time there is little that can be done medically. Most of the attempts at improving the appearance, which is so important to teenagers, are cosmetic in nature. A whole host of methods have been introduced to remove unwanted hair; depilatories (dissolving creams); waxing (removing hair with melted wax); electrolysis (destroying roots with electrical current); tweezers (pulling) and bleaching (camouflaging) are just a few of the common methods. Some work for certain individuals, and not for others, and vice versa, or for certain locations and not others. There are potential ill effects and complications, so I urge you to speak to a competent dermatologist and then a professional cosmetician before you embark on a course of "treatment". (Oops, my physician bias is showing!)

The same, in reverse, goes for a relative absence of hair. After one evaluates the physical condition and rules out any illness, then wigs, transplants, implants and other methods of increasing hair can be used. In all of these instances adolescents feel at a distinct disadvantage because they feel unattractive and unwanted. The skin and hair are so front and center that I have seen many adults who still shudder at the memories of embarrassment and humiliation associated with their own past perceptions of ugliness. The fact that the hair on Margaret's face is visible is only part of the story; the major issue for her is her self-image and self-esteem. Margaret's appearance *can* be helped — if her self-esteem doesn't improve as well, she should speak to a counsellor at an adolescent clinic.

34 **My son Christoper has acne. Not earth-shattering, or extensive, or even unusual, but enough to cause him grief. He scrubs his face with drying soap until it is painfully red. He avoids chocolate, sweets, greasy or fried foods, even milk (he read that it, too, is acneogenic). Yet still his zits come! He is good-looking, has friends of both sexes, does well in school, and is close to his family. What do you suggest?**

Obviously your son's acne is not a result of a lack of cleanliness or an excess of the wrong foods. The truth is that these are seldom, if ever, the culprits. The real causes of most teenage acne are heredity, constitution and stage of life. If his parents had acne, or if his bodily chemicals are such that acne flourishes, then cleaning or dieting will have a marginal or negligible effect. Sometimes facial scarring and nutritional deficiencies are caused by misguided attempts at zit eradication.

Why, you ask, does Christopher go about the elimination of this teenage affliction with such zeal? Because, in spite of doing well in most respects, he has some problems of self-esteem and self-acceptance. He has focused on this very visible part of him in the hope that once his skin is clear, so too will his self-image be enhanced dramatically. As a great seer once said, "This too will pass."

It might be wise to consult a dermatologist, just to make sure that there is not more here than meets the eye. Occasionally, antibiotics are successful in reducing the bacteria which help contribute to the acne. But leave that decision to the professionals.

35 **Leon is a terrific son; he's 17 and I couldn't ask for a more co-operative kid. He does well at school, and seems to enjoy his life. The only problem is, forgive me, he stinks! He seems to shower every two days (not often enough in my book), but the main reason for his body odor is the total absence of antiperspirant or deodorant among his toiletries. At times I cannot bear to be near him!**

I'm sure that you know that body odor tends not to be an issue prior to puberty. At that time sweat and other substances (such as sebum) produced by glands conspire to produce a new aroma in the adolescent (or into the home!) Young adolescents, eager to attract members of the opposite sex, and usually emulating their parents, begin to use the phenomenal array of chemicals designed to neutralize or please our olfactory sensibilities. We, in the Western world especially, have made a multibillion dollar industry flourish because of our need to reduce infringement on our smell receptors. Heaven forfend! And of course we've taken it to ridiculous extremes; there are sprays, roll-ons, sticks, soaps — scented or unscented — and so on, for every part of the body, designed to keep us pure (or at least smelling it)! On the other hand, any of you who've been in a crowded room in parts of the world where this stuff is not sold (or bought) or where body smells are acceptable, will understand the need for those particular substances.

So there are two extremes. Leon may approach one side, eschewing the use of these materials for one of many possible reasons. Do they cause him to break out in an allergic rash? If so, there are good hypoallergenic deodorants. It may well be that he does not think he smells bad. And if he has friends, and especially girlfriends, who not only don't avoid him but are attracted to him, he then has no evidence that he is giving off an unpleasant odor. I am assuming you are not overly sensitive to smell, that it is not a preoccupation of yours. That being the case, you can then broach the subject with him. Some people leave a new bottle of deodorant in their teenager's medicine cabinet; some try more subtle encouragement, perhaps a poem. My own approach would be to say, "Leon, do you realize that since you've become an adult, that you are *just like the rest of us*? Unless you wash more often and use deodorant you give off a strong odor that some people might find offensive." Consciousness-raising often works wonders.

36   **My 16-year-old daughter, Hazel, has everything she could possibly want — brains, beauty, friends and a loving family — but she is 50 pounds overweight. No matter what I do, she can't seem to shed these pounds.**

In the Western world we are absolutely obsessed with weight reduction. Indeed, 75 percent of our population is on some form of diet at any one time. It's mind-boggling! Between diet fads, farms, spas, camps and fitness fads, clubs, centers, programs and books, anthropologists in centuries to come will no doubt look upon us as bizarre, superficial, and/or idiotic. We seem to equate self-acceptance and self-esteem with perception of external attractiveness or beauty. What a myth! As far as your daughter is concerned, what do you mean "no matter what *I* do"? Losing those 50 pounds and keeping them off is ultimately going to be solely up to *her*. And it's not going to be easy. People are always losing weight and just about every diet works for a while, but the weight almost inevitably comes back.

Hazel has so much going for her. Am I to assume that she is as concerned about her weight as you obviously are? If she is not, I hope she can carry on as a happy, productive individual. But if she has caught the bug of self-rejection due to heaviness, then she has to fight this weight problem. There's no secret to losing weight: decrease caloric intake (smaller, healthier meals), and increase caloric expenditure (exercise). Do enough of both, and presto, weight falls. Some people find it easier to do this under the care of a physician or a clinic, others need a more structured approach such as that offered by Weight Watchers, Weight Loss Clinics, or TOPS (Take Off Pounds Sensibly). Still other people are most comfortable in a group program (which I happen to feel is the most effective therapy for any compulsive behavior), like Over

Eaters Anonymous. But both you and your daughter should be under no illusions about the difficult path she will have to tread.

37 **Angela, our 17-year-old daughter, is driving us crazy with her dieting! When she is on a diet, which is almost invariably, she can think of little else, and also insists that I cater to her whims in the kitchen. I try to, but I can't keep up to her. She has been on Pritikin, Rice, Beverly Hills, Grapefruit, Scarsdale, High Carbohydrate, Fit for Life, and other diets. Furthermore, she isn't the least bit overweight; she is slim and attractive! She isn't anorexic or bulimic, but she seems to be thinking of her weight and body constantly; nothing else appears to matter.**

What Angela is showing is a combination of society's preoccupation with the equation of slimness equalling attractiveness, and her own obsessional nature, which feeds into it perfectly. As I've said elsewhere (see Question 36), there are millions of people around the affluent Western world dieting at any one time. This is particularly offensive when we know that there are many more millions in Third World countries who are literally starving to death because of famine and drought. Still our narcissism continues unabated.

At least for adolescents, there is some semblance of an excuse, since they are dealing with questions about their changing bodies, their evolving self-images and identities. Teenagers feel a great deal of insecurity regarding their relative place among their peers; "Will I be accepted?" and "Am I attractive?" are almost universal teenage questions. Angela, however, takes it to ridiculous extremes. For her, nothing is as important as her diet rituals and her resultant weight. But she has a mother who goes out of her way to support her daughter's silliness. Why in the world should you even try to keep up with her? You know full well that she will soon tire of her present diet, only to have it supplanted by another fad, which will be The Answer to all her problems.

You also know that all of these diets are equally effective, or more accurately, ineffective.

You probably cannot reason with her right now, since she is obsessed with her campaign to diet. But you can stop your own contribution to her all-consuming passion. Let her fend for herself in the kitchen. While she likely will not listen to you, she may well be amenable to a conversation or two with a nutritionist or dietician who works with teens. Most adolescent medical clinics have such people who can explain to their clients just what works and what doesn't, and what is healthy and what is not — many of the diets are not only useless, but can be dangerous. They can make interesting dieting suggestions which young people often find fascinating. If *you* make them, Angela will write them off as useless.

One last thing: if her obsession with dieting has reached the point that she can't function in school, socially with friends or family, or in her usual activities, then I would be even more concerned. If this is the case, (and you don't suggest this at all), Angela should speak to a mental health professional at the same clinic.

38 **Our daughter, Carey, is 16 and ever since summer camp she has been on a health food kick — she pops vitamins into her mouth daily, won't touch meat, and only shops at health food stores, which increase our food costs enormously. Even her cosmetics have some vegetarian non-additive, vitamin, natural, hypoallergenic, non-toxic or pure designation! The whole thing seems ridiculous and exploitative to us. What do you think?**

Well, with all due respect to the thousands of people who are devotees of the health food habit or fad, I *do* have some reservations as to the validity of the claims made by the leaders of the various movements. Frankly, there are no good studies supporting most of their statements: longevity is not prolonged;

morbidity (disease incidence) is not reduced. A good, balanced diet without junk foods provides all the proper ingredients and vitamins for any person's health.

There is an almost religious zeal among many of the adherents of these concepts; it is a veritable way of life. As with all intense belief systems, the supporters feel wonderful, almost exalted by their experiences. This is one of the main reasons for the difficulty in assessing the true effectiveness of these health foods or drugs: *everyone* feels better. Whether this is a result of the substances themselves, or (as I suspect) of the intense conviction (autohypnosis) of the *righteousness* of their pursuits is not yet proven. There is a cultish aspect to their involvement; if you disagree, then "you don't understand", or you "haven't experienced", or "it is your failing". And as with other cults, the total involvement usually lasts for a few months, only to disappear as if it had never happened (although there are followers who adhere to the health food approach for many long years). Some of the health food-niks are also into naturopathy, holistic healing, and other alternate approaches to traditional medicines.

Carey will most likely give up her obsession with these products in fairly short order. You can wait it out if you are patient and tolerant. But if the costs become prohibitive, or if her fascinations intrude into your lifestyle, then you might have to put your foot down. In the meantime, treat her with good humor.

39 **Our daughter Belinda is 17 and is endowed with extremely large breasts. So large, in fact, that she is physically uncomfortable. Worse still, she is constantly teased, tormented or come onto by immature guys. At first it was a fun topic around the house, but she has become increasingly sensitive. Yesterday she came to me in tears, saying that some guy had grabbed her. She said that she wants to reduce the size of her breasts. Is it possible?**

Yes, it is possible to reduce breast-size surgically, although Belinda might want to consider the pros and cons with her doctor or an experienced counsellor beforehand. Large, pendulous breasts can and do cause a great deal of discomfort, including backache, tight bra straps, and postural difficulties. Reducing the size of the breasts can readily overcome these problems, but sometimes some supporting fibers are lost, leading to more drooping and sagging than the girl originally may have envisioned. I am assuming that Belinda is not overweight, since you haven't mentioned it. If she had a general weight problem, then weight loss would include a considerable reducing effect on her breasts, which have a significant amount of adipose (fat) tissue. But this does not appear to be the issue.

The complaint that guys are crude and aggressive because of the size of her breasts is not a figment of her imagination. Dolly Parton may well be talented, but you know as well as I the major source(s) of her attraction to comedians and many audience members. Many grown men are still erotically preoccupied with large breasts on their fantasized lovers, and Belinda fulfills their daydreams. The fact that these men act on their desires is a reflection of their immaturity and crudity. I don't want to condone the behavior of these dolts at all, but there is little that Belinda can do to eradicate their offensiveness. She can ignore them, walk away, or tell them off, but she is still left with the problem.

Given what you've said, she probably would be an excellent candidate for surgical breast reduction by an experienced surgeon. I want to add that, as legitimate as Belinda's concerns are, I could just as easily be getting a very similar letter from a mother of a girl who is convinced that her breasts are far too small. She might be worried about her daughter being teased, and wondering about surgical correction (including implantation of tissue or silicon) to overcome this problem. My answer to this mother would have the same common theme. If it is too stressful, and surgery works, then it might be considered.

---

40 **Our daughter, Brenda, is a wholesome 16-year-old, but she has a body and face that suggest someone considerably older. Even more**

important is that she is statuesque, voluptuous and really beautiful. Men are always admiring her, and I don't mind that. But they also ogle, leer, touch, make passes and offer various lecherous "services" to her. She is offended and even frightened. When she complains, people tell her to "enjoy it" or some similar message. How can I advise her?

When I suggest to you that there is little that you or she can do, it almost sounds as if I were condoning the behavior of these boors. I am definitely not. And the attitude that Brenda should either "grin and bear it", or even worse, "enjoy it" is particularly offensive to me. She *should be* offended, especially when the leers evolve into passes.

It is for this reason that there is relatively new sexual harassment legislation in most jurisdictions. What Brenda is facing is bad enough, but at least it is impersonal and anonymous. Can you imagine a similar situation in which she was harassed by an employer? There are numerous examples of this kind of power, control or threat game being tied to sexual advances.

You can tell Brenda about this legislation, and the reasons for it. You can give her a subscription to *Ms.* magazine, or tell her about other popular feminist literature, to acquaint her with the fact that she is in good company, and that this is part of a larger problem of sexism in society. You can advise her to avoid any behavior that could be construed as encouragement, that is, no eye contact, giggling, smart remarks, return glances, or overly tight clothing. This is a lot for a 16-year-old to digest, but Brenda will have to get used to it, and learn to not give these guys the time of day. As she gets older, she will become more adept at handling this harassment, and not allowing them to get the better of her or upset her so. What some women have done, given the right circumstances, has been to report a particularly offensive guy to his superiors or even to file a formal grievance. But strong action takes considerable confidence; some help and support from others can shore up their courage. Brenda is growing up, and learning about the less salutary aspects of some people is part of that process.

41   **Our son, Gary, (17) came to me (his father) last week with a problem which surprised me. He told me that he is convinced that his penis is too small, and that he is very afraid that he'll never be able to satisfy a woman. He wouldn't show me his genital area, although I obviously have seen his penis before. In all honesty, I find it on the small side, but I've seen smaller on many married fathers in the locker rooms of clubs I've belonged to. My reassuring him didn't help. He *has* seemed a little down lately, and I wonder how to help him.**

I'm sure that you know that Gary's concerns are extremely common among teenage boys, and even among grown men. And they certainly aren't new; teenage boys have always been worried about the relative size of their organs. Hence the almost universal mythology of penis size as a sign of manliness, or of exceptional talent as a lover. And it is a total myth, completely unrelated to either of those qualities.

Part of the problem is that teenagers are thrust into common locker rooms among boys their own age. The rates of development of growth (height as well as genital size) vary enormously. You could and do have anatomically grown men and little boys sharing the same locker because they happen to be the exact same chronological age. There is inevitable teasing and Gary may have been on the receiving end of this, which could account for his down mood.

You want facts? Penis size varies tremendously. A flaccid (soft) penis averages in the range of 7 to 10 centimeters in length (3 to 4 inches), but shorter and longer lengths are certainly seen. Even these dimensions are misleading, because the ultimate erect size also has a wide range. Sometimes a smaller penis ends up in erection longer than a seemingly more endowed member. The "average" range for erection is 5-1/2 to 6-1/2 inches, but again, shorter and longer have been readily seen. More importantly, the shorter penises function equally well during sexual intercourse. Size bears no relationship to ability as a lover. A good lover is caring, sensuous, tactile, responsive, sensitive and passionate. Oh yes, a penis helps, but its length is not the issue. Perhaps Gary should see a male counsellor at a local adolescent clinic, who, I assure you, has heard all this before. He'll also be able to ferret out what else might be on Gary's mind to account for his recent blue period. If he is close to your family doctor, Gary could just as well discuss it with him.

42 **Our two kids are 17 (Dean) and 18 (Lois) and I am scared stiff that they'll get AIDS. Both of them have healthy sex drives, and they are no longer virgins. Neither of them is homosexual, but I know that AIDS can be spread to hetero-sexuals, and that it is an epidemic. How can I get them to stop having dangerous sex?**

As you know, AIDS stands for Acquired Immune Deficiency Syndrome. Currently it is all the rage in the media, but it *is* a serious, even lethal disease. It has not yet reached epidemic proportions in North America, although it certainly may if there is no change in sexual behaviour, and/or no vaccine or cure is found — both highly unlikely, in my opinion. The disease is acquired through sexual relations with someone who is carrying the virus, and apparently, the virus has to enter the bloodstream through an available cut or abrasion. It is found in the blood serum, and in particular concentration in semen, in victims and carriers. There is no evidence that it is spread by sneezing or kissing, although the virus has been occasionally isolated in the saliva of those afflicted. It is most commonly transmitted be-tween homosexuals in the act of anal intercourse. Another way of getting this disease is via injection when using non-sterilized and contaminated needles, or from medically indicated transfusions with non-screened blood.

There have been screening tests available to check out blood supplies for transfusions since 1985, and to see if susceptible people are viral carriers. Needles can and should be properly sterilized. There are safe sex techniques currently taught and practised, which minimize the chances of introducing the virus into the partner's bloodstream. Indiscriminate, random, anonymous and promiscuous sexual practices greatly increase the chances of exposure to, contraction of and spreading of the disease. There has been a dramatic change in homosexual sexual practices as a result — bath houses and washrooms are now empty, whereas a few years ago, they were heavily frequented by members of the gay population seeking quick sexual fixes. Heterosexual practices are also changing rather dramatically.

As far as Dean and Lois are concerned, they have almost nothing to fear. It is true that heterosexual and female AIDS victims have increased significantly in number. As of now, if they have monogamous heterosexual relationshps with known, trustworthy individuals *and* they use a condom during sex, you can be almost totally assured that they will not get this disease. The long incubation period (years), and the fact that carriers of the virus will likely get the disease, make these last caveats mandatory.

There are, of course, no guarantees, but if Dean and Lois are careful (monogamy, *knowing* their partners, condoms, and so on), they (and you) should have no concerns. You can contact your local Board of Health, Public Health Department or General Hospital for further information.

43   **My 16-year-old daughter, Jennifer, has been living with me (her mother) for the past ten months, ever since my husband walked out on us. He left us with a huge debt; we had to sell the family home and moved into a nice apartment. Since then Jennifer has complained about monthly aches and pains, fatigue, crying spells, insomnia. She is also noticeably tense and irritable on those same days, which always seem to precede her period. Could this be PMS?**

This is actually a complicated question. PMS stands for Pre-Menstrual Syndrome, a conglomeration of varied symptoms which may affect more than half of all women during the few days prior to the start of the monthly menstrual period. The symptoms are similar to those Jennifer complains of: all the way from cramps to depression, from bloating to anger, from sweating to trepidation. Some people feel that PMS is "all in the head", that is, a disorder of someone who wants to feel vulnerable on those days. Some radical feminists see PMS as a figment of a male sexist mentality, which can then use it to explain any weaknesses of female leaders, for example. PMS is a real disorder, and further research will elucidate causes, effects, and new methods of treatment.

What makes it more complicated in Jennifer's case is that she may well be mourning the sudden loss of her father, and to a lesser extent, the come-down in lifestyle. If these are indeed symptoms of depression she is having, she should not be complaining of them on a regular, monthly basis. This can easily be monitored by her, and it will give her doctor a good way of establishing a baseline level of functioning. More likely, it is the interplay between the PMS and the depression which makes the former so excruciatingly unbearable on these few days each month.

Certainly, Jennifer should be seen by her family doctor. If PMS is the main diagnosis, there are some effective medications which can be used. Ditto for depression. The physician may ask that Jennifer receive a complete examination and evaluation. It sounds more formidable and formal than it need be. It can be informal and supportive, and young people invariably feel better after the experience.

44 **Debbie, our 13-year-old daughter, complains of stomach pains quite frequently. Her pediatrician, a wonderful man, has carefully investigated her problems, and gotten a couple of expert consultations, but they all feel that there is no basis for her complaints. Lately she has told us how tired she is, and we have noticed a dip in her school work. Could the doctors be missing something?**

Yes, and you probably know what it is. When they say that there is "no basis" for her complaints, they are, in fact, dead wrong. Debbie is unhappy about something she herself may not even be aware of, and her body is expressing in nonverbal form that unhappiness. Somatic complaints, lethargy, fatigue and diminished concentration are a common group of symptoms for some unhappy teenagers. And abdominal pains are particularly common emotional flags of which clinicians (and parents) should be aware.

I couldn't tell you why she is unhappy, but it is often related to self-acceptance and self-esteem. She is at the pubertal stage and may even be in a new school. There is considerable internal and external upheaval, and this is producing undue stress in Debbie. I would have to know about her relationships with family and friends, her personality and previous history, in order to go beyond this educated conjecture.

The first step is for you to speak to her about her life, beyond these symptoms and signs. Perhaps she'll tell you about problems of which you were totally unaware, of fears, unrequited love or loneliness, all of which can precipitate this array of unpleasant complaints. Failing this, you can ask your pediatrician to arrange an appointment with a staff member of a teen clinic or adolescent treatment center. The people there, no matter what the discipline (nursing, social work, pediatrics), are experienced, interested, and adept at getting to the core of emotional problems that masquerade as physical symptoms. That environment would be considerably less threatening than immediately referring Debbie to a psychiatrist or other mental health professional.

45   **Four months ago our 14-year-old son, Jock, was diagnosed as having Juvenile Diabetes Mellitus, for which he has to take daily insulin injections, and he was put on a fairly strict diet. For the first few weeks he was terrific, doing everything he was supposed to, and still doing well in school, seeing friends, and participating actively in sports and other activities. Then he started to**

slip, missing his insulin or forgetting to test his blood or urine glucose. More recently, he has let his diet go down the tube, loading up a number of times on foods which are strictly forbidden. Last week we had to take him to the hospital in bad shape. How can we help him cope with this life-long problem?

Jock's story is a common one. Not only diabetics who sugar-load, but hemophiliac adolescents who jump off high fences, asthmatic teenagers who smoke, or severely allergic young individuals who eat shellfish are part of the same syndrome. They are all victims of serious chronic diseases which need constant monitoring and treatment, and which significantly compromise their lifestyles. There is rotten timing of treatments, medications, tests, procedures, rules and restrictions. It is upsetting, frustrating and even infuriating; so unfair! And it is a reflection of imperfection and vulnerability.

Adolescents in general often have an "It can't happen to me" attitude. Some of them tempt and test fate by putting their innermost fears on the line (we call that counterphobic behavior) defying the admonishments of doctors, and rebelling against parental authority. And, of course, many teenagers are less cautious than their parents' generation. In Jock's case, it seems that all four rationales are operative: the frustration, the denial, the testing, and the lack of caution, not to mention Jock's personality factors and relationship with you, which give his behavior its own unique flavor and dynamics.

I am sure that the Diabetes Clinic at your local Children's Hospital (or department) has social workers and psychiatrists attached to it to deal with this very problem. I am not suggesting this because Jock is disturbed; rather, to the contrary, it is because his behavior is so typically normal for boys and girls who get hit by illness out of the blue and have to make sudden dramatic changes in their lives. He will do well once he goes through this temporary stage and learns to incorporate his illness into his life and identity. You both can and should discuss it with him, but your doctor can arrange an appointment with a trained individual at the clinic.

There are two further elements which will help him adjust to this illness. One is the knowledge that many have gone through successfully and the lessons to be learned from their coping skills and experiences. The second is the well-founded hope that a medical breakthrough, because of exciting research in this area, may soon render the constant injections obsolete.

46 **Our son, Jerry, has a recently diagnosed chronic bowel illness (Crohn's Disease), and he can't always keep up with the other kids in high school. The doctor has him under fairly good control, but he'll never be perfectly well. We are all very discouraged.**

Crohn's Disease (Regional Ileitis) is an inflammatory disease of the small bowel. It's painful, weakening and exhausting, because it continually flares up. This letter, however, could have been written by thousands of parents of young people suffering from other chronic diseases (rheumatoid arthritis, cystic fibrosis, hemophilia, retardation and muscular dystrophy are some examples) or handicapping conditions (such as cerebral palsy, severe deformities or perceptual handicaps). It is difficult not to get discouraged. I often marvel at the inner strength of many people I have met, the afflicted kids and their parents, who can be an inspiration for the rest of us. From these people I have learned that first there has to be an acceptance of the disorder and its inherent limitations. That is, after the initial shock, denial, anger, bitterness at the unfairness of it all — and it *is* unfair — followed by the sadness, born out of loss, and the realization that some desired levels of achievement will just not be accomplished, one has to come to terms with reality. Professionals such as doctors, social workers, psychiatrists, ministers, rabbis and priests can certainly be of help, but the most help comes invariably from people in the same situation. You can usually find this assistance through formal and informal self-help groups, other people who have been in the same situation. The social worker working with the doctor at the G.I. clinic can get you that help.

It's easy for me to sit on the sidelines and pontificate, but I've seen this so often. You and Jerry will learn to cope with this terrible disease, to challenge life again and win. You shall overcome! Some people find Harold Kushner's book, *When Bad Things Happen to Good People*, very helpful.

47 **We have four kids, ranging in age from 7 to 17. Norman is our youngest child and he has terminal leukemia. We've been working with his doctors and an excellent social worker, and we are prepared for the worst, as is Norman. Two of his siblings are compassionate and caring, and their sadness is not significantly interfering with their lives. But his older sister Raquel is furious with me. She feels that we have given up. She is angry at the doctors and especially at the social worker (whom she adamantly won't meet with again). We are baffled.**

Much more so than younger kids, teenagers have a realistic conception of the irrevocable nature of death. Unlike children, they do not personify it as scary, or see it as temporary, or view it as unreal. But they can certainly deny to themselves the inevitability of it when the specter of intense loss is staring them in the face. Adolescents are good at fooling themselves in a variety of ways ("It can't happen to me"). These deceptions are usually used as a temporary measure to protect themselves, and avoid facing an unpleasant reality — for a while. Because of these self-protective maneuvers, teenagers often handle their responses to the dying and death of loved ones in an unpredictable manner. I have often been asked about teens being too withdrawn, too sad, not sad enough, not caring, and so on, by confused and suffering parents.

Raquel is wrestling with the impending death of Norman in her own way. She is fighting against an impending, extremely painful experience (which I assume is unequivocal at this point). Her intense anger is born out of a sense of frustration and powerlessness. Whom is she to inveigh against? God? She is angry at you, her parents, for "allowing this to happen". It is obviously a sentiment of a much younger child, but as a mid-teenager, she is expected to regress to childish behavior at times, especially when in severe crisis, which this obviously is. As hurtful as her rage must be to you (coping with your own burden of sorrow), it is a temporary phenomenon. Perhaps Raquel could have a chat with the hematologist primarily responsible for Norman's care. He could provide her with the medical information necessary for her to understand the tragic, inevitably painful loss of her brother. You might also tell her that you understand her sadness, her intense anger; that you are angry, too, at the injustice of it all. You will find that her rage will dissipate as Norman's deterioration becomes apparent and when she has the facts to make some sense out of it all. Perhaps a counsellor could be arranged just for her so that Raquel won't have to share "yours".

Sex and Love

Is it true that love makes the world go round? Well, it certainly makes teenagers' heads spin and hearts skip a beat; it can wreak havoc with their common sense; and it certainly activates their hormones — not to mention their genitals. All this commotion occurs with the vicarious participation of parents, who may find their own memories rekindled, often to their concern and consternation.

Is there a dramatic sexual liberalism now? Is sex rampaging, ravaging, and rapacious? *Playboy* and the magazines like it were talking about a sexual revolution *many* years before there was even a hint of a change in the statistics. Was it a case of the tail wagging the dog? Do expectations in society and in the home of early sexual behavior determine the actual enactment of that behavior, as in a self-fulfilling prophecy? I happen to think so.

Of course, other things were happening in the late sixties and seventies that affected the sexual behavior of teenagers. There was a general movement towards freer expression of all kinds of feelings, sexual included. There were increasingly explicit depictions of sexuality in a variety of art forms (films, for example). The Women's Movement had the paradoxical effect of both liberating the female sex drive and needs, and also freeing up the procrustean attitudes of many men. Suddenly, sex was "in".

Sexual behavior has changed over the past generation. Both girls and boys engage in sexual activity at an earlier age and more frequently than in previous generations. Yet many of the old attitudes and beliefs remain constant. The adage that "girls use sex to get love, and boys use love to get sex" is still valid for sexually active younger teenagers. There are, however, many teenagers who are *not* sexually active. There is a large and growing number of young people who remain virgins and want to be that way until they are married, or they meet a special individual. But the pressure to participate, perform and produce olympian levels of pleasure remains a destructive undercurrent in certain media publications, and has been adopted by certain subgroups in the population.

Society's preoccupation with sexual matters, added to the adolescent's natural fascination with his or her new sexuality, makes for a potent mix. And problems do abound, including teenage pregnancy, sexually-transmitted disease (the most lethal of which is AIDS) and other byproducts of careless or destructive sexual behavior. But it is unfair to tar every youth with the same brush. Unfortunately, as with many other problem behaviors, the causes are phenomenally complex, and they seem to reside disproportionally in specific at-risk groups. Glib solutions, as in "Man the barricades!", reactionary attitudes and restraining legislation just don't work. Even sex education or family life education courses (the polite and more accurate euphemism) have varying degrees of success. These courses (which do discuss "plumbing" as well as relationships, values, responsibilities and feelings) produce a major change in knowledge; the students know a lot more about these issues after the course is over. They also tend to be more tolerant of others' sexual behaviors, more accepting of their variations and predilections. But in the area of *personal* behavior, there is almost no change whatsoever. Those teenagers who are into a sexually self-destructive mode, for whatever reasons, will continue on their unfortunate paths. They will only be derailed if a number of simultaneous needs are fulfilled: birth control availability, access to medical attention, supportive peers and communication with interested parents. Attention to all of these areas is necessary in developing a positive and healthy approach to sexuality.

The last item, parental involvement, cannot be stressed too much. Because of the sensitive nature of the topic and the current public preoccupation with it, many parents have absolved themselves of the responsibility of talking to their teenagers about sex. They let the school, magazines, or friends do it. Unfortunately, it doesn't always work. Sex and love are closely tied to values, feelings, and relationships, and the most effective place to get grounding in these vital aspects of life is in the family.

We lose sight of the fact that our young people *need* to talk to adults in order to learn about themselves, their potential, their limitations, their possibilities. If love is not reciprocated, if there is pain in a relationship, if sex is a problem, who better than mother or father to discuss it with?

What about the adolescents themselves? Accountability and responsibility have to be learned during the childhood and teenage years. Even if the support systems are all in place, we still can and do see young people getting into trouble sexually because of their own troubled psyches. Yet this group is a small minority, and even these individuals can be helped. Rather than simply leaving sexuality to our youth, we should be educating, communicating — and enjoying doing so.

48   **We are a group of very concerned parents of young teenage children who attend the local junior high school. Last year the school board introduced sex education classes for that school, disguised by the title "Family Life Education." Our society has enough problems with promiscuity, homosexuality, AIDS and teenage pregnancy without these things being encouraged in the schools. Don't you agree?**

Wow! You are concluding that sex education leads to the various "vices" you cite, and you lump some wildly different things together. There is no evidence that sex education leads to any of these phenomena. Rather, there is data to show that good Family Life Education courses certainly increase participants' knowledge about sexuality, romance and relationships, and also increase their level of tolerance of other people's behavior. The issue of changes in actual sexual activity is more complex. But it is clear that sex education courses, combined with open and early discussion of sexuality in the home, actually reduce the incidence of early sexual behavior and teenage pregnancy. They *do not* lead to promiscuity, homosexuality, AIDS or any other issues you might label terrible or immoral. By the way, if you are still wondering, I do not agree with you.

49   **While cleaning my son's room, I found a whole bunch of filthy girlie magazines, such as *Playboy* and *Penthouse*. They weren't hidden, just stacked on the floor of his closet. They are vile and obscene, and I am shocked that Grant would bring pornography into our house.**

What I have to say is not going to please you. I frankly find magazines such as the two you mention (and others of their ilk) to be, Hefner and Guccione forgive me, *boring*. There is no good evidence that the seductive and salacious poses of the young women in these glossy sheets do more than titillate some men. Reading such magazines does not cause them to become molesters or pedophiles, nor will it make them promiscuous or passionate. If you are concerned because it is demeaning to women, well, I won't disagree with you, although these nymphets have all chosen to pose (we have learned that some regret it in later years). "Worse" magazines do exist, which show actual scenes of brutality. While I am appalled by such material, censorship is anathema to me, and is ultimately more detrimental to society. Where does one draw the line? The Supreme Courts, working with proposed legislation in both Canada and the U.S.A., have been wrestling with this dilemma recently, and a few words here obviously cannot do this complex subject justice.

Yet somehow your concern about Grant does not seem to reflect a fear that the magazines are corrupting him, or even disapproval of the way the women are portrayed. Rather, I sense a kind of moralistic condemnation of open sexuality. This is, of course, entirely an individual matter. You are certainly entitled to set the values and moral code for your family and home. Mine tend to be more liberal, but that doesn't make them right.

Just be sure when you are castigating Grant that you aren't giving him the impression that sex and eroticism are dirty. Hopefully, he is not so preoccupied with the magazines that he does not read anything else or engage in other pursuits.

It's not smut; it's merely inconsequential garbage. He'll tire of this stuff soon enough. If he is obsessed with this material, as with most obsessions, the problem lies with the "obsessor". He would indeed need help, but not because of the nature of the material.

50 **I know that the common attitude that masturbation is bad for someone is nothing more than folktale, but we are concerned that Nick, our 17-year-old son, is overdoing it. He must retreat suddenly to his bedroom or the bathroom five or six times a day, for a few minutes each time. A couple of times, with the door ajar, I've seen him do it, but I've said nothing. I can't believe that it's**

not doing him any harm. We don't really have any other major concerns about him.

Well, at least we can agree that it is a myth that masturbation causes mental weakness, warts, pimples, poor eyesight or palmar hair. You are asking if a frequency of more than half a dozen times a day is intrinsically harmful. My answer is still, "absolutely not!" There is just no evidence to show that increasing the number of times will hurt the individual.

Now there are infrequent exceptions. A guy can masturbate often enough to cause redness and abrasions on the stalk of the penis. Likewise, a girl can do the same, or introduce objects into the vagina or near the clitoris that cause occasional problems. But in general, there is nothing to worry about. And the positive aspect of these mechanical injuries is that they slow down the frenetic activity. Masturbatory activity is so intense at this age because it is novel, it releases pent-up sexual energy, it temporarily reduces stress, and it is immensely pleasurable.

The operative word in your concern is "overdoing", or reaching a frequency that you feel is excessive. The truth is that anything can be done to excess, as in too much of a good thing. For example, an obsessively disturbed individual who masturbates continually, almost ritualistically, is obviously in trouble, but this description doesn't sound at all like Nick. Furthermore, somebody with such a problem would usually show other signs in his personality and actions of obsessive-compulsive behavior. Even in this hypothetical (but real) instance, however, the problem is not masturbation itself; rather, it is an ingrained personality disorder which uses masturbation to express itself. We have seen this behavior also — but unusually — in various forms of psychoses such as schizophrenia.

Lastly, the frequency of almost any human behavior varies enormously. We are all quite different in our biological rhythms and drives. Some people masturbate once a week, others once a day, and some even once an hour. It is harmless, save for the exceptions I mention, and in all instances the activity will "peter out" (forgive the pun) as the young people mature, and find fellow human beings to experiment with and to love.

51 **We are deeply religious Jewish people. We have a 15-year-old son, Mordecai, whom we have reason to believe is masturbating. Aside from health problems, which we are convinced are nonexistent, we do have strong moral and religious feelings against this practice. How do we broach the subject?**

Your letter could have been written by many religious Christians as well. Frankly, your question would be better directed to an orthodox rabbi. That is, it is not as much psychiatric and psychological in nature as it is philosophical and spiritual. You are not concerned about Mordecai's health, but you feel that his "spilling the seed" is immoral or sinful.

After reading the previous letter, you surely know where I stand. I don't consider this activity in the same negative light as you do. This issue obviously comes up on many occasions when I work with people of very different backgrounds and beliefs. I lay out for them what is considered to be developmentally normal or abnormal, what is acceptable or not, and what is of concern or not. The rest is up to the parents, who are masters of their own domain; far be it from me to attempt to impose my biases and lifestyle on others.

I *do* have concerns about equating masturbation with sin. But if you speak to Mordecai gently, in a non-confrontational, non-demeaning manner, and if the message is *not* that sex is intrinsically dirty or bad, Mordecai can be informed of your deep-seated beliefs (which I am sure he already knows in detail). In my own experience, the masturbation of kids such as your son (as with most others) tends to dissipate over months and years. But when confronted, the individual usually feels tremendous guilt, and often goes underground for a while, making sure that the masturbation is done privately, and with no tell-tale evidence left behind (stains, wetness, paper, and so forth). Others, of course, give it up, if their own beliefs supersede their urges.

52   I think that Women's Lib has gone too far. In the middle of a family conversation about sex, our 16-year-old daughter, Liza, told us loud and clear that she masturbates. I was shocked! I know that boys do it, but girls?! I certainly never did it, and I've had a good sex life with my husband.

Just because you never masturbated does not make your daughter's behavior wrong, (nor does it mean that she is right and you are wrong). I *do* feel that the consciousness raising of the Women's Movement has made women more aware of their bodies and needs, and legitimized or gave them permission to explore, experiment, and excite themselves in ways that they just wouldn't have a couple of decades or so ago. Girls still don't masturbate quite as commonly as boys, but it is an extremely common experience. And, as with boys, the variance in frequency is enormous (see Question 50). I like the idea that you are able to have open discussions in your family regarding sex, but I would hope that your response would be an enlightened one, rather than an uninformed and "shocked" one. I'm glad that you enjoy a good sex life. It (and her own healthy attitude) augur well for Liza's sex life.

53   I am a single mother with a 13-year-old son, Jeremy. His father disappeared years ago. Do I have to find a male "partner" to prevent my son from going gay?

Don't believe experts who tell you they know what "causes" homosexuality. They don't know, and neither does anybody else. There is absolutely no evidence to suggest that homosexuality stems from the lack of a father's presence; or from the influence of an over-bearing mother, passive father, or brutal father...the list goes on. If we were to accept that premise, given the number of single mothers today, gay youth would number over 40 percent of the population.

If you are in love, and you and your partner decide to live together, that's great. But don't live with a man for the sake of Jeremy's sexuality.

54 **I am in a real quandary. My son Phil is 19, a wonderful boy. But we (his father and I) think that he has homosexual tendencies, and we are terrified. He does not date girls, but is always with some male friends. Lately, he has become secretive about his whereabouts at night, and last week we found magazines in his room clearly catering to a gay audience.**

I obviously can't tell if your son is gay or not on the basis of what you've written. To make that kind of judgment would take a discussion with him regarding his experiences, fantasies (masturbatory and otherwise), dreams, attractions, and desires. Just the facts that he hasn't dated, has many male friends, and has those magazines do not add up to enough information to make that determination.

Phil's secretiveness may be as much a reflection of your increasing curiosity and even intrusiveness, as it is of his potential homosexuality. Even if he is gay, I'm not sure that there is anything you can do. When (and if) he is ready, he will tell you, and this revelation will depend upon his trust in you, his need to share, his degree of pain at keeping his orientation a big, dark secret, and his concern about hurting you. The fact that you are already "terrified" makes the latter a real possibility. (I'm sure that he knows where you stand).

I can understand your concern, if not your terror. Certainly, homosexuals have a rough road to travel because of society's ill-founded moral strictures, but many have led remarkably satisfying and successful lives. How he lives will be his business, but help, rather than panic from his parents, will make his, and your, lives a little easier. The fact that you describe him as "wonderful" tells me that he is a lot less concerned (at least outwardly) than his parents. While it may be premature, or even unnecessary, you would do well to read the late Laura Hobson's book, *Consenting Adult,* a novel about a mother's relationship with her homosexual son.

55   **We have an 18-(almost 19) year-old son, Steve, who is a freshman at college. He is a delight to us, but I am concerned about him. He has never gone out on a date. He is very attractive (everybody says so), does well at school, and has many friends of both sexes. Yet he doesn't go out with girls. He's probably still a virgin. I'm wondering if he's a homosexual.**

I can't tell you if Steve is gay or not, but there are no hints, at least in your letter, of homosexual tendencies. That is, he may be gay, but there is every reason to conclude that he is a healthy young man with a heterosexual orientation. Even if he hasn't yet had sexual intercourse, or even dated — so what? He is soon to be 19, and I can tell you that he is in good company. Statistics have shown that more boys and girls are engaging in sexual intercourse earlier, with more partners, and more frequently. But this does not account for an enormous number of adolescents who are not sexually active at an early age. There are many young people of both sexes who don't begin dating, romancing and exploring their sexuality until their late teens or early twenties. We seem to want to believe that all teenagers are all sexually active.

And what is the rush? We all agree that sex is wonderful, but people can and should be initiated into that activity when they are ready emotionally and intellectually as well as physically, and when the right factors — the partner, the mood, the opportunity, the location — are in place. Moving from the sublime to the ridiculous, drinking and driving are two other activities which we have rushed kids into, with dire consequences for many. You have a son who is a delight to you in all respects. Do yourself a favor. Leave him — and yourself — alone, and enjoy him as a person. His time will come.

56 **I was surprised and annoyed to overhear Darin, our 19-year-old son, regaling his friends with stories of his sexual conquests. He prided himself on never using a condom, and on his luck in never getting any of his "girls" (as he called them) pregnant. How do I broach the subject with him? I wasn't eavesdropping or snooping; their talk was rather raucous.**

Darin obviously is building up a "scorecard" in an immature and outlandishly macho manner. He not only sees his sexual relationships as notches in his belt, but he is sexist and irresponsible to boot. In this era of herpes, AIDS and other sexually transmitted diseases, his outdated, narcissistic approach to sex is potentially destructive to himself and his lover; it could even be lethal!

Condoms are readily available, inexpensive and safe. They are strong, lubricated and thin. They do not, at least physically, detract from the enjoyment of sexual intercourse. They actually reflect more caring and sensitivity on the male's part. They can and should be a fact of sexual life, especially if there is some degree of promiscuity, or indiscriminate copulation.

Perhaps Darin was merely showing off (in an offensive manner); it could be that he was not exactly being truthful, but was trying to score some points with the other neanderthals. I certainly think that you, as his mother, could easily broach the subject with him by saying something along the lines of "I couldn't help overhearing…". You could show him your letter and this answer. Darin certainly needs some confrontation and education.

57 **My daughter Linda is 17, and has a boyfriend who is a very nice guy; but she wants to go on the Pill. What should I do?**

By her request, Linda is telling you that she wants to have safe, sexual relations with her boyfriend, that she respects your relationship with her to the extent that she can be open and honest with you and that she wants to discuss the issue with you.

Linda can take the Pill without your approval or co-operation, but clearly she'd rather not. The fact that she told you is what's important; would you rather that she hadn't? It may well be that she is ambivalent, torn between her romantic involvement and carnal desires on the one hand, and her young years, values, inexperience, uncertainty about her commitment to her boyfriend and vice versa, on the other. It's your role as a mother to listen to her, to reflect to her what you hear her saying, and to give her the benefit of your love, concern, knowledge and wisdom — even if you disagree with her ideas. There's no guarantee that she'll make the decision that's right for her, but the odds that she will are much better with your helpful involvement, than without it.

No matter what you tell Linda, at least encourage her to speak to an approachable and knowledgeable doctor, who will discuss with her the potential short-and-long-term side effects before prescribing the Pill.

58 **My 18-year-old daughter, Victoria, unnerved me by asking my advice on birth control. She is adamant about not going on the Pill. I'd like to give her guidance, but I am worried about condoning and even encouraging her sexual behavior. What other birth control means are there? (I've only used the rhythm method).**

You would do well to appreciate her openness and honesty, and her trust in you. By giving her advice, you are facing a fact of both your lives. You can question her about her lover(s), her values and her relationships; but you don't own her body. She will appreciate your caring, even if you disagree with her practices.

As far as the technical suggestions are concerned, I can give you some basic information, but she should speak to a good family practitioner for a comprehensive discussion of pros and cons, effectiveness, side effects and her personal needs.

IUD stands for Intra Uterine Device. It is a small plastic object placed by the doctor into the cervix, which effectively prevents implantation of the egg. It may cause pain and bleeding, can contribute to infertility, and is not 100 percent effective (95 percent or more). Usually it is used after a woman has had a pregnancy.

There are also contraceptive foams, creams or jellies, which are put into the vagina before intercourse as a means of killing the sperms. These creams have a high failure rate, often because they are introduced much too early, or too late.

A diaphragm is a cup-shaped rubber cap that fits over the cervix, effectively blocking the sperm's route. It is often combined with the afore-mentioned creams to increase the "foolproof" nature of the barrier. It has to be fitted by a doctor, and there are fairly definite rules regarding time of application and removal.

There are other means, including the most ineffective of all, the one you have used, the rhythm method (having sex only during the non-fertile time of month), and, of course, condoms (see Question 56). These are effective, but require the co-operation of Victoria's lover. All the methods can be poorly effective when practiced poorly. Therefore, Victoria obviously has to be properly instructed (by the doctor). Her motivation and interest are clearly high, so that it should not be a problem.

59 **I have an 18-year-old son, Tony, (from my first marriage) and two daughters, aged 8 and 10. Tony is a good kid, although he and my new husband often don't see eye-to-eye. For the last few weeks, he has been taking a girlfriend (she is 16) up to his room, closing the door for a couple of hours and then taking her home. We are appalled.**

It sounds to me that in addition to being appalled, you are also paralyzed! Why do you let him do this? Do the girl's parents know? Is this what you want for your daughters? Or your son, for that matter?

Tony may be angry at you and his stepfather for real or imagined misdeeds; he may still be blaming you for the loss of his "real" father. He may be challenging you; he may be testing his sense of young adulthood and machismo and independence. But you owe it to yourself *and to him* to confront Tony and get him to stop this rather outrageous behavior. You can discuss, cajole and reason until you are blue in the face, but when all is said and done, this issue is non-negotiable, isn't it? There's nothing wrong with that. Limit-setting, demands, responsibilities and accountability are all parts of life and growing up. You impose these constraints because you love him, not because you don't.

60 **Our daughter, Corinne, is almost 12 years old and I'd swear that she is already a teenager. I tell my friends that she is 12 going on 17. She is past puberty, well-developed (very well), wears make-up, dates boys of 16 or 17 years of age and has older friends. She says she is bored with her own classmates. I'm afraid that she's going to get into trouble.**

Your letter will ring a bell with many other parents whose preteens are already acting years older than they are "supposed to". There are many reasons for this behavior. First of all, there is a pressure to grow up exerted by society, the media, the peer group, and even parents. We too often don't allow kids to enjoy their childhoods, but rush them along on an accelerated course into adolescence before they're ready. This is manifestly unfair to these youngsters, but it also puts them at risk, because they are not ready to withstand the pressures of that age group. There is another possible reason that Corinne is "12 going on 17". The variability in the rate of development and maturation of children and adolescents is phenomenally wide. Some 12-year-old females are little girls, and others look like grown women (ditto for males). Unfortunately, there is no correlation between intellectual and emotional maturation, and physical development. Lastly, Corinne may be acting in an older fashion as a statement of independence from you, her parents, even as an act of rebellion.

Whatever the cause of this seemingly precocious behavior, you are wondering if Corinne has a problem, or if it will evolve into more serious behavior. I'm sure that the specters of drugs and sex are of immediate concern to you. You can try talking with her, and sharing your concerns, but I'm not sure she'll understand your message (what exactly *is* your message?). Is she overly seductive? Does she give evidence of indulging in risqué or even self-destructive behavior? The major consideration in determining whether a problem exists would be how Corinne is doing in other respects: school performance, relationship with family and new friends, self-esteem and general mood. If all this is positively oriented, then I would suggest that there is little to worry about. If, on the other hand, Corinne's "cover" behavior is generally indicative of deterioration in other respects, then she may be on a collision course with impending difficulties. If the latter situation pertains, it might be useful to have Corinne evaluated at an adolescent clinic by a trained team of counsellors who work with this age group.

61 Our 17-year-old daughter, Caroline, is only moderately pleasant to live with when she has a boyfriend. Although she is young, this has been going on for years. With a "steady" in tow, she is happy as a clam; as soon as there are rumblings of conflict, or worse, when they split (invariably), Caroline becomes irritable, miserable and morose. Even for those infrequent periods when she is not involved with a guy, she spends her time longing, pining, searching and dreaming about the knight on a white charger. She performs adequately at school, has some friends, and a few interests (she plays piano, loves skating), but everything pales in comparison when a boyfriend materializes.

I'm not sure that even when Caroline has a boyfriend that she is such a pleasure to live with. "Moderately pleasant" doesn't sound like any great shakes, and from what you say, even those periods are few and far between. I probably don't have to tell you that most adolescents are very sensitive to romance, and especially the lack thereof. Some are more upset by "soap opera" relationships, and the trials and tribulations of starcrossed young lovers, or of unrequited lovers, have kept many a teenager (and their parents!) awake for hours at night. But when a teenager becomes totally preoccupied to the extent that Caroline has, I begin thinking of other issues which may be covered over or hidden by the romantic obsessions. It may be that she is overwhelmed by the presence or absence of a boyfriend because she measures her self-esteem entirely by the extent to which she feels loved or admired by a guy. We all need positive feedback in order for us to feel worthwhile and enhanced. The amount varies from person to person, from those who are more self-assured all the way to those who need almost perpetual adulation to convince them of their worth. Feminist behavioral scientists and clinicians have been saying for years that too many women assess their self-image in terms of the love of an important male, beginning with "daddy". Whether or not this tendency is universal, is debatable, but it is clear that for some girls at least, it is indeed true.

It may also be that Caroline has some other emotional problems, which she is not dealing with because she keeps herself and her family in a state of perpetual crisis over boys. These need not be serious problems; they are just not being dealt with. For example, Caroline's way of coping with a mild depression might be to invest her energies into the problems surrounding a relationship with boys. In a way, the constant uproar staves off the pain of her inner sadness. This is just one of a number of similar possibilities. It may be *because* of her problems that she has difficulty with boys. I don't want you to get the impression that this is inherently ominous. Caroline is not failing in school, she has friends and outside interests; all this is strongly in her favor.

I'm sure that referring Caroline to a psychiatrist would meet with strong antagonism from her ("What for, because I can't keep a boyfriend?"). Two possibilities of intervention spring to mind (I assume that you've spoken to her about your concerns, to no avail). One is to ask if she'd like to talk to someone about her apparent unhappiness. A counsellor or other staff member of an adolescent clinic would be less threatening, and potentially very useful. Another strategy would be to deal with it as a family problem. You can get a referral to a family therapist from your doctor, or you can see a counsellor at a branch of the Family Service Agency.

62 **My 16-year-old daughter, Susan, is 6 weeks pregnant and refuses to have an abortion. Her boyfriend (backed by his family) is adamant that she should have an abortion immediately and is no longer speaking to her. She is still in high school and all we can foresee is disaster.**

I've been through this dilemma many times with young women and their families. Essentially, a pregnant teenager has three choices:

1) she can have a therapeutic abortion;
2) she can give up the baby for adoption;
3) she can keep the baby.

Each option solves some problems, and almost inevitably causes others. There are no absolute rights and wrongs in this complex area, and there are usually painful feelings associated with any of the decisions. It boils down to a highly personal and unique set of circumstances and factors. The ultimate choice in some ways ends up being the least detrimental alternative.

In arriving at her decision, your daughter — and you — would invariably take into consideration her age and maturity; other aspects of her personality (judgment, responsibility, reliability, self-esteem, warmth, relationships, and so on); her (and your) value system, including morality and religious beliefs; her relationship to the baby's father; her future schooling and career plans; financial issues; social supports. Every one of these factors will play a role in your daughter's decision.

Certainly, you will have input and influence, but the final decision will be up to Susan. I would be dishonest if I said that it's her life and it won't affect you, because as caring parents, you are drawn into any difficulties she may experience, regardless of her choice. These unfortunate experiences are now so common that a bright side has actually evolved. School, social and medical services are usually available to support pregnant teenagers before and after their difficult decisions. These services can help minimize the pain and hardships, and also offer assistance in making the selected choice much more viable.

I don't know what Susan's final choice will be; I have seen considerable mind-changing and vacillation even after a decision is supposedly reached. It's important that your daughter should have the benefit of discussing her situation with counsellors and others who have worked with young women in similar straits, and who don't have an axe to grind one way or the other. Hospital departments of Obstetrics, teen clinics, Family Service Agencies, the Children's Aid Society, Public Health Nurses, and similar services can all supply such help. I won't pretend that the ensuing months (and years) will be easy; there will be relief, recriminations and regret no matter which way she goes. But if she has information, support and understanding, your daughter's pregnancy need not be a disaster.

63   **We just discovered that Leanne, our 19-year-old daughter, had an abortion last year (her sister spilled the beans), and we are hurt that she didn't share her pain with us. We are also furious that all our moral teachings went out the window. What do you suggest we do?**

Well, the reason you are hurt is exactly because Leanne correctly surmised your reaction: she feared your "fury". I would be hurt, too, if my daughter couldn't confide in me when she was going through a hard time. I'd certainly feel sorry for myself (as you do), but I'd be more concerned about her having to go through an inevitably difficult experience — and it always is — all on her own. If she was lucky, her sister and perhaps her lover helped her through it, although I know of countless examples of the guy suddenly disappearing before that traumatic experience.

Therapeutic abortions, as you know, are extremely common in our society, as in many others. Despite some very strict moral and religious prohibitions, this medical procedure is widely used by women of all ages in order to terminate an unwanted pregnancy for many different reasons. It is also a highly emotional issue, with extraordinarily strong feelings on both extreme sides, all the way from the very liberal group to the ultra-conservative group.

My own opinion happens to be more along the continuum towards the former than the latter, but I am certainly not an advocate of abortion-on-demand. Discussion, information, counselling, presentation of alternatives, social supports, and so forth, are all necessary before a young woman can make a crucial decision that she has to live with for the rest of her life. What Leanne needs — even now — is your understanding and empathy; not your anger. Finally, I hope that her sister told you in order to help bridge the obvious gap between you and Leanne, and not for some other, more selfish purpose.

64

Henry, 19, is a freshman in university. We just received word that his girlfriend of four months (Alice) is pregnant and fully intends to keep the baby. Not only that, she is expecting full co-operation, both emotional and financial, from Henry. He came to us in a panic, not wanting to give her either at this point (he insisted on an abortion, and she refused). She even threatened legal action against him. What should we advise?

Isn't it amazing that love and pregnancy, some of those inexplicably wonderful things about life, can be made into horrible experiences. Henry's girlfriend (ex-girlfriend, I expect, by this time) has made a unilateral decision for her own personal reasons. I assume that she is about Henry's age; and I'll give her the benefit of the doubt that she is mature and stable, and recognizes the problems inherent in being a single mother.

Henry, however, is in a quandary. Having been through this with teens in other, similar situations, I still have no preconceived notion of how it will go. Sometimes the girl decides to give up the baby; at other times, she goes it alone, demanding little or nothing from the father; but at times, there have been lawsuits directed at the biological father in order to extract some financial support. And of course, there are times that the pregnancy encourages an early marriage.

Most often under these circumstances, there is a sudden demise of the love relationship between the two, and that appears to be the case here. If Henry is adamant that he is not in love with the girl, and has no interest in being a father at this stage in his life, he has to make that loud and clear immediately. He also has to get legal advice, because this is a complex issue involving ethics and legalities and the latter vary from jurisdiction to jurisdiction. Your role is to support him in this stressful and confusing time. Much of this has to do, of course, with Henry's feelings. This is his biological child, and he may begin to feel a paternal responsibility, and even love towards the child, even if he continues to resent Alice. Of course, if Alice's parents were writing, my answer would be somewhat different (see the following letter).

65 **Our daughter Alice is an 18-year-old college student and is now also in her fifth month of pregnancy. She wants to keep and raise the baby, but is insisting that her ex-boyfriend Henry, the father of the child, provide emotional and financial support. He is furious with her, having urged her to undergo a therapeutic abortion (when it was possible). We can understand both their viewpoints, but of course we side with our daughter, who has threatened to sue Henry. What should we advise?**

Alice is embarking on a rough road. Single motherhood, especially in the teenage years, is difficult, and puts at risk both the mother and child, (in this case, both very young). I worry about Alice's schooling, her self-image, her fulfillment. But Alice is adamant, and has already passed the point of no return as far as the pregnancy is concerned. She may ultimately decide to give up the baby at birth, but I strongly doubt that this will transpire; there is no ambivalence in her stance at all.

There is no doubt that pregnant teenagers need excellent prenatal care and social supports. Both of these can be arranged with your help, and that of Alice's friends. But what you can extract out of Henry is a different story. Abandoned pregnant teenagers are not an uncommon occurrence. Too often we hear of young women who have gotten pregnant after an amorous relationship, only to have the guy either deny responsibility or disappear completely.

Alice most likely will have the sympathy of the court, if she pursues the litigation route, that is, she can probably force Henry — or more likely his family, at this stage — to contribute money to the support of the child. I would urge her to go for some counselling immediately. She has some important issues to ponder and needs information about support services, alternative plans, daycare, nannies, child care and so on. She also has to clarify her feelings toward herself, you, Henry and the baby. She has to be educated as to what having an infant is all about.

I don't want to pussyfoot. Almost invariably, a major part of the load will fall on your shoulders. Alice will want solace, support, advice, babysitting services and money. While you and we (society) have to do as much as in our power to help both of these children, showing compassion and support, and preventing deprivation and presenting opportunities, I can't help feeling somewhat resentful that the taxpayer has been "forced" into this situation. (I'm glad I got that off my chest.) I wish Alice all good fortune.

66 **Our son Ted has been dating the same girl, Judy, for two years. He declares that he is madly in love with her, and there is no one else for him,**

and that they will be married and live happily ever after. So what's the problem, you are asking? The problem is that Ted and his girlfriend are both 16 years old! Neither of them has ever dated another person (they don't want to), and he bristles at our suggestion that he date other girls. What should we do?

I have no magic answer to give you. You have, I am sure, conveyed to Ted that you feel that he is too young to make a major romantic commitment, that it is as unfair to Judy as it is to him and that he should experience other relationships even if he does end up with his present girlfriend. I am also sure that as thoughtful, caring parents, you have not berated him as much as you've wanted to, and that those times when you have expressed your concerns to Ted, as few as they've been, have been far too many for Ted. Forbidding him from seeing her is a possibility, but I have found that it seldom works, and often backfires. You could also threaten, make compromise deals, or offer incentives. All of these strategies and more have been tried — usually, but not always — to no avail.

My own experience tells me that in his present state of romantic ardor, you will not be able to reason with Ted, no matter how reasonable your arguments. He hears you; he knows your concerns; he just happens to think that you're dead wrong! When I've been involved in situations like this, I have found that time and fate are amazing healers. In the vast majority of cases, one or the other (or both) of the lovers begin to cool, or at least to look anew at the implications of the commitment. As they mature, the long-term implications suddenly hit them square on. Discomfort, anxiety and fear begin to mix with the passion. When this happens, there is an inexorable move toward separation, even if it is temporary. This will most likely happen with Ted and Judy.

If not, well, maybe they are meant for each other.

67   **Believe it or not, I think that our 17-year-old son, Frank, is having an affair with our next-door neighbor. Dorothy is 45, married, a mother of**

three and a good friend of mine! For the last three months he has been over there almost daily after school for an hour or two. He comes in quietly and sheepishly and doesn't talk about what he does there. When I ask him, he says that he likes talking to Dorothy. When they are here together, their eyes lock often.

Are you worried about Frank's health, psychological state, or his sense of morality? Or are you concerned about Dorothy's marriage? Are you angry that she is deceiving you, and leading Frank astray? You probably feel a little bit of all these emotions, right? You do sound most exercised about the deceptive quality to this relationship.

You realize, of course, that there is a humorous aspect to their affair. It is not the first time that I have heard stories like this, and they always bring smiles to the faces of listeners, professional or otherwise. Part of it has to do with the actual enactment of the common fantasies of adolescent boys to be led into the ways of lovemaking by older, experienced women. Many of your son's friends are probably jealous (if they know). I really don't see this relationship as lasting much longer; there are too many factors against its' continuing — not the least of which is Dorothy's marriage, and your friendship with her. Dorothy will have to consider whether it is indicative of a faltering marriage or of her own personal unhappiness. Or it may mean nothing. You can expedite the end of the affair, of course, by being confrontative, or even subtly telling Frank or Dorothy that you are on to them. But I'm not sure that you will get satisfaction from the telling and ending.

Why not wait a while longer until the excitement of their fresh sexual relationship wears off? You might even be able to look back at it and laugh eventually, with both of them. Furthermore, what are the possible consequences if you're wrong?

68 **Our 16-year-old daughter, Betsy, who is very sweet, is the object of the torrid passions of a 19-year-old guy, who is somewhat of a creep.**

They dated once about six months ago and she didn't like him at all, but he fell head-over-heels in love with her. Since then he has sent cards, poems, gifts and flowers. He phones her incessantly even though she won't speak to him anymore. Lately his infatuation has taken a new turn. He seems to be everywhere! He follows her on dates, visits her school and sometimes paces or parks his car outside our house. She is now getting a little scared, and we are angry. Should we intervene?

Betsy is being harassed, plain and simple, and there are laws against it. What started out as a romantic campaign to win her affections has ended up as an intrusive and frightening experience. And frankly, I don't know whether there is any legitimacy to her fears or not. There are plenty of crazies out there, and who knows what kind of distorted perceptions and thoughts are going through this young man's mind? I don't know where this obsession is leading, or if he is ultimately dangerous, but I don't believe in taking chances.

It is no longer a benign (but always painful) example of unrequited love, if it ever was. This fellow was on a date with Betsy on only one occasion, and on the basis of that less-than-satisfactory experience, he has turned it into a magnificent (for him) obsession. He is now obviously wholly preoccupied with her, although it is clear that it is more a product of his convoluted and, yes, disturbed mind than of reality. Whether or not this guy fits a psychiatric diagnosis, I can't say at this juncture, but it is clear that you are no longer dealing with a lover (if he ever was one). He is verging on the delusional, and he certainly has an obsessional disorder.

Finally and most importantly, you *must* intervene. Betsy can't get rid of this guy on her own. A clear, cold, unequivocal message from Betsy must be delivered to him (registered mail). It should say that if he bothers her again, legal means and/or police will be utilized to make him cease and desist. If he calls again, you tell him in no uncertain terms that *you* will *never* allow him to speak to her. Tell him that if he parks outside your home, that *you* will have him arrested by the police. All gifts or offerings sent are to be returned. Most important is that he should know that no longer will he be allowed to continue any sort of involvement with Betsy, and that the police are now on record as knowing that she has been harassed by him.

69 **Our 17-year-old son, Max, was arrested last week. It seems that he exposed himself in a park to three young girls who were playing there. One of the mothers of the kids saw him and called the police. There is a court date coming up in eight weeks, and we are terrified. It's not as if he's done anything else like this before, and he swears that he won't do it again. How do we convince the judge to let him off?**

I have no doubt that your son feels remorseful, and for sure he regrets that he got caught! The role of the judge is to interpret the law, treat the charged one fairly, with compassion as well as justice, and to protect society. If "letting him off" will accomplish those goals, then the judge will not make any further demands on Max.

Now put yourself in the role of one of the mothers of these girls. What would you want then? Wouldn't you possibly talk about the potential harm to your daughter, or other girls, or the progression of your son's behavior from exposing himself to child molestation (pedophilia)? If not, you are one of the few exceptions, because I have heard these very sentiments expressed many times, even by liberal, compassionate parents.

The judge will probably insist that your son undergo a psychological and psychiatric evaluation, and will likely reserve judgment (sentence) until he receives a copy of the full report from the professional(s). If Max were my son, I would not wait the eight weeks until the court appearance. Why not contact a good adolescent psychiatrist right away? You (and Max) will find it to be a fruitful experience. Max will explore all aspects of his life, not just the sexual — his moods, his relationships, his self-image — because these may well be related to the experience of exhibitionism (even if it is a single, isolated, never-to-be-repeated event). This action will certainly strengthen Max's case with the courts, and it may also reassure you, and Max himself.

70   My 18-year-old son, Andy, and I have lived alone for most of his life. Considering when I married and had a child, I am a young single mother (I am 35). My husband left me when Andy was a baby, and we haven't seen or heard from him since. I now have a career, a good income and support-ive friends. And I thought Andy was doing won-derfully. Last week I found him in my room, all dressed up in my underpants, a silk dress, and my shoes. He told me that he was just kidding around and not to worry. I know now that this has happened before, since I've noticed my draw-ers and closets somewhat re-arranged. I wonder if the "chickens have come hence to roost", and that living without a father has brought this on. Is he gay?

To quickly answer your questions, the absence of Andy's father probably has nothing to do with this behavior. I don't know if he is gay, but I strongly doubt that he was just "kidding around" with your clothes. Was he rehearsing for a mock fashion show, or a school comedy review? I suppose that these are possibilities, but he didn't offer them. I would guess that Andy has transvestite tendencies, that is, he derives sexual satisfaction and even re-lease from wearing women's clothing. We don't know the causes, but it is not more common among young men raised by single mothers. It is not seen in women. Many transvestites are not homosexual, but about one-third are gay. I wouldn't know what Andy's sexual orientation is on the basis of your letter.

What to do? If you had written a whole list of concerns regarding Andy's mood and behavior, I might have recommended some form of evaluation. But you have felt that he "was doing wonderfully", which to me means that he is performing well at school, has friends, and feels relatively good about himself. That being the case, I'm not sure that there is anything to be gained by a professional evaluation, unless Andy himself wants one (you can ask him).

Transvestism, with or without homosexuality, is usually not eradicated by a psychological "cure". Most transvestites live with their private pleasure. Many are successfully married; some of their wives know about their transvestism and others do not. Most are in the closet, that is, they hide their predilection from friends and outsiders. Some are open, vocal and visible, joining organized transvestite social groups. The important issue is how well the individual (in this case Andy) is handling this part of his personality, and how he is doing in other spheres of his life.

71 **Ron is our only son, and we have a big problem. He's 18, but he is very unusual. He actually acts like a girl; at times I could swear by his actions that he really is a female in drag. What makes matters worse is that he has told us that he *feels* like a girl, and wants to become one. Is he gay?**

Your son is *not* a homosexual, which is defined as someone who maintains his maleness yet is sexually attracted to those of the same sex. He also is not a transvestite, a male who gets sexual pleasure from dressing up as a female. Ron sounds as if he is wrestling with the condition of transsexualism, the intense desire to become a member of the opposite sex. Actually, it goes further than this; these individuals actually feel that they *are*, in essence, of the opposite sex, but they are wrongly encased in the body of the same sex.

As you may know, some of these transsexuals undergo a series of sex-change operations, which essentially change their genitalia from one sex to the other. But prior to this arduous, complex surgery, which takes place at a specialized medical center, an intense series of physical, chemical and psychological investigations are set into motion. The highly trained team has to be certain that the indications are valid, and not due to an individual's neurotic needs or confusion. If they are satisfied as to the need and the appropriate criteria, the surgery will proceed. At the same time they receive the beginning of lifelong opposite sex hormones, since testicles and ovaries cannot be manufactured. In addition, ongoing intense counselling and psychotherapy is usually indicated.

I don't know if Ron fits into this last category or either of the two others. But at age 18, he probably has a better than average idea of which way he is heading. It would be wise for him to be evaluated by a team at a Human Sexuality Program at a University hospital in or near your home town.

72 **I've had a terrible case of genital herpes for about ten years. I'm worried that my teenage kids will get it, because maybe I was already infected when I gave birth to them. The disease has ruined my sex life with my husband and I would hate to feel that I've caused the same fate in them.**

I assume that with your long-standing infection you already know most of what there is to know about herpes. But just in case, let me acquaint you with some facts. It is a sexually transmitted disease (STD), and quite common. Sores and pain are fairly common symptoms in severe cases, but many cases are relatively mild, bothersome, temporary, but not horrendous. Your own case is obviously a severe one.

It is definitely not hereditary; it is caused by a virus, which is spread via intimate contact with an infected area. This virus is a variant on the one which causes cold sores. It is highly unlikely that you were infected when you gave birth to your children. Infants who are born during active herpes are actually at high risk, since the virus can be lethal to them at that point.

I wish that I could do something for your own long-standing infection. I have to assume that you are in close touch with your doctor, since there are new medications on the market which minimize the pain and suffering. Unfortunately, the virus is not (as yet) destroyed by these drugs. Lastly, you can rest assured that you *have not, are not* and *will not* cause a herpes infection in your teenagers. (For a discussion of AIDS, see Question 42.)

Family

Whoever first coined the expression, "Be it ever so humble, there's no place like home", was not merely referring to the physical place of residence. That is a minor aspect of this truth. The saying really refers to the security, warmth, comfort and nurturance of the family.

Human beings, like all higher members of the animal kingdom, are social creatures. They need other people to share communication, affection and intimacy. I know that you can all think of exceptions, but loneliness and isolation are usually terrible experiences to endure.

I am not holding up the nuclear family (Mum, Dad, 2.5 kids) as the only or even the best way to live. What with divorce, reconstituted families, single parents, communal living, and so on, "family" refers to variations on a theme of living and belonging to and with others.

We all recall with nostalgia at least some elements of family gatherings, of experiences with parents, or brothers and sisters, cousins, uncles. Blood is thicker…, especially when there is trouble and tribulation.

Teenagers change things in families, almost overnight. For one thing, they are bigger! We suddenly find ourselves in the company of these "space-occupying humanoids"; new elements of noise, mess, music and language intrude into our heretofore cocoon-like existences. Things we took for granted are knocked topsy-turvy. Teenagers don't like our organization, rules, food or values. We are once again beset with concerns about drugs, sex, school, careers and other stuff we put aside, at least as problems, years ago. What's going on?

For all these issues, families with teenagers are alive. There are only a few short years of excitement and arousal, worries and wonder. Enjoy them.

73 **We have no control over our 17-year-old son, Bradley. He comes and goes as he pleases, never helps around the house, and is rude to us. Yet everyone thinks that he is a gem — bright, warm, charming, co-operative. Somehow we're missing the boat!**

That boat is going to be empty! Not only are you missing it, but so is he. It may be irrelevant, but how did you ever allow that son of yours to get away with this self-indulgent arrogance and nastiness? You can't convince me that all of this disrespectfulness started overnight. Somehow, over the years, Bradley bamboozled your husband and you, and has not been held accountable for his abuse.

We have responsibilities as parents to love and support our children, but if we do so without imposing limits, demands, and expectations, we are not fulfilling our mandate. Limits are part of loving. You have to live by them, I do, so why in the world shouldn't he?

His attitude will catch up with him eventually. People who admire him so much don't have to live with him; but even they will eventually see through him. However, I don't think that you should wait for that fateful day. Lay down the law: rude? No allowance! Disobedient? No privileges! No help? No car! And so on. A boot in the buttocks is a beautiful metaphor. Let him learn that his parents are united, that they have enough self-respect to prevent him from acting like a punk to them, enough strength to confront his abuse, and enough caring to teach him how to act towards loved ones.

74 **Our 13-year-old daughter, Terri, thinks that we are the most horrible and strictest parents imaginable, maybe because of a curfew we impose. She can go out on school nights only if her homework is done, and she has to be home by 9 p.m. On Friday and Saturday nights, she can stay out until 11:30 p.m., which we'll occasionally stretch**

to midnight. She's a good kid, but this issue has been a heated one for a few weeks.

Stick to your guns. Your limits for a 13-year-old are not at all oppressive. I take it that Terri's friends are allowed to stay out late, which causes problems for her. Acknowledge these difficulties, but after explaining your reasoning for your rules in your home, make this a non-negotiable issue.

Adolescents are testing the limits of their bodies, their space, their power and their autonomy. They experiment, they push, they argue. They do need more independence, and matching responsibilities, but they also need limits. I have them, you have them, Terri will have to learn sooner or later that she can't do everything she wants to do simply because her friends are doing it. That doesn't make it right, does it?

I don't want to sound maudlin, but she will come to appreciate your limit-setting as merely another expression of your concern and love for her.

75 **We are fortunate in having a sweet, responsible 16-year-old daughter (Tracy). Believe it or not, we haven't had any problems with her. Until now. We recently moved to a new city, and the issue between us is curfew. She quickly made some new friends. They evidently are allowed to stay out till midnight on weekdays, and up to 3:00 a.m. on Friday and Saturday nights. She accuses us of being too strict, even mean. Are we?**

No, I don't think that you're mean. Parents are certainly obligated to set rules of behavior for their children, and that includes adolescents. Curfews vary from family to family, and I am reluctant to second-guess other parents on the hours and limits they set.

But in this case I think that you are right. A teenager in mid-high school should not be coming home at midnight on school nights, nor should a carte blanche for 3:00 a.m. weekend curfews be given. Such freedom seems to me to be an invitation to further behavior which pushes against limits and responsibilities. I can sense your worry about drugs, sex, unfinished homework, and so forth. While these fears may prove to be unfounded, my own feeling is that you should not give in. If Tracy is as sweet and responsible as you say she is, she may well thank you (deep down) for your concern and controls. The only other comment I have is that your recent move has likely been tough on her, and she wants to please (and hold onto) her new friends. The curfew has to be set in a climate of understanding and empathy. She'll appreciate it.

76   I am a single mother with two teenage daughters, aged 14 and 16. I don't like their constant talk about boys, clothes and make-up, but for some reason nothing bothers me more than their use of the telephone. Between the two of them, they can spend around four hours a night on the phone, and I am fed up. What can I do?

Part of what you're talking about is your level of tolerance; some parents wouldn't mind, but I agree with you. The hogging of the phone is a metaphor for insensitivity, self-centeredness, and shallowness. I assume that you've discussed, reasoned, cajoled, confronted and threatened, all to no avail. It is most difficult to lay down the law as a single parent, no doubt about it, but it can be done. Hopefully, you have enough appreciation of yourself that you will not allow them to walk all over you. Further, I hope your relationship with them is otherwise positive enough that they will understand (at some point) your non-negotiable stance.

The stance? If they can't limit their calls to thirty minutes each per night, then no phone. They can purchase another line — with their own money. Then let them fight between themselves for the hog-of-the-night award.

77 **Phillip and Peter are our two sons, aged 16 and 15, models to the outside world of sweet, loving boys. Our present problem is that their constant bickering at home, which was always bothersome, has recently escalated into open violence. Surely this is not what's meant by "sibling rivalry"?! My husband and I have a bad marriage, and there is seldom peace in our home.**

Sibling rivalry, a trite, overused, cliché, refers to the jealousy a toddler feels at the arrival of a demonstrably loved infant who usurps his primary position. What you are describing, on the other hand, is protracted, unresolved fraternal emnity, which at best is very sad, and at its worst is potentially dangerous. It may sound melodramatic, but serious injury or even death could result from their explosive, mutual anger.

It is obvious that there is a high level of tension in your family. In such a strained situation, even seemingly minor issues can trigger altercations. There is a sensitized reservoir of anger in your household, which doesn't take much to tap.

I don't know what Peter and Phillip argue about, but the specific content of the conflicts is probably irrelevant. What *is* important is that they are using each other to avoid dealing with gut-level, painful issues at home, and their increasing frustration and powerlessness. So they exercise futile attempts at power and control with each other.

I urge you to seek some help for your family, which is a social system in distress. A family therapist at the Family Service Agency, or a professional referred by your family doctor would be able to see the four of you together, and each of you individually, to make a cogent evaluation of what can be done to overcome the debilitating discord.

78 **How do you handle a kid who will complain, whine or demand persistently and relentlessly until he gets his way? Our son Scott is only 13, but he is the most argumentative child I have ever seen.**

> **He just doesn't take no for an answer. My husband and I finally give in just so that we can get some peace. He is like a steamroller, and we can't seem to stop him. But his teachers love him, and he is a gem with his friends. He seems to save his "best" behavior for us.**

I'm sure that there are some readers who are shaking their heads, wondering how you can let a 13-year-old child run your lives to such an extent. My gut reaction is frankly similar, but I've seen kids like this, and they are truly remarkable in their ability to frustrate and upset their parents. Scott is unusual because generally these kids are provocative and argumentative with other authority figures (like teachers) and even with friends. They quickly can find themselves ostracized and rejected by peers and others because they are so hard to get along with. Scott at least appears to be able to pick his spots. This ability doesn't make him any more lovable, but it is actually a good sign. If he was completely out of control in this regard, I would be inclined to offer a poorer prognosis.

As it stands, there is some cause for optimism, but paradoxically, it will cause Scott some grief. Because there is considerable control involved over where and when he exhibits this immature behavior, you will have to make it perfectly clear to him that it is unequivocally unacceptable, and that the issue is non-negotiable. Further misbehavior will be subject to punishment.

This is obviously a hard-nosed approach, and frankly, such strategies appeal to me in many circumstances. Of course, I also believe in the power of encouragement, in rewards for good behavior (positive reinforcement) and in support and compassion. It may well be that sessions with a family therapist would be tremendously useful to you. You would all discover what Scott is trying to accomplish (successfully) through his childish behavior, what upsets him at home, and why you capitulate. (The latter forms a big piece of the puzzle.) But even family therapy should not detract from the fact that Scott should not be allowed to get away with his persistent pushing.

79 **We happen to have a 19-year-old son, Derek, who is brilliant, popular, multi-talented and ambitious. You know, the type who has it made. Unfortunately, he is also arrogant, narcissistic and manipulative with his parents. Last weekend he brought home some classmates from college (Yale) and proceeded to treat us as social pariahs; he was rude, sarcastic, critical and generally miserable to us whenever his friends were around. We have sacrificed for this boy over the years, and he rewards us with disrespect and disdain.**

Yes, I know the type. Derek sounds like the kind of guy who uses people because he believes they are expendable, even those he supposedly loves; the kind of individual who takes advantage of and exploits people and feels entitled to do so; and certainly the kind of guy whose parents gave him everything because he could do no harm in their eyes, until it was too late.

You are certainly not doing yourself a favor by putting up with this disrespectful, demeaning behavior. You aren't even doing Derek any good; he has already adopted an approach to you that speaks volumes about his likeability.

I am of the impression that he has been walking all over you for years, and you have been putting up with his callousness and ingratitude. By your tolerance and silence, you have, in fact, been implicitly supporting his inexcusable behavior.

Show him your letter, or tell him directly how you feel, how hurt and disappointed you are. Finally, tell him that further support, financial and emotional, will be contingent on the respect and love he shows you. If Derek can't muster these feelings for you, let him at least muster his own support.

80 **Please let me know if we're out of line. Our two kids (14 and 15) keep telling us that we're way too strict. In a nutshell, they're not allowed out on school nights, they have to be in by midnight**

on Friday and Saturday night, they have to keep their rooms neat and tidy, and help with some household chores. They're not allowed to smoke or drink, swear at home, or be rude or disrespectful. It seems that some of their friends don't have to abide by any such rules. Are we wrong?

No, you are not wrong. I keep telling teenagers and their parents that mothers and fathers have a right and a responsibility to set rules, regulations, and constraints. The bottom line is "it is their game; they can determine the way it is played". Teenagers need love, caring, nurturance, support and so on, but they also need to learn that there are set limits to their autonomy. Restrictions are part and parcel of growing up and learning about a sense of self. You have them, I have them and there is every reason to impose them on our youth. This goes for any social system anywhere, in any type of family.

I am assuming that your rules are set in a context of privileges and warmth. That is, if your home atmosphere is wholly and solely "thou shalts" and "thou shall nots", then no matter how minor the demands are, they will be seen as oppressive and will be resented. The specific rules you have cited as examples don't in themselves seem unduly stringent. My own rules for my teenagers are only slightly more permissive than yours.

That I may agree or disagree with you, however, is unimportant, since there is so much individual variability from family to family depending on values, traditions and attitudes. But I find your kids' depiction of you as "way too strict" to be somewhat inappropriate.

I'm often amazed at the number of grown adults who come back and thank their parents for imposing rules during their teenage years. Even if your kids' friends have a much easier time of it with their rules, you'd be justified in sticking to your guns — as long as the rules are not senseless or cruel and there is an offsetting atmosphere of affection, plus room for some privacy and autonomy. One cannot set rules (and enforce them) for all behavior — it would be unrealistic and destructive. Space to make mistakes is clearly important, but your rules are not entirely unreasonable.

You might consider a compromise position, which allows them, for example, to go out on school nights for special activities, or impose a 10 p.m. weeknight curfew. The bottom line, however, is that your kids will have to comply.

81 **I know that my 14-year-old son, Anthony, who has been a joy to us, has been visiting our family doctor, but neither of them will tell me why. I am going crazy trying to guess, and my imagination is running wild!**

Well, as a parent of adolescents, I can certainly sympathize with you. My imagination would run wild (as you say yours does) all the way from sexual issues (homosexuality especially, right?) to serious medical illnesses. Medical confidentiality is one of the most important characteristics in a relationship between a doctor and patient. It has to do with privacy, propriety, and trust. So too, the relationship betwen an adolescent and his parents is based on these qualities, as well as on parental love and responsibility.

Whatever Anthony's emotional or physical problems may be, you can rest assured that if they were serious enough, if the timing was right, and if both of them felt that your knowing would help the situation and reduce your anxiety, you would be told. Obviously, these criteria don't (yet) apply.

Nobody is trying to pull the wool over your eyes. There is no malevolence, or nefarious motive. You are being left out until such time that it is advisable, necessary or worthwhile to tell you. Until then, stay cool, and enjoy your son.

82 **Our 13-year-old daughter, Carol-Ann, belongs to a wonderful youth group run by the local "Y". About fifty kids in the group went to a weekend retreat at a rural center set up to study nature, and they were also to focus on relationships and**

> **some (minimal) Christian teachings. They were accompanied by adults whom we know and respect. When she returned two days later, Carol-Ann had a big red hickey on each side of her neck! We were (and are) very upset. Obviously the supervision was too lax, and there was a lot of bad behavior going on. We are now wondering about sex, drugs, and other terrible things. Carol-Ann has said nothing except that it was a great weekend. She says the hickeys were just a bunch of boys and girls kidding around, but we doubt it.**

Why are you so convinced that Carol-Ann is lying? Has she given you other cause for concern about her misbehavior, or the group's dubious demeanor? It sure doesn't sound like it from your description of the group ("wonderful"), the retreat's purpose ("Christian") or the adult chaperones ("respect"). Actually, Carol-Ann's brief description of how she came to have those souvenirs is their most common origin, or method of application. It usually involves a group of boys and girls playfully wrestling with each other, holding "victims" down, and bestowing lovebites. I would be willing to wager that Carol-Ann is not the only young person from that weekend funfest to have these momentos. If she were involved in passionate sex — which is obviously what you fear — I doubt that you'd see these tell-tale signs. They are more comical than cause for concern. You are making a mountain out of a molehill. If you still have significant worries, why don't you phone the adults for confirmation or refutation of your fears? They'll likely laugh at you.

I do have one reservation. What is the basis for your mistrust of Carol-Ann? It sounds as though she doesn't deserve it, and you might want to examine your relationship with her with a family counsellor.

83   **While reading my 16-year-old daughter Ellen's diary, I discovered that she is on the Pill and is**

having sex with the boy next door, an 18-year-old neighbor whom I liked until that moment. She also wrote that she got stoned recently. She has been a good student, popular, loving and dutiful. But it's obvious that Ellen has serious problems. We want to punish her so that she will learn her lesson, but we don't know how.

You describe Ellen as "a good student, popular, loving, dutiful", fairly laudatory adjectives all, and yet you are convinced ("it's obvious") that she has "serious problems". All this worry on the basis of a sexual relationship with a young man whom you admittedly "liked", and a recent experience with marijuana. Your solution to her terrible problems? Punishment. This is how you help someone you love? Frankly, I have strong doubts about the validity of your assessment of Ellen's psychological state.

I don't know if your daughter is ready at her age to have a sexual relationship. Some 16-year-olds are, and many aren't. But I do know that you, as her parent, have a serious problem with trusting and trustworthiness. Snooping seldom, if ever, pays off. It usually raises more conundrums than it solves. You have a bright, socially adept, loving daughter, who will become a lot less so if you keep invading her privacy.

84 **Our 13-year-old son, Pierre, marches to the beat of a different drummer. He speaks in an articulate, clipped fashion; he reads voraciously; he avoids sports. He is interested in science, the arts, computers, the world. He has no close friendships and no interest in girls. While he does not seem unhappy, we are very concerned about his future.**

Your son *is* different, but I feel like saying, "so what?". I don't want to make light of your obvious concerns, but perhaps you should look at his considerable strengths instead of bemoaning what you see as his deficiencies. Pierre sounds like a bright, inquisitive, intellectually-oriented youngster. Rather than denigrating his non-conformist nature, perhaps you should be extolling his virtues.

It is hard enough for a kid to be different from the dominant peer group — that child is often ostracized or ridiculed — without his parents playing a similar, if more subtle, role. Encourage Pierre's unique strengths and pursuits. There are schools and groups for gifted children and adolescents in most urban centers. There he could not only pursue his own interests, but he would meet others his age with similar feelings and ideas. You would then find that his problem with social isolation would gradually evaporate.

Why does his hero have to be Dr. J. or George Brett? What's wrong with Einstein?

85   **We live next to a family of "surly-birds". They are well-to-do, ostentatious and arrogant. The father drinks heavily and the mother dresses like a teenager and is always flirting. They have three teenage kids. The 18-year-old daughter is scowling, tough, and she smokes and drinks. Ditto for their 17-year-old son. A 13-year-old son seems the softest of the five, but we can see him changing. Is this behavior all hereditary?**

As far as I know, there is no gene for surliness and arrogance. The old adage that says "the apple doesn't fall far from the tree" is most apt here. Clearly, the tone and style are set by the parents, and the children have adopted what is most familiar and likely to be rewarded. Nor is this unusual. I think if you look at other families you know, you'll see strong behavioral and personality similarities between parents and teenage kids.

It is difficult to separate what is genetic or hereditary from what is environmental or learned. It is the old Nature-Nurture controversy. This distinction is especially difficult to make in adolescents and adults, in whom behavior patterns tend to be complex. There are factors of temperament — our rhythms, reaction times to stimulation and stress, pace and activity, — which are subject to heavy genetic influence. Not only that, but in each individual there is a remarkable consistency and predictability in these temperamental factors over many years, from infancy to adulthood.

Does this mean that our fate is sealed at birth? Not at all. It is what occurs in the interplay between constitutional (bodily) factors and our environment which determines that fate. Nor is it cast in stone. People can and do modify, change and improve on their self-destructive patterns, if they *want* to. I guess this is one of the reasons for the existence of a thriving mental-health professional industry. In the case of your "surly-birds" (an excellent label, by the way) their external arrogance may well preclude any desire to change, unless they are confronted by painful reality. Sometimes, of course, that very arrogance covers up feelings of inferiority and insecurity. But at a distance, who can tell? I doubt that it is worth your while to help them.

86

We are moving to another city (400 miles away) in a couple of months and our 14-year-old daughter, Heather, has been complaining for weeks about it. She does not want to leave her close friends. At times she cries, at others she sulks or is irritable.

I assume that you are moving because of a better financial or personal situation, and also that the move is non-negotiable. Your daughter has to hear both messages, loud and clear, so she knows that her misery and animosity is not going to change the situation.

But Heather is at an age when friends are of the utmost importance. The closest friends share deep secrets, feelings, fears and fantasies. To have all this security swept away is frightening.

It goes without saying that you have to explain to her the necessity for the move. Even if she's upset, the fact that you are discussing it with her will make her feel good — eventually. You must also show her that you do understand her feelings, and that you know why she is so unhappy. I don't want to minimize the difficulty of a major move for anyone. It is disorganizing and disorienting for a while, until you learn your way around and become comfortable.

Moving is often tougher on adolescents — they are thrust into new schools and have to make new friends. They are worried about being accepted and liked, they fear rejection and embarrassment. Your daughter can be reassured that though it will be hard at first, she too will overcome.

There are steps you can take to make the move easier on Heather. It is a good idea for the two of you to visit the new high school well in advance of her first day. Some progressive high schools even have welcoming committees. If not, you could enlist the aid of the principal or vice-principal: they would (usually) be pleased to greet and reassure Heather, and to introduce her to some friendly students. If you have any contacts in the new city, visit them with Heather, especially if they have teenage children who could show her around. Visit the outstanding attractions of the new city: try to accentuate what she is *gaining*, not what she is losing.

87 **When is a teenager ready to move out? Sandy, our 15-year-old, says that she can't stand us and wants to go on student welfare. We have been fighting with her constantly for a few years now, and frequently I'd like nothing better than to see her out. She poisons the atmosphere and brings us and her younger sister and brother down. She has friends, does okay in school, and as far as we know, is not into drugs or sex.**

It sounds like Sandy may be out soon whether or not you (or she) wants it. That is, if this antagonism keeps up, something is going to give. She is either going to fall apart or get out rebelliously (through drugs, sex, school avoidance or similar escapes).

Unless, of course, you two are such terrible people that she wants to leave to avoid the abuse you shower on her. I obviously can't tell if this is (or isn't) the case.

In any event, a family assessment is clearly in order. All of you would be seen as a group and individually by a professional family therapist; in addition, Sandy would be assessed by an adolescent therapist. There are adolescents who can manage on their own. Most cities offer high school students who can't live at home a living stipend and regular visits from a social worker employed by the school board. The purpose of the family diagnostic evaluation would be to see if anything can be done to keep Sandy at home and avoid tearing the fabric of the family. Failing that, her level of functioning would have to be examined. She might be better off in a group home, with other kids around her age, and with a trained supervisory and/ or therapeutic staff (depending on the nature of the home) of child care and social workers.

The term which was used in the '60s and '70s to describe teens who left home early and assumed total adult responsibility was "emancipated adolescent." Sandy will not be emancipated simply by physically moving out. Emancipation, in this context, implies a kind of emotional and financial independence and maturity, an ability to live away from one's family. And it would be sheer nonsense to suggest that the vast majority of 15-year-olds could manage so autonomously. Sandy will need help if she is going to succeed in this difficult endeavor. I hope that it proves unnecessary.

88   We are fortunate that every year at Christmas and in summer our family goes on a vacation together. This year our 16-year-old daughter, Natalie, has informed us that she'd prefer not to join us on our yearly jaunt to New York City, but would rather go with another family on their vacation so that she could be with one of her best friends. They've invited her, all expenses paid, to the Caribbean. I am angry about it, but Natalie can't understand why I'm upset. And

she is adamant about her preferences. Am I wrong to demand that she accompany us (as I want to do)?

The level of affluence in your family is obviously higher than in most, but the problem you are confronting is common to families at all socioeconomic levels. When do we insist that our adolescents accompany us on our family outings and when do we allow them to be the ultimate arbiters of the importance of our family vacation?

This issue has something to do with your perceptions of the integrity and the sanctity of the family, of the obligation the family members have to each other and of the answer to the question in the last paragraph. But your anger may be more a product of bruised feelings and your sense of being rejected by your daughter, who not only is not willing to accompany you on an enjoyable family ritual, but who is actively stating a preference to you. She is "adamant" about her choice, and is perplexed by your tightening of the apron strings at this age in her life. She sees this different vacation plan as a natural and not unreasonable request from a blossoming young adult, and probably views you now as somewhat stodgy, conservative or even unfair.

Certainly, if the trip takes on major significance to you for some reason, her desire to go with her friend will have to be dampened. A wedding, a funeral, a graduation or some similar event would clearly supersede Natalie's trip down south. Is your family's winter vacation of that measure of magnitude? If it is that important to you and your spouse, then who am I to say that you're wrong? But if there is considerable room for doubt, perhaps you could reassess your own adamancy. If you insist that she come with you instead, your vacation may not be quite as wonderful an experience as you would like it to be.

89 We went off on a lazy weekend to New York City, leaving our house in the care of our 16-year-old son, Ian. His 18-year-old sister is away at school, and our housekeeper had that weekend off. We returned a day early, in the morning, to find our

**living room a shambles — broken lamps, ciga-
rette butts, stained furniture and rugs — in a
general state of disarray, with a slew of bodies
sleeping throughout the house. We kicked them
all out, but our son complained that we came
home too early, that all would have been cleaned
up if we had kept up our side of the deal! He also
blames a few outside trouble-makers.**

Obviously, a drunken bash ensued at your home, with your son's
active involvement. This is, unfortunately, not a rare occurrence
in the absence of both parents. There is invariably alcohol abuse,
which seems to disinhibit the group, and mob psychology takes
over. The kids egg each other on, and sometimes the party is
crashed by outsiders. At a minimum, Ian and his friends have to
clean up the mess, or pay for the clean-up and complete restitution. Whether or not you wish to institute further punishment
against your son will depend on many factors: your general
reaction to your children's misbehavior, Ian's previous history (is
this new or recurrent behavior?), and his demonstrated sense of
remorse are a few important examples. Sometimes the police are
called in, even after the event, in order to survey the damage,
admonish the participants, and occasionally to lay charges.

90 **We are a middle-class family, very committed to
our three teenaged children. Obviously we would
like what is best for them. We recently moved
to a new town because my husband's company
transferred him, and we suddenly find ourselves
in a very uncomfortable position, playing catch-
up with our new neighbors. Parents here send
their kids to the top schools, lessons and camps,
all in the finest designer clothes. We just don't
have that kind of money, nor those values. And
then we wonder if we are doing our kids a disservice. Maybe we should take out a bank loan,
or re-mortgage or even sell our house?**

You are *not* doing your kids a disservice. Parents have always compromised and sacrificed their lifestyles in order to better the opportunities for their children. But one could argue in your situation that your desire to put yourself in financial jeopardy merely in order to create three more Yuppies is doing them no good in the long run. I even question the public perception of the "top" schools or camps. Of course, there are exceptional individuals and organizations, but most fall into a general above-average category. Your kids can get a terrible education at an elitist school, or an excellent one at a solid public school. Likewise for camps, lessons and universities (looking ahead). As far as designer clothes are concerned, well, the less said about that the better.

We all compromise our lives to some extent for our children, but there are limits. What your children do with the opportunities you offer is up to them. The seeds are planted in the home (family), and earlier (genes), but then the kids themselves take over. Motivation, drive, ambition, commitment, energy, curiosity — they can apply these qualities anywhere. Your values, love and commitment will do much more for them than will needless sacrifices.

91 **My husband and I are having a strong disagreement about our son Martin's Bar Mitzvah (the Jewish ritual when a boy turns 13). I would like a simple ceremony and party at home, but my husband wants an extravaganza. He wants to outdo all the other boys. Not only will it cost a fortune, but I think it's in poor taste. I'm not even sure it's an important ritual.**

From my name, I am sure that readers will deduce that I'm Jewish, so that I am quite familiar with Bar Mitzvah extravaganzas. My own feeling is that the Bar Mitzvah ceremony (like the confirmation ritual, convocation or even, for some, the Sweet Sixteen party) is a most important ritual. Ceremonies mark developmental milestones in a formal manner. There are actually few occasions in life of unmitigated, communal celebrations of pure, unadulterated joy. They signify a recognition of a graduation or a successful mastering of one era of life, and the eve of embarking on another adventure. These rituals, be they religious or purely social, are never-to-be-forgotten. It is better that they be remembered with warm feelings and fond images.

Now that we've established the importance of Martin's celebration, your question boils down to one of taste. Martin's father wants ostentation, you want simplicity. What does Martin want? What can you afford? Who is your husband trying to impress? Why are you so nonchalant about the whole ritual? I would ask you all of these and other questions in order to resolve the conflict. One thing is sure; Martin will remember and savor this day of commemoration and celebration no matter whether you spend $250 or $20,000. Both have been done. Some of your guests will disagree with whatever choice you make. But most will join with you in sharing the warmth and spirit of the occasion, no matter what you do. Surely you and your husband (and Martin) can work it out.

92 **Our 16-year-old son, Rich, spends money (which neither he or we have in abundance) like it is going out of style. He borrows from friends, uses (abuses) our credit card, "forgets" our change, and so on. Luckily, he hasn't stolen. Nothing but the best for him; he'll buy only expensive designer clothes, gourmet foods, or luxury items. Now he is in debt, but we still can't get him to stop.**

What do you mean you "can't get him to stop"? I am incredulous that he has access to your credit card; but it sounds like he has you (and others) bamboozled. Are you afraid of him? He's only 16 and already set in a pattern that is self-destructive, and yet he seems to be almost rewarded for his terrible behavior. Why don't his friends put it on the line with him? How can he not return change to you after purchases made with your money? Most importantly, how does he get away with all of this deception and abuse?

Somehow he's decided that only expensive items are worth having (at least, he may have some sense of aesthetics, design or fashion); maybe he's been given a feeling of entitlement. Did you feel that the sun rose and set on him when he was a young child? Is he trying to live up to his name? Unfortunately, he hasn't learned responsibility or accountability. And you don't seem to be able to set any limits on his irresponsible behavior.

Merchandise which is inappropriate or which he can't afford should be returned. He should not have use of a credit card. Debts have to be repaid forthwith. If he has to get a hard job to pay back his friendly creditors, then so be it. If he has to be punished, that too may be necessary. Rich must learn to stop this terrible spending in the name of narcissism. You say nothing of his mood or psychological state. If Rich is unhappy about his behavior and wants to change, a psychological evaluation is in order. If he doesn't change soon, the next step will be police involvement. You can tell him I said so. And if you haven't got the wherewithal to impose the limits that he so sorely needs, then perhaps you should call the youth bureau of your police force and enlist their help.

93 **We have a terrific 17-year-old son, Bob, but we can't understand why he seems to have money to burn. For the past year he has never been without a roll of bills. It isn't that he isn't generous with his money; he gladly shares with friends, buys us gifts and is generally financially helpful. But he won't tell us the source of his income. He just says "I earn it", and changes the subject.**

There are only a limited number of sources of such a cache of cash in the hands of a male adolescent. One is the misguided generosity of his parents; clearly this is not the case. A second is a wealthy girlfriend who is bank-rolling him, a decidedly unlikely situation. A third is theft of money, or of hot merchandise which is then sold for profit. A fourth involves the extortion of money from others on the basis of blackmail or threats of violence. Fifthly, and not uncommonly, he could be dealing in illicit street drugs. And lastly, he could be hard at work at a legitimate after-school and weekend job.

There is nothing in your letter which smacks of an antisocial lifestyle; you describe Bob as "terrific", generous and helpful. But I must say that his secretiveness concerns me. Surely, if he had a respectable job, he would not hide information about it from you. I have known a number of high school students involved in criminal behavior, who on the surface maintained a facade of honesty and morality for even their closest family and friends. We can all be fooled. I obviously have no way of knowing where Bob gets his largesse, but I suspect it involves some illegalities, or at least some shenanigans.

He is still under the age of majority (in most jurisdictions), but even if he were over 18, I would say that you and your husband have no choice but to confront him and demand a cogent explanation for his new-found and inexplicable wealth. If he is engaged in any illegal activity, he obviously has to stop immediately because of the criminal aspects, as well as the danger of being caught. That he could be involved in something so lucrative and covert for over a year without his parents finding out at least a hint about the activity tells me something about the level of communication and sharing in your home, or rather the lack of it. Visits to a family therapist may be in order, even if Bob is holding down a legitimate job.

94 **We were, I thought, a happy family. Successful careers (I'm a features editor, my husand, an engineer), an older Yuppie lifestyle, two adolescent boys (Michael and Jordan), many friends. Were, that is, until a close friend of mine gave me hell for ignoring the sadness of our older son, and berating me further for a lifelong clear favoritism that I've shown our younger child. Clear, it seems, to all our friends, and worse, clear to my older son especially. My husband, who is not**

implicated and who never says much, says that he "tends" to agree. Michael is a good kid, but he hasn't got Jordan's looks, talents or brains.

You sound as if you are sitting on a powder keg. You have worked so hard at this image of familial utopia that you have lost sight of the forest for the trees. There are clearly communication and emotional problems in your midst, which you are suddenly having to face. How is it that your husband hasn't confronted you on this issue? Are you so dominant, or is he so passive, fearful, uninvolved or insensitive? Why has it taken so many years for this secret to be revealed? Why has it been so apparent to everyone else? And surely there were clues for years in your older son's behavior that you obviously ignored.

Now I'm berating you, too. I don't intend to blame you for your son's depression — if he *is* depressed (I don't know) — it may have nothing to do with you. Parents feel guilt-ridden enough as it is without having shrinks indict them as responsible for their kids' problems. No, I'm being critical because you and your husband have been so caught up in the process of making it that you have not (yet) been able to help your son.

You must speak with Michael, and ask him about his feelings. You have to find out about his depression and his feeling of being relegated to a lesser level of importance compared to his brother. The chances are that he believes the message that he is not as worthwhile. Beliefs about ourselves in childhood and adolescence often remain part of our lifelong adult baggage no matter what we learn to the contrary. Meanwhile, you have to confront yourselves pretty seriously. Is your friend right? On the basis of you letter, I'd say that she is.

Ask Michael if he'd like to speak to an objective counsellor or therapist. Sessions with a family therapist would clearly be helpful; they would serve as an entrée to getting help for Michael — and you. Such sessions would benefit all of you. Jordan would learn about his "favored" status (which I'm sure he already recognizes) and your husband would finally see his role (or rather, the lack thereof) in your family situation.

95 **We have three teenaged daughters, who give us the usual blend of pleasure and problems. Only one gives us cause for serious concern. Our middle one, Tess, feels that she is unfairly treated by us, that we favor the others and that she never receives as much affection, attention or gifts as do her sisters. She is always jealous, and on the lookout for examples to prove her case. She has felt that way ever since she was a young child, and we have tried to reassure her all along. We've bent over backwards in an effort to show her that she's as loved and respected as the other two, but she keeps carping and complaining. We're getting tired of it, and we can't seem to convince her.**

Your letter brings up a number of overworked, hackneyed clichés that I'm sure you have already considered. The so-called "middle-child syndrome" which describes the squeeze play between the first (and thus, most important) and last (and thus, most babied) children, with the middle one(s) left out of the goodies. Certainly we have all seen elements of this syndrome from time to time, but as a general rule it just does not hold water. There is no good evidence to show that middle children (of three) are in any way detrimentally treated, hurt or harmed, or that they are a more vulnerable group. Another commonly abused concept is "sibling rivalry", which originally referred to the first baby's resentment of the arrival on the scene of a pretender to the throne, but has since been extended to include any degree of competition or jealousy between sisters or brothers.

You don't mention in your letter whether Tess's jealousy pervades her entire life: does it affect her relationships with friends, acquaintances or other family members? Since it is a preoccupation in the family, it would be helpful to know if it is a generalized obsession. The problem with someone who "doth protest too much" is that their obsession becomes a self-fulfilling prophecy in two ways. First, even if it isn't so, she believes it so strongly that she acts as if it were fact; and second, if she bothers people long enough, she will indeed turn them off. And you are sounding annoyed and frustrated. It is not comfortable to be constantly monitored and criticized, and whatever validity there may or may not have been to her "carping", you both are tired of it. The other kids are, indeed, more fun to be with.

Tess has won the battle, but she may now lose the war, unless she gets some help. If you suggest to her that she see a psychotherapist of some kind, she will have further evidence of your singling her out for mistreatment. She will see it as a lack of confidence in her, and her insecurity will be further encouraged. I would suggest that you approach this jealousy as a family problem (which it is) rather than her problem alone. Tell her that you can't take her constant complaining, that you are willing to admit your mistakes and that you want to see what can be done to improve her and your situation. A branch of the Family Service Agency or your family doctor can refer you for this type of counselling. Saying "we are all going" will make this a non-negotiable and non-blaming project.

96   **I am the father of a beautiful 16-year-old girl (Madeleine) who is doing well in all respects. My problem is with my wife, Gloria, aged 39. Ever since Madeleine reached puberty, Gloria has acted more and more like a teenager, almost competing with our daughter in words, clothing, music and behavior. The worst incident was when we were at a holiday resort last month and my wife had a bit too much to drink and got up on the dance floor and started dancing lewdly with Madeleine's male friends! I was furious, but Gloria rejected my criticism, calling me "stodgy and old". She has been irritable with me over the past four months, although I can't see what I'm doing that's any different. What gives?**

Gloria is obviously going through a rough time, and is unfortunately hurting others (you and Madeleine) in futile attempts to deal with her problems. She is likely feeling the pinch of her age.

As the mother of an alluring mid-teenager with forty rapidly approaching, she is reassessing her identity as a woman, and unfortunately, much of self-esteem is determined by a sense of personal attractiveness. Feminist researchers have made this point repeatedly: because of early and repeated conditioning, too many women evaluate themselves in terms of important (to them) male opinions of them. Gloria, for some reason, feels that she may have lost her attractiveness to you, or perhaps she takes your caring for granted. She is (most likely unconsciously) threatened by young nymphets (as represented all too well in the person of Madeleine) and is trying to convince herself that she is still sexy, seductive, and captivating to men both young and old. Unfortunately, she ends up making somewhat a fool of herself, and I am sure she feels worse about herself the next day.

Her cuttingly insulting remarks to you indicate a reservoir of anger which she has been harboring towards you. Perhaps she want to shake you out of your complacency. There is an air of desperation in Gloria's sad and vain attempts at personal re-affirmation.

I wish that Gloria could talk to other women who have gone through the same problems. You might try to gently nudge her in that direction. Perhaps you could suggest to your wife that she see a psychotherapist, preferably female, to work on her concerns about herself and her marriage. There may be some involvement of you and Madeleine, and perhaps some surprising revelations about her feelings that Gloria has not yet shared with you.

97 **What do you do with a teenager who won't leave her mother's side? Mandy is our 14-year-old daughter, and although she is happy, she seems to be tied to my apron strings. She goes to school all right, but that seems to be the end of her activities. She won't go out with girlfriends (even when they call her), or take part in any activities, or have any fun. She seems happy enough at home, but adamantly refuses to go out unless it involves shopping or doing other things with me, which she genuinely enjoys.**

This is the kind of situation which can either be of considerable concern or, paradoxically, might not be a problem whatsoever. And, from your letter, I can't tell with certainty which it is. Let's take the upbeat possibility, and that is that Mandy is a youngish 14-year-old, very close to her mother, secure within herself and happy with her life. She gets enough social interaction at school to satisfy her, and prefers at this stage the warmth, intimacy and love that she gets from you. She is developing and maturing at her own pace, her own interests are slowly evolving and over the course of the next months and years she will gradually increase her contacts and experiences to include friends and other activities.

That was the good news; now the bad. A couple of possibilities exist. One is that Mandy is so inordinately tied to her mother in an intense mutually dependent relationship (symbiotic) that she cannot separate for fear (on an unconscious level) of doing damage to you both. If this is the case, she might be getting mixed messages from you (as in "go — come hither"). Another possibility is that she is so intensely shy and insecure that she is extremely fearful of going out with people. So she stays home where she is not challenged, and she is safe. For completeness we should include the chance that Mandy is very disturbed with a major psychiatric disorder, schizophrenia, for example.

Certainly, if any of the negative descriptions pertain, Mandy needs a good psychiatric assessment, and corrective intervention would be indicated and necessary. But let me urge you to hold off for a while before you sound the alarm. From the tone of your letter, I surmise that Mandy is actually doing quite well. She goes to school, has girlfriends calling her, and has a good relationship with her mother. More importantly, she seems to be a happy young person, quite content with her lot. My hunch is that Mandy is marching to the beat of her own drummer, and feels relatively good about herself and her life. She may simply need a bit more time to move away from mother and surely you can give it to her.

98 **I'm in a bit of dilemma. My husband Alec's pride and joy has always been our only son Jack, or perhaps I should say *his* son. Jack is 14 years**

old, a very nice boy, and I've had a good relationship with him all along — but it has been in spite of Alec. For as long as I can remember, Alec has been trying to cut me out of the relationship. He would undermine me, criticize me, take Jack on excursions alone, put him to bed, and so forth. Now that Jack is an adolescent, Alec seems to live his entire life through his son's experiences and especially his successes. At first I thought that a close father-son relationship was a good thing, but this one, I feel, has gotten out of hand. And I am odd man out! Am I wrong to be concerned?

No, you're not wrong, on a number of counts. Your husband's living so thoroughly vicariously through his son points up the lack of fulfillment in his own life, and it must put enormous pressure on Jack to achieve, excel, produce, and so on. Alec will be shattered when Jack begins to pull away from him as an adolescent should. And if Jack doesn't develop an autonomous identity, independent of his father, he will lose out. The problem as I see it is to make Alec recognize what he is doing, and to take steps to rectify it. If he can't do it himself, he might need some professional guidance to help him let go. "Separation — individuation" is the term given to the process by which young people become separate, independent individuals. In this case, Alec has as much need to accomplish this separation as Jack does, and if he can't or won't do it, he is going to end up hurting his pride and joy. I frankly doubt very much that Alec will either admit that he has a problem, or seek help for it.

But there is another equally serious problem, which might serve as a vehicle to get Alec into a family therapist's office, and that is the state of your own relationship with him. Words like "cut out", "in spite of Alec" and "undermine", show vividly that your marriage is in deep trouble. Jack may be the fulcrum, the pivotal issue around which your differences become crystallized, but it could seem that you and Alec have to take a serious look at your own shaky union. It will likely become more openly embittered when (and if) Jack does achieve his separate identity. I think that it's time you confronted Alec about his destructive behavior. If he can't or won't admit what he is doing in relation to Jack, he will have a rougher time denying what he is doing to you. Professional help is highly indicated if you are to salvage a mutually respectful and loving relationship. Right now it is nothing of the kind. You might also want to ask yourself why you put up with this denigration for so long.

99
We have three terrific sons, aged 19, 17, and 13. The problem is that I have always — and continue to do so now — treated my youngest child, Joey, as my baby. I allowed him to keep (my wife said "encouraged") his baby blanket and his baby language much longer than the other kids. I have hugged, kissed and fawned over him, and still do, much to my wife's chagrin. Actually, he's her "baby" too, but she feels that I overdo it. I doubt that I'm doing him harm, but I guess that I have to hear it from a "pro".

Well, being a "pro" hasn't prevented me from doing very much the same thing with my own youngest child. And I have heard an identical story (variations on a theme) from many other parents. It is not only the parents who savor what they consider to be their last child (although sometimes they're fooled); it is often the older siblings who dote on the youngest family member, so that he or she receives extra attention from all sides.

One of the few times harm is done is when the extra caring crosses the boundary into infantilization, that is, the extreme dependency engendered when the "baby" is not allowed to do anything for himself. The adolescent is then left with the feeling that he can do nothing on his own. It can be equally harmful when that youngest child is given positive responses to every request, whim or demand, which is as good a definition of a "spoiled child" as any I've heard. Lastly, if this youngster is not only savored, but favored, it gives him a message of personal specialness which is seldom merited, and may cause resentment in his siblings.

I can give you the same advice as I give myself. There is nothing inherently wrong with "loving up" your youngest child. Joey will remain your baby for the rest of his life. Just monitor yourself, and make sure that the three traps I've mentioned are avoided.

100 **We have been blessed with a wonderful daughter. Doubly blessed, in fact, because Mary (17) was adopted in infancy when we learned that we couldn't have our own babies. She was told around age seven or eight that she was adopted. She listened and never said another word, nor asked a question about the situation. In the ensuing years she thrived in all respects; we couldn't be more pleased with her. Last month she started asking questions regarding her past: her mother, her father, where she was born, under what circumstances and so on. Her questions were relentless, and we had few answers. She seemed pressured to find out, and the tension between us was palpable. This has continued, and she has told us in no uncertain terms that she intends to find her "real" mother. Have the past years and our relationship with Mary been an illusion?**

No, your relationship has not been an illusion. But Mary is wrestling with her identity and her sense of self — and a large part of defining who we are entails learning about from where we came — that is, our past. Without a sense of their history, young people have a tough time in looking forward to some kind of future, establishing a value system, and maintaining a feeling of continuity and stability in their lives. It is no accident that *Roots* was such a popular book and television series.

Mary has come of age. She may have been reading about the growing momentum among adopted individuals to discover their biological origins. This movement is being formalized via legislation and adoption procedures in many areas. Of course, there are built-in safeguards: the adopted son or daughter (aged 18 years or over) has to want to find his or her mother; the adoptee is the only one who can initiate the search. In addition, cooperation of both the adoptive parents and the biological parent(s) is sought, and in many jurisdictions, is mandatory. The natural mother has to (also) want to meet her child.

Adopted kids, even in the most loving of families, often have all kinds of fantasies as to who their biological mother was and is, and why they were given up for adoption, no matter how often and well they have been reassured. Nowadays, there is even some initial written communication between the natural mother and her infant, to be given to the latter in late adolescence.

Mary is trying to establish her identity. She may well have been discussing her feelings and needs with friends. She most certainly is going through the same exciting and agonizing process as other kids her age, of discovering what she is all about. It may be that something specific happened which precipitated her almost aggressive approach to you. Likely, these thoughts and fantasies have been fermenting and festering for some time, and before she had the requisite level of energy and courage to broach the subject — it was blurted out in a barrage.

I've been through this quest more than a few times with adoptees. In my experience, there is always some degree of surprise, relief, excitement, disappointment, joy, sadness, love and anger felt by the various people concerned. I have yet to see one instance of a loving relationship with adopted parents destroyed by the process. Of course, conflict-ridden relationships or disturbed individuals can upset any family. But in general, I think that you have nothing to fear.

Mary does not love you less, she is not moving away, she is not rejecting you. She is merely doing what she has to do for a sense of completeness. It is for this reason that most jurisdictions now encourage this process, if the adopted mother and the biological mother agree to participate. If your relationship with Mary has been as good as it sounds, then you have nothing to fear. Often, meeting the natural parent is a let-down; sometimes it is rewarding, occasionally even enriching; at times it is extremely painful. But *your* relationship with *your* daughter is secure. Encourage her in her quest, but let her know how much you care.

$\underline{101}$ **I married an older man who is now 69 years of age and the father of Johnny, who is 17. My husband now has Parkinson's disease, and is nearly incapacitated. It may sound crazy, but Johnny is too good. He is so devoted, so responsible, so caring, that he spends all his free time helping his father and me. He seldom goes out with friends and he even phones us from school to see how we're doing. He acts more like our parent than our child. What should we do?**

There may well be a difference between what you should do and what Johnny allows you to do. First, however, you should examine your own motivation, and the messages you are giving to your very dutiful son. It may be that rather than your parent, as you suggest, he has assumed the role of your surrogate husband. Do you convey to him your need for his presence and his caring? Is any guilt induced by you if he decides to go elsewhere with friends?

For an adolescent, wrestling with emancipation, independence, and autonomy on the one hand and dependency on the other, he is taking his devotion to an extreme. At this time, he is also dealing with his sexuality as a large part of his identity, and doing "husbandly" things may fit in with his needs at the moment. At some level there may be resentment for having to contribute so much at home, but guilt can consume him so completely that he actually ends up doing even more.

This description may sound like a cynical view of his sense of responsiblity and altruism. He may well be making all of this effort simply because he is concerned and wants to be of maximum help. But this lack of his own social life concerns me. At his age, peer group involvement is actually enjoyable and very important. Is part of Johnny's sense of obligation also a way of avoiding or escaping social interaction?

To return to what I said in the first sentence, you certainly should express to Johnny the very concerns you've raised in your letter. And you can show him this answer, if you want. He may, however, not want to hear what you have to say. He may reject any suggestion that he is overdoing it, or doing it for the wrong reasons. But, as in so many other circumstances, consciousness-raising is very important. You will have planted the seed of self-examination, and I'll bet you'll see at least a modest change.

102 **Our 5-year-old child (Sander) has been diagnosed as autistic and retarded. My husband has a great deal of difficulty accepting this diagnosis; he sees it not only as a condemnation of Sander, but of himself, too. Partly as a result of this feeling, he has removed himself completely from dealing with Sander — he doesn't play with him, come with us to the doctors, or even want to talk about him. If not for my older son Marc, 15, I would be at my wit's end. Marc has taken over completely; he's dedicated himself to helping me with Sander. I have to blink sometimes to see that he's not my husband. Is this situation going to be a problem?**

You are bringing up many issues simultaneously. Believe it or not, your husband's reaction is not that unusual. While most men can handle these crises, I have often seen fathers who are simply unable to accept critical illness in a child, who deny, avoid, withdraw, or even crack under the pressure. Most often their wives will increase their degree of nurturance, caring and energy in order to ensure that domestic life continues, and the sick child is cared for. Your husband needs some more time in order to face and accept the reality of Sander's illness. A counsellor could be of great benefit to you and your husband in coping with Sander and the inevitable strain on your relationship. I am sure that a visit with a social worker or other mental health professional could be arranged by the doctor(s) in charge of Sander's case.

Counselling would also ease the burden on Marc. This young man is playing the role of husband and father, albeit somewhat modified. While his help is welcome and indeed needed, his own needs have to be considered. I am sure that he is helping you with the best of intentions, and generosity and altruism are certainly qualities we wish to inculcate in our adolescents. It does him no good, however, if he inadvertently drives a wedge between you and your husband. At 15, he is in the midst of defining his sexual identity and his mature (adult) relationship with his parents and the opposite sex. It would also concern me if the degree of Marc's involvement with Sander and you is such that it detracts from his activities with friends, or from his school performance or from any other important experiences he should be having at this stage. You have to be wary of falling into the trap of expecting Marc to take care of everything.

While Sander's illness is a serious one, with tragic overtones, I am sure that you have come to realize that you are not alone — there are local and national organizations of all kinds helping families afflicted with these problems. Research has shown that there can actually be a positive effect on adolescents who are raised in a home with a sibling who has a serious psychological or physical illness. If Marc's involvement can be kept within reasonable bounds, you can all benefit from his contribution.

103 **Our 4-year-old cat (named Silly) is dying of irreversible kidney failure. At the moment he is messy and smelly. The vet has urged us to put him to sleep, but our two teenagers are adamant that we not give up on him. You'd think that a close human being was at death's door, the way they are carrying on! They both look wan and haggard; they take turns stroking him, and even crying. I point out to them that it's only a cat and that we'll get another one, but this seems only to upset them more. They call me callous.**

No wonder that they're angered and hurt by you. It is not an accident that literally millions of people around the world adopt household pets to enrich their lives. When the relationship is working well, both the master and the pet benefit greatly. The pet owner receives devotion, someone to love and stroke and nurture, a modicum of predictability and simplicity in a frenetic life, and an unequivocal sense of belonging. The pet receives that love and nurturance, and, certainly in the case of dogs, returns it in gobs of joy.

Adolescents are no less bewitched by the loving offered by a pet. For many of them it is incorporated into the definition of their identity. It may sound silly, but the question "Who am I?", which is being pondered during these teenage years, is often clarified by a loving relationship with a dog or cat. Teenagers with low self-esteem or those who feel lonely are often energized and fulfilled by their pets. "Hey, I can love, and I can be loved!" are common implicit lessons.

Actually, I am somewhat surprised by your lack of feeling for Silly (this pet obviously was not a source of solace or succor for you) and your lack of compassion for your kids' mourning an imminent loss. It could be that cleaning up after a cat who can no longer take care of itself is a chore, but surely the kids will do it, if it is too much for you. Yes, at least in this context, you *are* callous.

104

I am the mother of four children (aged 20, 18, 15, 14) and the two older ones are away at college. I have recently taken a full-time job (as a social worker) after having worked part-time for many years. For the first time, I am not at home to greet my children after school, and I feel terrible about it. In this day and age I know that this situation is not unusual, but it is certainly new in our family. The two younger children know it, and have expressed their dissatisfaction with my absence, as has my husband. When I do come home from work, I am too busy cooking and cleaning, and then too tired, to give them much time. I am so guilt-ridden.

When people refer to "latch-key children", those kids who let themselves into their homes after school, they usually mean youngsters between, say 5 and 10 years of age. It is not an unimportant problem, and it is a growing one, with the increasing proportion of married women in the workforce.

But the situation you are describing is considerably different. Your affected children are adolescents, and I am sure that they don't come home right after school anyway. There are extracurricular activities, friends, lessons, sports and so on to occupy their time, if they are in any way typical. You are also a professional, who has waited years to resume her career; there aren't too many men who will put their careers on hold in order to satisfy the needs of their families. This kind of sacrifice seems to be entirely the domain of women. I don't hear about your husband cutting down on his hours at the office. You are also falling into the trap of trying to be a superwoman. Child-rearing, cooking, cleaning, full-time job — and that's all you've mentioned to me. I'm sure you've deleted athletics, paying bills and balancing books, looking after your husband...pant, pant! You can't do it all, nor should you expect yourself to, nor be expected to by your family. Your guilt, or anger at yourself, is misplaced. Instead of taking you for granted, or complaining that "mummy's not here", your kids and husband should be pitching in with the domestic chores.

I think that it's time you sat down with them and told them the (new) facts of life.

105 **When I see what some of my friends have gone through with their kids, I dread the time when mine reach their teenage years. A couple of these kids put their parents through the wringer and then had the gall to move out and have nothing to do with them. I can tell you that's the last they'd hear of me! Life's too short to have us grovelling to our kids, especially if they treat us like dirt.**

I happen to agree with your last sentence, in general. I tend to be open and loving with my kids, but there's no doubt whom we all consider to be "boss". Grovelling, however, shouldn't enter into it from either side; if it's there, something terrible is going on in the relationship. In working with families, there have certainly been times that I urged them to encourage their out-of-control, disdainful, destructive adolescents to leave. And certainly, I know of many teens who have left on their own because of frequent altercations at home, or because there was something "out there" that was better.

Obviously, it makes a huge difference if we're talking about an 18-or-19-year-old versus someone who is 14 or 15. There are all kinds of variations on the theme of kids who move out, but as general rules, (i) they come back eventually, and (ii) they come back when the chips are down. Evolution or God has arranged things so that blood *is* thicker than water. All other relationships pale in significance when we are in dire need, and so it is with teenagers. I have seen countless "emanicipated adolescents" who when pregnant, strung out on drugs, under arrest, or physically or emotionally ill, call out for "mummy" and "daddy" in a cry for help. It happens even with teens who have terrible histories of miserable lives with their parents. And these same rejecting parents respond with nurturance, support and love.

Of course, there are exceptions, and perhaps your examples are some. But I encourage parents to never close the door irrevocably. Lines of communication should be kept open. It is a particular tragedy when there is a permanent schism between parents and their children, a terrible loss for all.

Marriage and Divorce

For all the current cyncism about the necessity for and the longevity of marriage, there are few viable institutions which have stood the test of time as well and have withstood the multiplicity of stresses inherent in our society. Teenagers in our culture still revere romantic love as a forerunner to the stability of marriage. They fantasize, idealize, and dream of perfect relationships for themselves and they are very sensitive to the nuances in the relationships between their parents. They do best when their parents are in loving, happy, mutually respectful marriages.

Although separation and divorce are commonplace in most countries of the Western world, for the adolescent children involved, each break-up is fraught with poignancy and pain. There is no escaping the unhappiness. The best one can hope for is to mollify, to minimize the inevitable gut-wrenching anguish and suffering which occurs when a mother and father split because of irreconcilable differences. A dream is shattered, a myth is destroyed. Grieving and mourning take place in a process somewhat akin to that which occurs upon the death of a loved one. People recover, but we should be under no illusions about the difficulties. On the other hand, teenagers nowadays often find themselves in new families with the sudden addition of a new parent, and sometimes, new siblings. Just as they are getting acclimatized to living with one parent and visiting with another — and this process of adaptation can take years — they find themselves having to learn to live in an entirely new social system. If one of the unsettling characteristics of adolescence is change, and with it, unpredictability, these new arrangements only serve to add to the cacophony in their lives. The difficulties need not be seen as oppressive or ominous, but as with divorce itself, parents have to understand that there are problems inherent in any family re-organization. They can be rectified, minimized, or even prevented at times, but only when the eyes of the participants in those dramas are wide open.

Marriage, fortunately, is here to stay. So, occasionally, is the necessity for divorce. Legislation making divorces more difficult to obtain would not solve the issue of marital problems. Marriages are not actually made in heaven, they take ongoing work as well as commitment; they can be joyful and pleasurable, to be sure, but there are also inevitable difficulties and even pain: understanding these facts should give young people a more realistic view of what the institution is all about.

106 **My husband Will and I will be separating because of "irreconcilable differences". Because of the new *Family Law Act*, and sensitive lawyers, our separation has been planned and even peaceful. Until recently, that is. We both want our 13-year-old daughter to live with us exclusively. She doesn't want to choose sides, and lately Will and I have been at each other's throats over Jane's custody. How do we stop all this fighting?**

The road to hell is paved with good intentions. Trite but true. I can't tell you the number of times I have seen the best laid plans turn into conflict and misery over the very issue you are describing — child custody. The fate of children and the division of money and property has always brought out the worst in the combat units in disputed divorces. Now that the latter has more or less been resolved with the new legal climate (no fault, equal division of assets), the former has remained as the last battleground for the war between adversaries.

No, it needn't, and shouldn't be that way. But I have seen many examples of what has started out as planned joint custody and complete visitation rights deteriorate into an unmitigated brawl, with lawyers in respective corners calling the shots. And who are the losers? The very individuals the conflict is aimed at protecting: the children. You and Will should avoid your lawyers for a while. Accept the fact that you both want what is best for Jane, and that you respect each other as parents, or at least accept that she needs you *both*, and as often and as much as possible. That has to be a "given". With that in mind, it would be wise to seek the services of a "divorce mediator", a relatively recent arrival on the professional scene. He or she will help you avoid the very problems you are now encountering. Jane will have a tough enough time going through this wrenching process with you, without the added burden of having the two closest people in the world to her in a "knock-em-down-drag-em-out" battle. You should know that as difficult as it seems to you, the complexities of this period can be ironed out. It will take time and effort, but mainly, motivation and good will. It can and should be done, for all your sakes.

107   After a long stormy marriage, my husband and I
      recently separated. Two of our three teenage
      children were devastated, while the third seems
      not to care in the slightest. What is the normal
      reaction?

There are no "right" reactions for teenagers in the throes of a divorce between their parents. They are filled with regret, sadness and fear, although they are also relieved that the daily battles may be over. And even if splitting parents prepare their kids for the break-up, reassure them of their love, arrange complete access to both mother and father, and convince them that the separation is not their fault (a common feeling), there will still be varying degrees of internal upheaval.

You can't predict from your kids' different reactions just how they're handling your separation at the moment, or what it means for the future. This is a process that takes months and years to work through. Kids who seem to fall apart at first – and why shouldn't they, it's very sad, isn't it? – often shore up their defenses, re-integrate, and do well, that is, they make the best of it and get on with life. Some others, who seem not to care, have difficulties later on. I cannot predict the outcome of the process for your kids. You and your ex-mate still have a responsibility to love, support, be available, teach, model and say "no" to your kids – all the usual duties of parenthood, in or out of marriage.

108   My husband and I are having serious marital
      problems. They seldom explode openly, but they
      are often smoldering beneath the surface. The
      tension in our house is high, and the air is gloomy.
      Both of our teenage children seem to be barom-
      eters of our conflict, and especially of their fa-
      ther's mood. If we're (he's) okay, they're up; if
      we're at each other, they are quiet, even sullen.
      Is this normal?

I take it that yours is a rhetorical question. That is, you surely know that it's normal for kids to pick up the vibes in the family. And often they act accordingly. Some adolescents will be fairly transparent, as yours are, in their reaction to their parents' problems. Others will try desperately to interject levity and effusiveness into the house. Still other teens will just remove themselves from the situation, preferring the company of friends. And lastly, some will demonstrate their reaction to parental conflict by developing their own problems: school failure, depression, antisocial behavior, drugs and so on. Kids have an almost biological inner propensity to maintain the wholeness of the nuclear family. They don't want to see either parent hurt, and from a less altruistic point of view, they want to avoid their own deep pain.

However they may express their barometric readings, they are telling you that you must get your marital act together. There are many talented marital and family counsellors around who could evaluate your relationship, and work with you to ameliorate the problems, if possible. It is likely (and advisable) that your kids would be involved too, so that they are not kept in the dark, and they become part of the solution.

I don't have to tell you that separation and divorce are sometimes consequences of severe, long-standing marital conflict. Counselling will not guarantee a happy marriage, but it will give you a clearer idea of its chances for survival, and help you all to cope whatever the outcome.

109 **My husband and I separated a year ago, after 20 years of marriage. Without getting into the whys and wherefores, it was the best thing we could have done for us, as opposed to our children! They had a tough time in the first few months, and have gradually begun to settle down, accepting the fact that we both love them and are devoted to them. My problem is that I have met a terrific guy whom I genuinely like. The first time he came to our home, my teenagers were so rude that I was astounded and ashamed. I yelled at**

them afterwards, but neither wanted to discuss it with me.

Many readers who have gone through a separation and divorce will recognize this mother's experience. Your children are still wrestling with the meaning of their parents' break-up *for themselves*; the disillusionment, the destruction of an ideal, even a mythology of marriage. These notions die hard. Kids also cherish, we have learned, an ever-present hope, even an expectation, that you and their father will get together again.

Alas, it is not to be. And this new man, as wonderful as he may be, is not only an intruder, but a clear message to your kids that their dream is unalterably shattered. He is the nail in the coffin of the marriage, so to speak.

You should be allowed to date, obviously. It may be premature to bring him home, but it depends on the readiness of your children. It is important that you speak to them openly and honestly about your own needs and intentions. But you should also convey to them that you are aware of their pain and sadness, and can understand their initial rudeness. It may take weeks, even months, for them to come to grips with the changes in their lives.

Just as these changes are inevitable, so too is their eventual acceptance and even enjoyment of the new situation. They'll start talking to you about all this emotional commotion soon; just give them an opening.

110 **My husband and I have been divorced for two-and-a-half years, and we are now each in new relationships. While it was a difficult period for our kids, we both felt that we all handled it well. We shared the custody, and the girls were free to choose with whom they wanted to live. The problem is that they use the power like a club. If they don't like one parent's rules or style or what-have-you, they opt to move in with the other, and vice versa.**

It sounds like the girls are having a field day at your expense, but of course this is not the case at all. As teenagers, they are *still* in that difficult period of adjustment after divorce. With both of you in new intimate relationships, it may well be that they are desperate to try to reunite the family unit before it's too late. Teenagers seem to suffer longer after a divorce than the younger kids, and even the parents; they also harbor hopes of reconciliation much longer. They may be angry at both of you, and they could be using the flexibility you have given them to punish you for hurting them so. When their parents are basically in accord, this problem can be managed gingerly (yet with difficulty). But when they are at odds, they can wreak havoc, play one parent off against the other, and use your mutual distrust to their (dis)advantage.

When children reach adolescence, custody assignment is in many ways more complicated, since the preferences of the children are more cogently and maturely based. In your case, the girls seemed to have a good relationship with each of you, so that even that decision was fraught with internal conflict. They didn't want to hurt either of you. You also realize that they are each wrestling with their own sense of autonomy, and their relationships with the opposite sex, both of which impinge on parents even at the best of times. We should not let them off the hook, but we do need to understand the various pressures buffeting them. Nevertheless, your backing down in the face of their threats is actually fueling these fires.

You and your ex will be doing your adolescent daughters a favor if you can maintain even the semblance of a united front. If their well-being is top priority for both of you, then it behooves you two to lay down your arms, at least as far as your kids are concerned. I know that bitterness sometimes reigns supreme in post-marital exchanges (what with deep hurts, rights over money, lawyers' machinations, and an adversarial court system), but even feuding ex-mates can provide some stability for their kids — if they want to.

111 I have been married for over 20 years to a wonderful woman, but I don't love her the way I would like to. I am deeply in love with somebody else

(my wife is unaware of this development, but suspicious). We are a visible family, well known in the community. Our marriage from the outside has seemed to others idyllic, even to me, at times, except that I have been known to see other women, and my wife and I have bickered incessantly for many years. I would like to make a go of the marriage, even at this stage, if possible; or to start over, and allow her the same opportunity (she is still beautiful and vibrant and has many friends and a career of her own). My problem is the four kids, all teenagers. While they have seen the tension between us, they would be terribly hurt by a divorce, and we just don't want to cause them pain. Neither of us is keen on seeing a marital counsellor, but we'd do it if absolutely necessary. We both feel that it lends an air of inevitability to the demise.

You are on the horns of a dilemma, partly determined by the situation, and partly because you have boxed yourself in. You don't want to hurt the kids, you don't want to see a marital therapist — you want a quick fix to make everything rosy and peaceful. Well, it is not going to be that simple. What do you mean by "the way I would like to"? Surely you are not comparing the blush of romance to a long-standing marriage! You seem quite sure that your new love is unlike your previous flings, that you no longer love your wife and that your marriage has been tense for years. In embracing this certainty, you have more or less closed your mind to the possibility of rekindling any romance in your marriage.

There is no doubt that you are embarking on a painful, protracted process. You *will* hurt your kids, and your wife, not to mention yourself, and your lover. You have to judge whether all this pain is worth it to you. You can explore this question in individual psychotherapy, to straighten out your own head regarding your needs, conflicts and priorities. At some point (soon, it appears) you are going to have to level with your wife, and tell her where your mind (at least) has been for these past few months and years.

I am not presenting this advice as an admonishment, nor am I telling you to live unhapily for the rest of your life. Only you can decide that. Certainly, exploratory marital therapy is highly recommended. But if you are going to split, be aware of the inherent difficulties and try to make the process as least destructive to your kids as possible. Ludicruous as it sounds, you will need your wife's co-operation; she will need your honesty and support. Divorce mediation may be a necessary step for you to consider at some point after that decision is made.

112 **Both my fiancée and I are divorced, and we each have two teenaged children living with us. Our divorces were messy and painful, and all the kids suffered for a while. But they and we seem to be doing well now. We are deeply in love and want to marry. We're concerned, however, about creating a new family and increasing the stresses on the kids once again. What should we do?**

This particular situation, so uncommon a few years ago, is now a relatively common phenomenon. The name affixed to these new assemblages is "reconstituted families". In your case, two families of four members each become one family of six members. There is no doubt that it will take a while for the new alignments, dynamics and balances to evolve before a state of relative calm and equilibrium is achieved. Until that time there will be wariness, tentativeness and some degree of stress — all of which are inevitable.

So many family therapists have been involved in attempting to handle the attendant problems that a considerable body of knowledge has been built up regarding the dos and don'ts of reconstituted families. The resultant clinical findings and the ongoing research have provided some preventative measures. Certainly, preparatory discussions and shared experiences are important questions which can be addressed *a priori*. Spend time talking and engaging in activities together. See how it feels; "wear it" for a while.

All of this preparation can be done on your own, particularly if you are both sensitive and aware. Some people involve a family counsellor at this stage to facilitate the smooth integration of the families. Others, of course, don't involve a therapist unless specific problems arise. Whichever route you choose, you can feel confident that this is all eminently "do-able". The best of luck to you.

113 **My wife Aimée and I are seriously thinking of splitting. We've drifted apart over the past few years, and I'm involved with another woman. Aimée is furious and has insisted on not only telling our friends and my professional colleagues, but also our teenagers (Rob and Janet) about all my many past indiscretions and malfeasances. I feel humiliated and publicly degraded. But the thing that bothers me more than that, is that our kids have needlessly been burdened with disrespect for and even dislike of their father. I am still living at home, but I am now very upset.**

The old saw, "Hell hath no fury like a woman scorned" is apparently operative here. In an attempt to justify your splitting to herself as well as others, Aimée is pulling out all stops, seeking allies and support. She is obviously deeply wounded as well as angry and vengeful. If you get hurt in the emotional traffic, so be it, from her perspective. The long-suffering wife should not be expected to show compassion and tolerance for her husband. She has also been deeply humiliated, so that your concern over the response of colleagues and friends rings hollow, and certainly won't get you empathy or sympathy from her.

The issue around the children is another story, I'm afraid. Aimée's desperation and anger have allowed her to not only involve them prematurely, but destructively. Nothing is gained by warring spouses attempting to poison their children's minds against their perceived adversary. As acrimonious and venomous as mutual feelings and outbursts become — and they certainly do — there is still no reason to involve your children. Furthermore, such involvement makes attempts at reconciliation (if it should come to that) extraordinarily difficult, because their mistrust and disrespect for you has to be overcome as well as Aimée's.

I hope that you are exploring the reasons for your "malfeasances" during the course of your marriage, and why you were so vulnerable to falling in love with somebody new. You may discover that the problems in your marriage were significant and involved you both. It may be that marital therapy should have been attempted many years ago. It may be too late now, but I notice that you are still living at home. Why the delay? Lastly, having been through this many times with others, my advice is don't burn any bridges irrevocably. Hearts and minds do change....

114

My wife and I have been divorced for many years. Our children were 7, 5, and 2 at the time. They were financially and materially well provided for, but I must admit that I was emotionally estranged from them and their mother for many years. Our divorce was acrimonious and extremely bitter. I think that we did everything wrong. I was immature and selfish and my ex-wife was constantly hostile, a terrific recipe for disaster. But after years of psychotherapy I've fallen in love with a wonderful woman, and I feel like a new man. Moreover, I am soon to remarry, and I'd like my kids (now teenagers) and even my ex-wife to come to the wedding. The problem is that they adamantly refuse. They don't even return my calls. What can I do?

I'm not sure there is much you can do in the short run. There are obviously deep and unhealed wounds, still festering and causing pain. Just because you are now ready to let bygones be bygones, and raise the flag of peace, is not enough reason for them to declare a similar stance. They want to be convinced that you are ready to enter into difficult discussions with them about the past, present and future. Before you get annoyed at me, I hasten to add that they must be prepared to make the same effort. Separation and estrangement are not one-way streets.

Furthermore, to them, your new marriage is akin to a red flag (as opposed to the aforementioned peace flag). They see you as having abandoned and deserted them, destroying the nuclear family as a direct result. Whether this is the whole truth (it seldom is) is irrelevant. Human beings — especially teenagers — like to deal in absolutes, rights vs. wrongs, good guys and bad guys.

Extend invitations to them, by all means, but they may choose to refuse, or not even bother to answer. But if your commitment to rapprochement is a real one, then don't make the wedding the ultimate test of its possibility. Call, write and invite, not in a grovelling manner, but in a generous, warm, caring, yes, even loving spirit. Sometimes a lengthy letter, followed by a meeting, works wonders. At other times it falls on deaf ears, or causes merely a temporary thaw in a permanently frigid atmosphere. Still another possibility I have seen is the fracturing of the wall of unaminity. That is, one or two kids might be willing to try to rekindle the love that was there (albeit quite differently now), while the others continue to "hate" you. Be prepared for all eventualities.

I hope that the rest of your emotional life is more peaceful and rewarding than the last decade.

115 **We have a wonderful marriage and family scene. Nan and I have been married for 21 years and we are still deeply in love. But in our two teenagers' school classes, approximately half of the kids are from divorced families. How do we ensure that our kids' marriages will be as successful as ours? It seems impossible in this day and age, when there is an epidemic of divorce.**

Well, you know as well as I that there are no guarantees in this world. It is fairly obvious — and well documented — that the best predictor of a good life in the future is a good life in the past. A child from a broken, battered, abusive background is much more likely to repeat that scenario than one from a loving, wholesome family. Similarly, a young person who has grown up in a family such as yours will try to emulate his or her parents and the atmosphere they helped create.

Your kids have known the love and security which is associated with a cohesive, warm family, and they will attempt to replicate those characteristics in their own homes and families. Of course, much will depend on their own personalities, and the kinds of people they fall in love with and marry.

What we are discussing here is obviously "odds", and if I were a betting man, I would say that you are in good shape. You have less to fear than most people; your kids will certainly try hard to avoid strife and schism.

School and Work

Do you realize that our adolescents spend an average of 10,000 hours each (!) in school during their teenage years? Small wonder that so many parents are preoccupied with what their sons and daughters are accomplishing in those hallowed academic halls. School not only provides for formal education; it also is a natural laboratory for the study of the self in relation to other young people. Attendance is crucial for the development of an individual's identity: mind, manner and morals.

We have long decried the lack of involvement of some mothers and fathers in the educational process of their children. But many parents are actually overinvolved. Some live through their children's successes vicariously, and take each failure very personally. They nag, cajole and demand relentlessly. Homework assignments, studying, tests and exams receive inordinate attention, and can become the focus of power struggles between the generations. These parents often see educational achievement as the ticket to success for their offspring, and can't abide by what they see as underachievement or laziness.

Where should we draw the line between ignoring and berating? One can argue about the excesses, the people who use their kids for their own sorry purposes, and exaggerate the premise of educational success. But that premise is basically correct. The farther one goes educationally, the greater one's chances for success. Sure, there are exceptions: individual interests and talents, contacts and mentors, life experiences and even luck can play major roles. But the single most important variable determining eventual socioeconomic standing is education. Certainly, for those who have major financial worries, the poor, disenfranchised, immigrants — school is the surest way out of the morass of misery.

Not all kids fit into high-level academic programs. The diversity in our society must be reflected in the flexibility, variety and array of schooling available. There are already different "tracks" or academic streams for kids with different talents and interests. There are vocational schools, which teach young people a variety of trades. There are also "alternative" schools, with much looser curricula, catering to some teenagers' difficulties with structure and conformity. Apprenticeship programmes, working for academic credits and private sector involvement should all be introduced. Once a youngster has been matched with the school appropriate for his or her specific intellectual level and other skills, the life of the parents will become much easier (if they can accept the match). Our kids are not all destined to become Einsteins, Pavarottis or Trudeaus (or even Sinatras or Springsteens), but the opportunities for maximizing the potential that each kid has should be provided by the school system.

116   **My husband and I are at odds on the choice of school for our 14-year-old son, Newton. I would like him to go to a residential private high school and my husband would prefer (to put it mildly) a good community high school a few blocks away. When I think of prep school, I see excellent education, fantastic facilities, a chance to live away from home, excellent contacts for later life, and the opportunity to develop a strong sense of self. My husband, on the other hand, sees spoiled kids, arrogance, indulgence and elitism.**

You sound too intelligent and thoughtful to believe that I can come up with a magic answer, especially in the area of who is "right" or "wrong" here. I just find it fascinating that nowhere in your letter do you mention what Newton is like, and what type of school *he* would prefer. Surely this omission is no accident! The personality and preferences of the student are crucial determinants in these deliberations; indeed, my decision would be much more dependent on Newton's own qualities than upon his parents' biases. Some kids thrive in prep schools, others are eaten up by that system. The same is true of the public school system. And it is unfair to talk about prep schools or community high schools as stereotyped entities. We know that schools, public or private, vary startlingly in their general atmosphere, approach to students, degree of rigidity or flexibility, scholastic versus extracurricular demands, uniformity of student body and other qualities. You also know that the type of school selected is no guarantee of scholastic success. If the choice could be narrowed down to good or bad, you would have a clear direction. But you have a choice between two positive alternatives, so the question to ask is which school is more in keeping with Newton's strengths and needs, and will help mold him in a way that you all want.

Both of your depictions of these different schools are based on your own stereotypes and fantasies. As far as your premature conclusions are concerned, there are elements of validity in both points of view. It behooves you to do some visiting of a variety of prep and community schools, with Newton along as the major player. Speak to educators and parents, and then see if some kind of compromise can be reached (for example, an egalitarian progressive school with high standards and a serious student body). All sorts and shades of schools do exist. There is no reason why Newton can't have an excellent education and a pleasurable one — nor any reason why his parents can't both be pleased.

117 Our son Barry goes to the best high school in our area; he's bright, has friends and seems happy and active, but he's failing. He just doesn't do enough work. We've never had this problem with him before. Any suggestions?

There are many reasons for kids doing poorly at school, and I'd like to mention a few even though they aren't necessarily applicable to your son. Sometimes high school students get a rude awakening; after a relatively easy time in elementary school, they may be unprepared for the workload or the difficulty of the new system. Occasionally, they are confronted with a whole new group of classmates and their unease or shyness preoccupies them and interferes with their concentration or school work. For others, poor performance is merely a continuation of many years of the same experience. Obviously, some young people are just not cut out for an academic curriculum. Lastly, a high school student who is depressed or significantly disturbed, or who has a terribly disruptive family life, will have a great deal of trouble keeping up in school.

So much for the generalities. Now back to Barry. He is not new to high school; he has a stable loving family; he is happy, has friends and is active. Also, the deterioration in his school work is a relatively recent occurrence. Something is obviously going on. It might be that he is just disinterested, or rather, that his interests lie elsewhere (sports, girls, drugs). Perhaps he is newly involved with a group of kids who share an anti-school ethic, in which doing school work is seen as "selling out". It could also be that he is covering up some preoccupation of which you are totally unaware.

Obviously, you have spoken to Barry about this problem, and he hasn't enlightened you at all. It might be a good idea to speak to his teachers, and hear how they perceive the situation. For example, are there any areas of strength (and good marks) at school? Do any of his studies turn him on? A meeting with the school vice-principal or guidance counsellor that also includes Barry might be most beneficial. Aside from learning more about the situation and getting advice about how to correct it, such a meeting is an invaluable exercise in consciousness-raising. It means your son will learn that you care very much about him (as if he didn't know!) and that you mean business. You, on the other hand, will learn more about him as an autonomous human being, and increase your low-key sleuthing into other aspects of his life.

Luckily, Barry has options in his life. Unlike some other kids who are doing poorly, he has all the potential to do well. He has to learn about accountability. You can offer incentives, rewards and punishments, but you can only do so much cajoling, threatening, pushing, supporting, encouraging and nurturing; the rest is up to him.

118 **On the surface our son, Dan, seems like the answer to a parent's dream, and friends have told us this with a certain degree of envy, especially in light of their own children's poor school performance. Dan, on the other hand, is an exceptional student, consistently at the top of the class. So why am I concerned? Dan eats, sleeps and drinks his studies. He has always done so, but now it is worse than ever. (He is 17). He doesn't socialize, except in school, but even there he's mainly in the library during his spares. He takes part in no social sports, although he does long jogs daily. He says that he has to do well in high school in order to go to a good university. He tells me that he is happy with his life, but I have my doubts. I think he's overdoing it.**

What your letter points out is the phenomenal variability among kids (and parents). Your friends are envious not just of the superficial picture you think they see; they probably know what Dan is like, and yet they are still impressed. I can hear them wishing that their kids weren't into drugs, sex or school avoidance. "If only I could have a child like Dan!," they think to themselves. They don't know that his mother is worried sick about that same young man!

Dan is a serious kid, maybe even somewhat obsessional, with a single-minded purpose, a dedication to academic excellence and achievement. To try to fit him into a mold that doesn't suit his personality would not do him (or you) any good. It's true that he's missing out on some enjoyable experiences, perhaps even developmentally important ones. But he is fairly set in his ways, and satisfied with his functions, and that is really the important issue. He also has time to broaden his horizons.

If his obsessional studying was marked or accompanied by failure, reclusiveness, sadness, sleep problems, poor concentration or other troublesome symptoms, we might be dealing with something more disturbing, or even pathological. But Dan doesn't seem to show these or other related indications of inner turbulence or torment. Maybe his personality makes some people uncomfortable. Maybe he won't be a popular individual, or full of fun and frolic, but I think Dan is going to surprise you; *his* still waters will run deep.

119 **I am the father of Sean, a 14-year-old boy who is a joy. He is doing well in most respects except one, and I am afraid that it is my doing. Ever since Sean was a little boy, I have helped him with his homework; often to such an extent that I have ended up doing it all, including projects and special assignments. While I resented this at times, I must admit that I enjoyed much of the homework, and especially felt proud when Sean brought home As for "his" work. Well, now he is in Grade Eleven and can't be encouraged to do his own work. He says that he "just can't", and is**

annoyed at me for not helping more. I am too busy now and frankly, his work is beyond me in some respects, but I don't know how to get him to work on his own without getting angry at me.

The tone of your letter suggests to me that given the time and facility, you would still be doing Sean's homework. You are certainly proud of your As. Luckily for both of you, you have neither, so that Sean has little choice but to do his work himself. It is sink-or-swim time, but that has more to do with circumstances than with your resolve.

Sean has had a good thing going for many years, so we can understand both his bewilderment and fear of having to work autonomously, and his anger at you for letting him down. But your help has had the paradoxically painful effect of making him question his own abilities. With each A came another dollop of self-doubt.

You must tell Sean exactly how you feel. You can show him your letter and this answer, if it will help. He must know that you have confidence in him, that you "helped" him so much less for his needs, than for your own selfish, self-aggrandizing needs. It was you who needed the As. Tell him that.

Sean likely needs some help now to build up his scholastic confidence, someone to coach him. But that person must definitely not be you! The tutor should be an individual who is familiar with the work, to be sure, but especially one who can make young people comfortable and bring out the best in them. With a bit of encouragement, practice, experience, some failures and more successes, Sean should get his confidence back. His father should be somewhat contrite.

120 **I overheard a conversation between my 15-year-old daughter, Melinda, and her friend last week that upset me. They were talking about a male teacher of theirs as they would discuss one of their closest boyfriends. When her friend left I asked Melinda more about it, and she revealed**

that she is madly in love with Mr. Salant ("call me Gerry"). I have met this guy at Parents' Night; he is good-looking, single, in his early thirties. I don't think that he is at all aware of Melinda's secret passion, but her total preoccupation with him bothers us.

What you are describing is a remarkably common picture: young teenaged girls falling in love with older teachers, idealizing them, imbuing them with all kinds of wonderful character traits, and of course, fantasizing, fantasizing, fantasizing. "Where we would go, where we would stay, what would we be wearing, what would he say, when (how) would we make love", and on and on.

The objects of these girls' affections are unavailable, which keeps them safe, and they can indulge their wildest romantic and erotic dreams to their hearts' content without fear of being put to the test. Usually the crush lasts from weeks to months and then dissipates into nothing, or becomes less fascinating with the availability of boys closer to Belinda's age.

Sometimes attractive teachers don't realize that they have this power over some of their impressionable students, and compound their blissful ignorance by blithely making "come hither" statements: "Call me Gerry" is a friendly, warm, informal invitation. On the surface it is innocuous, but if it is stated in a context of direct eye contact and warm body language, it can be misconstrued by girls with stars in their eyes.

Of course, there is always that very rare exception, the teacher who knows exactly what he is doing, and who is trying to seduce a young student. One could try to put a benevolent light on this behavior by classifying it as a Lolita complex, as in Nabokov's novel, but it is pedophilia. Parents should put this unlikely possibility on a back burner, and monitor their daughter's progress. Speak to Melinda, and gently tell her how inappropriate her behavior is. She will, in all likelihood, be offended — but you will have done your job.

121 **Adam is our only son. He is 16, in his third year of high school and he is a confident, outspoken kid. The problem is his teachers. I've felt this way for a couple of years, but I've never made a fuss until now — when they kicked him off the football team after he argued strongly with the coach. They have continually picked on him, making him stay after school, or giving him extra assignments. They accuse him of being disrespectful. We've always taught him to stand up for what he thinks is right; so what if he gets excited at times? Don't you think the school owes me an explanation, even an apology?**

I agree that an apology is owed, but not quite the way that you want it. Frankly, Adam sounds obnoxious, and it is obvious that he has been getting encouragement from you. It is one thing to be assertive and outspoken, but it is quite another to be arrogant and offensive. If this were an isolated incident, I might give him (and you) the benefit of the doubt. But the charges against Adam involve multiple teachers over a long period of time — there is agreement and consistency — or as social scientists are fond of saying, consensual validation. There is no excuse for rudeness and that is exactly what Adam has been showing to his teachers in the guise of offering legitimate arguments.

He sounds like he has an axe to grind. There is no reason he has to have a chip on his shoulder, and actively seek out confrontation with his teacher. You are half right: the school does owe you an explanation, but it is you and Adam who owe them an apology. And he needs help.

122 **I can't believe that I'm still concerned about Gary's truancy. When he was younger, he occasionally skipped classes, but he's now 16! Surely he should be beyond this stage by now. We have been informed by the school that he missed a total of 47 classes last semester alone. This is**

our main concern, although we know that he occasionally uses drugs and gets into some other trouble. But let's face it, all kids do that; we just don't want him to get kicked out of school.

I'm afraid that I can't buy your "boys will be boys" argument. It just isn't so that "all kids do that". In fact, relatively few do and they are largely a troubled group. While truancy is your primary concern, Gary, it seems, is involved in other potentially destructive behavior. And this involvement is not at all unusual. More often than not, high school students who chronically skip classes are also more frequently involved in smoking, drug use, school failure and other disturbing manifestations of anger and rebelliousness.

Your terse letter does not inform me about Gary's personality or the nature of the "other trouble" that he has been getting into. But if he's missed 47 classes in one semester, and has been using drugs, it is not far-fetched for me to assume that unless there is some intervention, your worst fears are indeed going to be realized. He will no doubt be out of school very shortly if this keeps up. It is all well and good that the school "informs" you that your son has been skipping classes, but is this truly the first you've heard of it? If so, then the school is sorely derelict in its duty. You should have been called a long time ago, with warnings and consequences for Gary for further absenteeism. There should have been interviews with you, Gary and someone official from school. I actually find it almost incredible that none of this apparently took place. There is blatant irresponsibility here. The most irresponsible party, however, is Gary, and unless he is held accountable, he is going to fall on his face, or elsewhere.

Depending on what else is going on with him, Gary may need a comprehensive psychological evaluation. But that action is down the road a bit. First and foremost, it is necessary for you and the school to confront his behavior, and impose stringent demands for him to live up to, that is, he must go to school, he must not use drugs, he must not get involved in "other trouble". This may sound silly coming from a psychiatrist, but compassion and understanding should not preclude getting Gary on the "straight and narrow". There have to be expectations and limits set for him, just as there are for all of us. This action is not in the service of retribution and punishment; rather it is in the service of love and education. If Gary "can't" live up to minimal expectations, some further intervention may be indicated.

123 **Our 15-year-old son, Mark, refuses to go to school. He's been a gentle, sweet, responsible boy, so that truancy is the last thing we'd expect from him. He has never been in any kind of trouble, and we are furious at him. We've tried to force him to go, but he seems to crumble in panic. It's baffling.**

Mark has not suddenly become bad or irresponsible. And your being "furious" is going to do him more harm than good. You are describing a complex and common syndrome, or abnormal behavior pattern, referred to as "school phobia". However, it is only common in younger children. A phobia is an irrational fear, one for which there is no valid cause. Between the ages of five and ten, school phobia is usually related to the difficulty the child has in separating from the mother and the security of the home. (Before settling on this explanation, it is important to rule out other causes, such as fear of failure, or of punishment after a misdemeanor, or even fear of a bully.) School phobia is readily correctible by bringing the child back to school, even against his will at times, and demonstrating that there is nothing to fear. School personnel are familiar with the problem, and can be useful in working with the child and the parents. Sometimes, a few counselling sessions are necessary and helpful.

But Mark is in a different age group. School refusal in adolescence is in fact indicative of more serious problems, and coercion is probably the least effective strategy to overcome them. The panic which Mark feels when you attempt to force him is not manipulative; it is agonizingly real. The obvious questions have to be asked, of course, but the school phobia may well be a symptom of severe emotional distress for which psychotherapy and even medication are in order. At the very least, Mark should have a comprehensive psychiatric evaluation as soon as possible. This can be arranged through your family doctor or Mark's pediatrician.

124 **Jody is our 16-year-old daughter who suddenly announced to us that she wants to quit high school. It's true that her marks have never been anything to write home about, but we never expected her to quit. She says that she hates school, and will never go back. She says that she wants to work (although she has no marketable skills). She doesn't seem unhappy; in fact, she appears downright relieved with her decision. We are miserable.**

Like you, and most readers of this book, I would like my kids to finish high school, go on to university and be successful in their chosen careers. (If we could also add wonderful marriages, children and health, they — and we — would have it made.) Often our kids follow these guidelines as if properly programmed by society, their parents and themselves. Sometimes, however, our best laid plans are supplanted by our kids' agendas. And they may well be inimical to our own. Jody knows exactly how you feel, and yet she sounds very adamant about her decision.

Your letter raises many questions, although it does answer a few. It is clear that Jody is not depressed; I presume that she is not dropping out because of mental illness. Furthermore, school has never been a place where she has enjoyed success, at least from an academic perspective. I would want to know if she is socially successful and what her interests are. Are her friends dropping out too? Is she heavily into dating? Has she been involved with drugs?

Answers to these questions would better tell us what exactly we are dealing with. Because you don't mention any of these issues as problems, I am going to assume that Jody wants to get out because of less pathological factors. Sometimes young people know better than we do what is best for them, and Jody may be one of those individuals. Certainly, this move entails a discussion with the school authorities — her teachers, guidance counsellors and vice-principal. They obviously have a vested interest in keeping kids in school as long as possible, yet they may surprise you; they may feel that Jody and traditional schooling are incompatible. They may suggest some alternate forms of training and education which are more in line with Jody's own particular strengths and interests, with which they should be very familiar. At the very least they can impress upon her the necessity for getting some specific trade or skill training. There are also special high schools which cater to specific interests and levels of academic ability. Rather than cause a major confrontation with Jody by forbidding her to quit and forcing her to return to an unhappy (for her) setting, you should try to work with her and the school to find a mutually satisfactory solution.

125 **We have a problem that is entirely of my making. I am the father of two great kids (15 and 17), but I can't seem to stop myself from keeping after them to do their homework, keep up in school, study, and so forth. My wife has a much more laissez-faire attitude (which actually infuriates me) but I keep on their cases. This pressure has caused more than a few unpleasnt altercations, as you'd expect. Still, I can't help feeling that they can do better (they are both above-average students), and that their future successes will be closely tied to their prowess at school.**

It sounds from the tone of your letter as if you don't like the battles which ensue as a result of your hounding your children, but that you still feel both reasonable and good about doing it. You've provided for yourself a rationale which justifies your behavior to you. And indeed, there is a correlation between scholastic success and later achievements. There are many exceptions, of course, in both directions, but as a general rule, your assumption holds. No doubt, if you could avoid incurring your kids' resentment, you'd carry on quite happily doing exactly the same thing.

But they *do* resent it. Their conclusion is that you don't trust them, respect them or have enough confidence in their sense of maturity and willingness to take responsibility for their own schoolwork. You haven't suggested that they are irresponsible or untrustworthy. In your case, while mild encouragement may be desirable, demands and badgering are obviously unnecessary and ultimately destructive to both your relationship with them and to the very goal which you are trying to achieve. If your kids were really angry and wanted to rebel against parental (paternal) values (and they all do, to at least a small extent), what better way to do it than through school performance?

I trust that you are not fighting your differences with your wife through your teenagers. You sound angry at her, and I doubt that it stems merely from her attitude to their schoolwork. Perhaps you should discuss this with her directly and get some help if necessary. Lastly, you *can* stop yourself; you just don't want to. The rest is up to you.

126 **Do you believe that high school students should work part-time? My husband and I want Charles, our 16-year-old son, to get a job after school, to help defray the cost of his entertainment, travel, clothing and books. Charles tells us that none of his friends work, and that his school work will suffer if he doesn't have time to do his homework or study. We find this hard to swallow.**

How is this for an answer? Yes and no. For example, if Charles is a good student, and has got gobs of time on his hands, the answer might be "yes". If he is a struggling student, who has to work arduously for every mark, the answer might be "no". If, on the other hand, Charles is heavily engaged in many extracurricular activities, the answer can be yes or no, depending on your values and priorities. Another consideration is your own financial status; if you *really* need his monetary assistance, the philosophical questioning becomes almost irrelevant.

Ultimately, it is your own system of values, and what you want to inculcate in Charles that is all-important. Do you want him to learn the value of a dollar by working? Is budgeting his own income something you consider important for him to learn? Do you feel that your son should experience contributing his share of money (chores, responsibilities) to the family?

I happen to feel that affirmative answers to all of these preceding questions are indicated; but this doesn't mean that all high school children should work at part-time, after-school jobs. Like so many other issues, "it depends" becomes the modus operandi. It depends on the individual's personality, schedule, intelligence, energy level, motivation, and other demands on his or her time. It certainly also depends on the principles, persuasive techniques, and pressure on the part of parents.

127   **Our 16-year-old daughter, Melanie, has wanted to get a job for years in order to earn extra money. School has not proven too onerous for her, she participates in extracurricular activities and has friends. We acquiesced, and she got a job at a fast food outlet with flexible hours and good pay. Last night, she didn't go to work, and was very upset. We pressed her and she said that she was reluctant to return because her supervisor was constantly making extremely suggestive remarks to her. He evidently was implying that she either "come across" or she'd be out of this job. How should we handle this?**

Sexual harassment in the workplace is, unfortunately, a common occurrence, and usually along the lines of Melanie's experience. That is, a male in a superior postion makes sexual overtures to a female with the implied or even explicit threat that her job is on the line. Some sexual bantering does, of course, occur between employees and employers in the workplace, and it is often mutually active and enjoyable. But even that seemingly harmless teasing can be taken too far. There are also some individuals who take offense at any hint of sexual overtones. Sometimes, sexual harassment is an overstated depiction of what was intended as a joke and occasionally it is maliciously charged. That just about covers the waterfront, right?

Melanie, however, seems to be in a clear-cut harassment situation that can't be allowed to go on. She could quit her job to escape her tormentor, but then he wins and she loses, and other victims will be harassed by him. As soon as you are sure of the facts, you have a responsibility to phone this guy's boss, or write him a formal letter of complaint. Provincial Human Rights Commissions often have to deal with cases along these lines, as do Labor Relations Boards. You and she could even launch an official complaint through one of these bodies.

Whether this fellow is castigated, fired, exposed, or otherwise punished is largely up to his superiors, and how far you want to take this charge. He has to, *and can* learn that his behavior is unconscionable and cannot be repeated. And Melanie has to see that she can be protected by the law.

128 **Our son, Peter, is in his senior (last) year of high school. He is an above-average student, but not outstanding. He is also a lonely young man. He has announced that before going on to university he wants to work and travel for a year. We are opposed to this for just about every reason one can think of, but especially because he'll lose time compared to his friends and peers. What do you think?**

Once again, I have to give you an "it depends" answer. This isn't obfuscation, but rather an indication that many decisions for adolescents regarding both specific, novel activities and timing are contingent upon a number of factors. Beware of glib, easy or "right" answers.

If Peter is mature, responsible, reliable and stable; if he genuinely doesn't know what he wants to do in university (especially if he's planning to go to a school with rigid, early demands for commitment to majors); if he is planning to pay his own way; if the time is to be used for thinking and experiencing, as well as for pleasure and time out; if nothing dangerous is being contemplated — if *all* the answers are acceptable (they seldom are), then he should have your blessing, even your encouragement. There is a term used in contemporary psychology to account for this hiatus, the "psychosocial moratorium", sort of a cooling out period. Only you know where Peter fits on a scale for each of these criteria. Usually, most of them are met to some extent, but there remain a couple of issues that are ambiguous and worrisome to most parents in this situation. After all, the time off is being taken because of some problem in the area of commitment to a direction.

All kinds of approaches have been used. Certainly, discussions between you and Peter regarding your feelings are essential, but I assume that they've already occurred and ended at an impasse, or even worse, with recriminations. Many more young people contemplate taking that break than actually do it, and support rather than opposition from parents certainly plays an important role in that decision. Your responsibility is to convey your misgivings, but *hear him out.* Find out what others think of your concerns. You may be surprised to hear how many express to you their support of Peter. Remember too, that if you come down really hard against this idea, it may *not* dissuade him; or if it does, you may be held accountable (by him and by yourselves) if the year doesn't go right.

Finally, the least of "my" concerns would be the ensuing loneliness if Peter does take the year "off". It really doesn't work that way. He can still be friends with those a year ahead of him, and he can certainly make new ones.

129 **I have a son, aged 16, and a daughter who is 17. Both are bright and want to go to Ivy League schools. The problem is money. I can only afford to send one of them to a top university. The other**

will have to make do with a lesser school. There is no doubt that my son will go to the better school because he needs it more, being male. My wife is furious with me, but don't you think that she's dead wrong?

At least you are progressive enough to allow your daughter to go to college at all! You are being sexist and unfair. If you are dead set on an Ivy League school; if there is only enough money to send one child there, and if no loans or scholarships or self-earnings are forthcoming, then I suppose you have given yourself no alternative but to choose one child over the other. I could argue that you've boxed yourself in, that there are many excellent but less expensive schools, that you could apply at one of the special sources of funds that exist to help students offset the cost of university. But I'd rather talk about your selection procedure, which is where your problem really lies.

You are immediately relegating your daughter to what you perceive to be an inferior educational experience merely because she is female. She won't need the contacts, the career, the achievements or the income: isn't that what you believe? I know many successful women, and others who weren't given the same opportunities, who would disagree vehemently (even violently) with you. Your wife may even be one of them. I will not deny that significant emotional and behavioral differences exist between men and women, but they have nothing to do with intellectual capacity, independence and career options. In this day and age, even given that women are still the primary homemakers and child-rearers (let us face facts), they can and do achieve pinnacles of success in all kinds of endeavors, despite the obstacles (including parents with attitudes like yours) that are placed in their way.

If you feel it is necessary to choose (again, there are other, better approaches), the child who gets the opportunity to attend the Ivy League school should be the one who merits it most, on the basis of scholastic records, talents, interests and aspirations; not because of biological sex assignment.

130 Our 18-year-old son, Tom, is entering an excellent university this fall and while he is looking forward to it, he hasn't the faintest idea what he wants to take, and it is of concern to him. He's considering everything from Premeds to Law, Engineering, Business Administration, Political Science or Psychology. The problem is that this school demands a commitment to a major, or a dominant subject area, in the freshman year, and he's just not ready!

Tom is in good company, and the school he chose should rethink its rigidity. While a focussed education offers a substantial improvement over a superficial smattering of minor courses, there are many successful examples of happy mediums, ranging from a delayed major selection, to more flexibility in the major (in course selection). Thousands of kids are not ready to make that commitment, not only because of their own stage in development, but society is now so complex and changing so rapidly that the plethora of choices is mind-boggling.

Be that as it may, unless he changes schools, Tom will have to try and keep as many options open as possible while meeting the criteria of this academic altar. An array of factors go into choosing a career line, including an individual's likes and dislikes, personality characteristics, academic strengths, parents' careers, personal experiences (work, people), mentors and models, and the process of exclusion, luck and serendipity. It may take Tom a year or two to "find" himself, or to enrich his experiences to the point of further evolving his interests. It may necessitate a year off to work or travel, and experience more of life, this year being the so-called "psychosocial moratorium". It may even involve making mistakes and switching faculties of schools. I have seen all of these approaches work countless times.

Others approach their decisions more methodically, by going to professional career counsellors or vocational services for advice. There they take an array of standardized interest and aptitude tests, and are counselled by a trained individual. Some have found it to be a useful exercise. It will not make the decision, but it usually corroborates, hones, focusses or reinforces previous areas of interest, and occasionally, reveals new and exciting directions.

Tell Tom not to give up: patience, experience and motivation will save the day.

131 **Carla is 19, my oldest and brightest child. She really took me aback yesterday when she said that she is considering quitting college. She has so much potential to be a top-notch lawyer that it would be a tragedy if she gave up this dream. Her father died a few years ago, and he would have liked nothing better than for her to follow in his footsteps. I considered law school too, but I had to go to work since we didn't have the money for me to continue. How could she do this to us?**

Whoa, wait just a minute! To whom, exactly, are you referring when you say "this dream"? I can't tell if it is yours or your late husband's, but I am pretty sure that it isn't Carla's dream. And what exactly do you mean by your last question? What is this "to us" business? It sounds like you have been laying a guilt trip on your daughter, whereby she is obligated to fulfill the dreams of her parents, to carry on the tradition of her late father, and to vicariously fulfill her mother, who didn't have the same opportunities.

There are many reasons for college students to drop out of school, either temporarily or permanently. Often it is for the best, sometimes it is not. But nothing is irrevocable, especially at Carla's age. From this vantage point, and with very limited information, I of course have no idea about the rest of Carla's current life, whether she has friends, is happy, has other interests, and so forth. It is clear, however, that she is having some serious misgivings about pursuing a path set out for her by others. She may be coming to the realization that in order to be her own person, and to define an autonomous sense of identity, she has to take an independent stand. Even if she returns to this original dream of yours, it will be because she wants to — her motives will not be found in a morass of guilt and moral obligation to her parents. Besides, she told you that she is "considering" quitting — a far cry from the act itself. She may have launched a trial balloon to see your reaction, or even to get a rise out of you. And she succeeded.

132 **My husband and I are hard-working retailers (we have a successful luggage business). Our problem is our son Graham, who is 21 going on 13. He's done a smattering of college courses, has a few unimpressive friends and seems to be drifting and aimless. Not only has he no idea of what he wants to do with his life, but thinking even about this coming summer seems beyond him. He seems to resent our questioning him, even when we are purposely gentle and treat him gingerly. We are at a loss, and he continues to be aimless and disorganized; even he isn't happy doing nothing. He just seems so unmotivated that we are quite confused, and frankly, annoyed. We told him that we won't continue to support him for his entire life, but he remains stagnant.**

Graham is at the stage of life when he has to confront questions such as "Who am I?" "Where am I going?" "How?" and "Why?". These existential queries are no different from those you ask yourselves, but it is in late adolescence that some critical decisions have to be made. They may not be irrevocable, but they sure feel that way at the time. As we get older, and our life circumstances change, we continue to confront our sense of identity, which is what these questions are all about.

I often argue with those who decry contemporary life as oppressive to youth, and who say it is terribly difficult to be young today. However, they are right about one thing: our world is changing so rapidly in the latter half of the twentieth century that there is a kind of unpredictability about the future that besets all

of us, and particularly our young people. Add to that the phenomenal myriad of choices available and you have a potentially
confusing situation. The majority of our youth handle these
complexities of life with relative ease; but for those who are less
resourceful, unsure of themselves, or somewhat obsessional,
that confusion can be absolutely paralyzing and debilitating. This
degree of the problem is not common, and a psychiatric label has
actually been applied to it: "Identity-related Disorder".

I would have to know more about Graham to be sure, but
certainly he shares some of the characteristics of that condition.
The clue is that Graham himself is not happy with his inactivity.
At least if he were enjoying the laziness and relaxation, we could
be critical, and even wish sometimes that we, too, could do
absolutely nothing. But Graham is manifestly in pain and that
suggests that he is spinning wheels, unable to take a stand, to
make a move or a commitment, and he is clearly suffering.

Graham needs help. He should see a career, educational or
vocational counsellor who can advise him on some paths to
pursue based on his talents, interests and limitations, which are
measured on a battery of tests and interviews. But this counselling may be a premature step. If Graham's emotional state is
such that he perceives failure at every turn, he should see a good
psychotherapist, one who is adept at working with young people.
Graham does need shaking up and confrontation. But he also
needs compassion and support, and insight into the causes of his
stagnation.

133 Our son Ed is 18 years old and although he's
extremely bright, he's been out of high school
for two years. He went from school to school,
always with the same story — obstreperousness,
misbehavior, failure. He finally quit and has had
a series of jobs. He's gotten into some debt, and
alienated a few employers along the way, and we
figured this was going to be his pattern. But on
his own, he started seeing a psychiatrist a few
months ago, who referred him to an educational
center. After testing him, they said that Ed had a

previously undiagnosed learning disability which had led to his scholastic problems and misbehavior. Now they've recommended a tutor and remedial counsellor to help him in his plan to return to high school and then go on to higher education. Is it all possible?

I assume your query means that you doubt that one can diagnose a learning disability at the age of 18, and that you mistrust Ed's newly found dedication to success in school. It is true that in this day and age, learning disabilities (in areas such as reading, writing, hearing and processing information, alone or in combination) are usually picked up in elementary school. But there are plenty of kids who still fall between the cracks and are never properly evaluated and tested. They develop a terrible self-image in the context of school, because it represents a sense of failure and misery, and they never receive proper remediation. Ed may well be one such example. He also has shown some signs of difficult social behavior, which often goes hand in hand with learning disability.

Yet something has turned around for Ed. Perhaps he was confronted with the results of self-destructiveness; or maybe it was his intelligence that made him realize that there was a real possibility that he was going down the tube. It could be that someone got to him with well-chosen words of advice or admonition. Whatever the case, he sought and received help. He is now on a corrective path, one fraught with difficulties and fears. He is returning to a threatening setting, and he'll be with students at least two years younger. He needs all the encouragement and help that he can get. Notwithstanding your familiarity with his personal history, and your suspiciousness of his motives, he deserves your (guarded) support at this juncture. I hope that he makes it.

134 My nephew Paul has contacted me about problems he is having with his father (my brother). Paul has had some trouble with a learning

disability during his years in school. He is now 18 and very bright, but he never finished high school. He started getting remedial help a few months ago, and is seeing a psychiatrist, too. He's presently enrolled in correspondence courses and holds down an arduous three-day part-time job. His goal is to go on to higher education. Paul is up early on his workdays, but he sleeps in until nine o'clock on his days off. Even on those days he studies alone for four to six hours, but the sleeping in infuriates my brother. So much so that they recently almost came to blows. My brother calls Paul "lazy", and keeps throwing his previous failures in his face. I don't want to paint my nephew as a paragon of virtue because he can be difficult, but he doesn't deserve his father's anger.

Something is missing here. Surely the nine o'clock sleep-in a few days a week in a schedule which is full and hectic can't be the sole source of conflict between Paul and his father. I agree with you, at least based on your rendition of what has transpired there. Nine in the morning is just not that late. What has to be filled in are the other grievances which your brother is still harboring against Paul. They may be based on intense past experiences and memories, or on present provocations, about which Paul didn't tell you. If neither of these situations applies, then your brother is an irrational ogre, which you haven't suggested either.

If Paul's plan is going to work — and it's ambitious and difficult — he's going to need all the help he can get. Your brother has actually been doing a lot for his son; remedial education and psychotherapy don't come cheap. But if the conflicts and altercations continue, Paul's best laid plans will be laid to rest. Something must be done to ease the tension.

It is a tough role for a brother/uncle. Strong recommendations from you when you assuredly don't know the whole situation will not be met with appreciation, least of all by your brother. You don't need that kind of reaction. But it would be entirely appropriate for you (with Paul's permission) to tell your brother of Paul's talk with you, and even to express your concerns regarding the difficulties between them — without choosing sides! Unless, of course, you are totally convinced of the rightness (and completeness) of Paul's case. You can recommend that your brother talk with Paul's psychiatrist to try to clarify the areas of conflict between them. What Paul needs now is some peace in his life, so that he can successfully pursue the hard path he has chosen. But your brother also deserves some consideration and a tension-free atmosphere. It sounds as if they could use the help.

One last thing: I often advise adolescent kids to talk to uncles and aunts at times to help overcome a roadblock with their parents. We can all recall a favorite uncle or aunt whom we spent time with, enjoyed, or even confided in — and perhaps still do. Paul intuitively recognizes in you a source of acceptance and support. You can be instrumental in helping him and his father to build a better relationship.

135   **Megan is 17, beautiful, brilliant and talented. This last characteristic is what is giving us trouble. The problem is that she passionately wants a career in the theater, and we are dead set against it. She has to make choices soon, and we already are having bitter arguments. We know a few people in that field; we're not too keen on them and especially uncomfortable with their lifestyles. Also, it's so hard to make it in the theater. What do you think?**

I must say that I've been through this problem many times over the years with friends, acquaintances, patients and clients, and heard common dialogue that is entirely consistent with your letter (and feelings). Many parents feel that the stage and screen as a way of life is too unpredictable, nonconformist, unstable, and even corrupting and dangerous. Examples to the contrary are often seen as rare exceptions, even when they meet them in person.

I'm afraid that there is little you can do at this point except help Megan to find the best opportunities for education and experience. By "choices" I expect you mean post-secondary education and/or experience. I assume that in your discussions and arguments you've told her exactly how you feel, and yet she is sticking to her guns. The theatre bug is not easily eradicated, and it either has to be worked out of the system, or fulfilled to the point of flourishing and growth. It seldom dissipates quickly, nor can it be banished out of existence.

Megan will have to embark on this journey. She may change directions a few times, but at this stage, all you can do is help her with the "bon voyage".

136 **Our son Robby is 21 and in his last year at the city university. But he is still living at home, and we think that this situation is unusual and unhealthy. He has never lived outside our family. He hated even the idea of going to sleep-away camp; he never slept at a friend's house. He is doing well at school, has many friends of both sexes, takes part in activities, gets along with us, and seems happy enough. But he must be in deep trouble, or he may soon be there. Do you think that he has a mother complex?**

What in the world do you mean by a "mother complex"? Do you mean that he is so wrapped up in his devotion/dependency/love for you that he cannot bear to separate for fear of leaving you with your husband, or of meeting new worries? If that is what you mean, I don't hear a shred of evidence for such a conclusion. Frankly, if I can read between the lines of your letter, Robby sounds very well-adjusted indeed. So for the first quarter (or so) of his life, he has enjoyed the ambience of the family. He's liked the warmth, love, security, convenience and support he finds there. I expect that he also appreciates the free food, laundry, maid service, car, room, and so on. So what?

I also take strong issue with your assumptions that Robbie must be in "deep trouble", or that his living at home must be "unhealthy". It often amazes me that we have such rigid ideas of dos and don'ts for our children, even as young adults. We may pay lip service to large individual differences, but the fact is that we all too often stereotype, classify and pigeonhole young people as if they were all alike. Some kids love it at home, and are slower to move out than most. That doesn't by definition make them pathological. It doesn't even mean, paradoxically, that they are in any way less emancipated or less able to act as independent adults.

I would indeed be concerned if Robbie was doing poorly academically, socially or psychologically. But by your own reports, he appears to be doing well on all of these fronts. I would recommend that you and your husband appreciate and savor what you've got at home (as Joni Mitchell sang, "You don't know what you've got 'til it's gone.") because he will be leaving in due course. Without a mother complex.

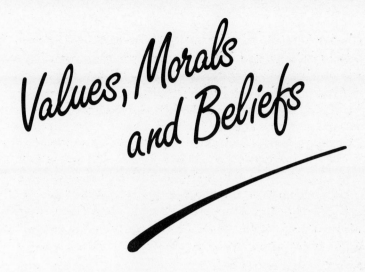

Values, Morals and Beliefs

"Ya gotta believe!" We seem to take two quite opposite points
of view when it comes to the values and beliefs of young
people. Either they are credited with having no interests
beyond cosmetics, consumer crazes and cash (not to
mention carnality) or they have ascribed completely to lofty
ideals, higher morality, and social commitment. The first
group are seen to be the bellwether or harbingers of the
demise of our civilization, the latter a signal of our
potential salvation. As usual, neither is entirely right or wrong.

Just as with adults, there is a whole range of teen
involvement with issues of morality, ethics, philosophy and
religion. The gamut is run from no interest to preoccupation.
We tend to do our teenagers a disservice by not catering to
their need to have something on which they can "hang their
hat". Many parents never have discussions with their
teenagers about their opinions and beliefs. I am not a religious
person, but I do feel that the rituals and routines which
make up a family's traditions are extremely important in
helping to define a young person's identity.

Actually, young people are potential ideologues. They want
easy answers to highly complex existential issues. Believe it
or not, they are comforted by simplistic rights and wrongs, dos
and don'ts. Our world has become so complicated that
even many of our arbiters of ethical philosophy, our religious
leaders, give highly ambiguous answers when there are

plaintive pleas for dogma. Hence the phenomenal attractiveness of so called "cults of unreason" to some young people (a small percentage of total youth). As unreasonable as we may find many of them, they all provide answers, a rigid moral code, and a sense of security, albeit temporarily. Historically, one does not have to look any farther than the great revolutionary movements of bygone eras — or even of our own — the activist masses and mobs tend to be the youth of the particular day. Hitler's Brownshirts and Mao's Red Guards were predominantly made up of adolescents.

Now, I'm sure that you find that information disconcerting or worse. So do I. But young peoples' needs for belief and belonging can be harnessed for "pro-social", as opposed to anti-social purposes. Adolescents can be mobilized to, and do, oppose nuclear war, demonstrate against various wars, support Greenpeace or other environmental causes and so on. I am not saying that these are all by definition just causes; merely that by example, modelling, discussing, teaching and yes, arguing with our youth about our own particular religious, moral, ethical, philosophical, political or social attitudes and stances, we inculcate in them a better sense of who they are and what they are all about. They see that there is more to life than money and materialism; that caring counts. They grow up into citizens with senses of social and moral responsiblity.

137 **We are originally from Pakistan, but we have been in Canada for over 20 years. Our 15-year-old son, Sanjay, came home from school yesterday with a bloodied face and torn clothes. Some toughs had taunted him, by calling him "Paki" and other nasty names, and insulted him and his family in horribly crude terms. He defended himself and was beaten by three of them. What bothers us even more than this specific incident is that Sanjay tells us that these insults have come his way many times, and from a variety of kids, not just these three. Sanjay is a quiet, warm kid, and for him to defend himself must have taken a tremendous effort and extreme provocation.**

This is a terrible story, and unfortunately, a not uncommon one. There is no country on earth free of prejudice. And this social disease is obviously not restricted to the young; they learn it from their adult models of behavior. Treatises have been written on the subject, attempting to explain why human beings react poorly (with fear and ignorance) to what they perceive as strangeness, threat or even danger. They translate their fear and insecurity into critical and aggressive thoughts (frequently), words (often, but generally only with friends) and deeds (least often). Sanjay has been a victim of this most infrequent yet most dangerous manifestation of prejudice.

I wish that I could tell you to rest assured that it won't happen again. But derogatory epithets will be hurled at other times by misguided fools, and with enough social support, and perhaps fueled by alcohol, louts will take out their frustrations on Sanjay (or Ng, or Moishe, or Ivan....)Without a doubt, a thick skin to certain barbs will have to be developed, but it sounds like Sanjay is already pretty good at not rising to each ugly provocation.

Certainly the school authorities and the police must be notified. The hoodlums should be apprehended and punished, with enough publicity to give other like-minded goons cause for reflection. You will also find that there will be an out-pouring of sympathy and support for Sanjay from many young people who genuinely want to be accepting and friendly. It is not just a question of "tolerance", which to me connotes "putting up with". It is more an issue of people of different racial or ethnic backgrounds getting to know each other, and developing a mutually positive regard whenever possible.

This might be a good opportunity for the school to institute a learning program on prejudice, with guest lecturers, workshops and discussions. Teachers, students and parents could be involved. This approach has been tried before and has proven to be beneficial to all participants. Actually, despite the depressing fact that xenophobia (fear of strangers) and prejudice exist at all, it is reassuring to see just how warmly people embrace each other when they do get to know one another — but it takes education, work and motivation.

138   **Our 16-year-old daughter, Candice, is a wonderful, wholesome girl, lost in a school and a neighborhood full of yuppies. She does have some friends, but the fact is that we can't and won't compete with the "materialism uber alles" mentality. The prevailing ethic seems to be "Buy, acquire, collect, travel, wear, drive, eat, play with the best, most expensive, and ostentatiously impressive!" Cardin, Gucci, Cartier, BMW and Polo are just a few of the names we hear bandied about with abandon. It is Rodeo Drive revisited. How do we keep Candy unsullied by this sad superficiality?**

Not only is this lifestyle superficial, it is also the height of narcissism, the epitome of self-serving shallowness. It is destructive to the sense of identity of those young people to whom you refer, and it will prevent them from ever participating in our society with a sense of contribution, altruism, caring or generosity. It's every man (woman) for himself! It is not easy to withstand this attitude when one is surrounded by a sea of selfishness. You must hope that Candice will by this time have acquired a more generous and well-founded sense of values from her family and others, which will protect her from this onslaught of yuppiedom.

You describe her as "wholesome" and "wonderful", so that clearly many of the values which you hold dear have been passed on, appreciated and adopted. There is an uncanny consistency in our personalities over time; the attitudes already inculcated in Candice will remain as inherent parts of her personality. Furthermore, while you decry the school and neighborhood, you are also unfairly stereotyping *all* the kids and their parents. Surely there are more than a few who believe that there is more to life than acquisitiveness and material style. Just as you have met substantive and impressive individuals, so can Candice. In any high school there are kids of all kinds, including warm, earthy, caring ones; Candice will have to be on the look out for them. She could join clubs, church groups and activities which are more in keeping with her own interests. This doesn't mean that I view her as a serious, boring, moralizing type; she can be fun-loving, appreciate music and dating, and enjoy other teen pursuits. But she should try to find other kids who share her wholesomeness.

Allow me to make two last points. Some apparent yuppies are actually nice kids, swept up in the accoutrements of style in order to placate, ingratiate or conform to others, to group pressure. They would like nothing better than to shed the silliness.

Finally, Candice and you have to make sure if she is having some social difficulties that it is not solely due to the clear difference in values. Sometimes we are blinded by preconceived notions as to what the problems are all about, and we do not see other possible reasons for them.

139 **Our 15-year-old daughter, Andrea, came to us with a problem with which we are having difficulty helping her. There is a group of girls that she has wanted desperately to accept her and finally, after many months, she is on the inside. No sooner did it happen when she learned that these kids are into some pretty serious and dangerous behavior, all in secret. They have been stealing, smoking grass heavily, and doing some**

> **very malicious rumormongering, all with considerable planning and titillation. These are all middle-class kids from good families whom we know. Andrea still likes them but doesn't know — nor do we — if she or we should inform their families, the school, or even the police.**

Here is a group of kids who seemingly have everything going for them, and through personal problems, boredom, and mutual encouragement, have formed a sort of planned anti-social gang (remember Leopold and Loeb?).

On the surface the solution seems so straightforward. "Of course", we should think, "here is a group that is doing terrible things and they have to be stopped for their own sakes as well as for the benefit of their victims." The other side of the coin is that Andrea will not only lose these friends, but she may well be persona non grata, ostracized by them, and possibly by others as well. The unwritten adolescent code of behavior declares that no tattling or squealing is condoned or permitted. If they are reported by her, you or even anonymously, these girls will assume that their newest member has blown the whistle. If she stays in the group, she will be expected to participate in these activities; her refusal will ensure her extrusion. Andrea cannot win in this situation; either way she will be hurt and the first thing she must do is face this unpleasant reality.

Your dilemmas are deciding the "right" thing to do and how to minimize Andrea's pain. As hard as it will be, Andrea should gracefully withdraw from this group of girls. They may not understand or like it, and Andrea, if she is strong enough, might say "Look, I like you, but I just can't get involved in this type of stuff. I'm not going to say anything, but it's too unpleasant for me here". Or if this explanation proves too difficult, she should just turn down invitations to join them, and not initiate or reciprocate calls and plans. I recognize that this is a major task for her, and I don't want to minimize the difficulties, but in a way she has little choice. If she doesn't do so, she is courting and encouraging participation in their nefarious games. It's just a matter of time before these girls get caught, exposed, humiliated and punished. If not Andrea, then someone else from within will tire of this behavior, or perhaps have a moral reawakening. Another possibility is that they will be found out by a member's ineptitude at being covert and dishonest all the time. Finally, they might well be caught red-handed doing one of their dirty tricks.

Andrea might ask herself what is so special about these girls that she needs their acceptance above all others. Or rather, what is it about her that has made her so "desperate" to join them?

140 We have been a regular church-going family for years. Every Sunday morning we (my wife and I, and our three children, aged 15, 12, 11) go to services, and then out to brunch with my brother's family. Recently, our 16-year-old daughter has refused to come with us. She says that she finds it "boring", a "waste of time", and says that none of her friends go. We are concerned that she will get into trouble, and that she will be a bad influence on her younger brother and sister.

I'm sure that many readers will empathize with your lament and worries. The truth is that the vast majority of teenagers, even from religious families, do not attend church on a regular basis, if at all. Most of them see the church (synagogue, mosque, ashram, and so on) as irrelevant to their concerns and lives. They find that what reaches them at that stage are their friends, music, sexual titillation. They worry about their bodies, competition, acceptance by others, shyness. These are generally issues that are just not addressed in most formal religious programs. Adolescent self-definition and rebellion certainly can play a role, but I wouldn't emphasize the negative aspect of these factors.

Even when the church makes a pointed effort at involving their youthful members via special programs, they often fail, because the sustaining interest just isn't there. But you needn't despair. Many adults return to their places and organizations of worship after an almost inevitable lapse of a few years. Your statement that your daughter's avoidance of church is a necessary prelude to "trouble" is somewhat baffling. There is simply no evidence for this conclusion. If she's been a good kid until now, and you offer no information to the contrary, there is no reason why she should change now. She is well aware of her parents' values, and they will be incorporated into her psyche and relationships.

Your concern regarding your younger children is well-founded, but the general rule is that they will pursue the course they were going to follow in any case.

Don't despair.

141 **We are a Christian, church-going, God-fearing family, but we are not religious zealots. Nor do we proselytize; "live and let live" is our credo, although we have strong views on morality. But we are deeply upset by our 17-year-old son Lloyd's atheism. Not only does he not believe in God, but he insists on ridiculing our beliefs and worshipping practices. He publicly repudiates religion, and by extension, his parents. He is intolerant of us, and arrogantly puts down religious doctrine. We have asked him to stop, but he doesn't listen.**

Not only is Lloyd rebelling against his parents, but he has chosen the most sensitive area in which to prod them. And he is doing it with a vengeance. He chooses atheism rather than strong belief, and then he engages in an arrogant campaign apparently aimed at discrediting his mother and father. As you know, some degree of testing, arguing and disagreeing is common and even healthy in teenage relationships with their parents. In defining an autonomous identity, it is important for some adolescents to "stick it to" their closest authority figures, mum and dad. It is not because he is an atheist that I say this. We live in a free country where we can choose to believe what we want. It is Lloyd's *manner* of opposition which concerns me.

Lloyd has clearly taken his rebellion too far. While religion serves as the focal point for his conflict with you, there is something else going on at a deeper level. Either he is unaware of this deeper problem or he can't deal with it consciously. More important than his atheism (at least to me) is his callous treatment of you both. I would have to know more about him, and your family's relationship balances, before even hazarding a guess as to why he is so anti-religion and anti-parents.

But his manner is verging on insolence. He is clearly out to provoke you; and you are, equally as clearly, unable to control him. You say that he won't "listen", which means that Lloyd seemingly does as he pleases. Religion aside, there is a control and discipline problem here. You cannot allow a 17-year-old to walk all over you; it is demeaning and destructive to you. It is also destructive to your son, believe it or not. I know nothing other than this negative aspect of your relationship. Are there any redeeming features? Can you exert control by discussion, or confrontation? Restrictions? Grounding? Withholding his allowance? But none of these methods can operate in a vacuum; they are dependent on a pre-existing relationship. Perhaps a few sessions with a family therapist are in order. I know that the Christian community has therapists with whom they are most comfortable, but I doubt that Lloyd would accept that recommendation. A branch of the Family Service Agency or a referral from your family physician will get you the proper help.

142 Our 19-year-old daughter, Margaret, has found religion. No, she hasn't joined a cult or any other such nonsense. But she has gone back to our Roman Catholic roots; she regularly goes to Mass, confession and other rituals. What makes this unbelievable and disconcerting is that her father and I (divorced now for seven years, but friendly) left the church many years ago, and are on the far side of agnosticism (nearer to atheism). What gives?

One can offer all kinds of conjecture here. Margaret is "getting even" with her parents for destroying the cohesive family unit.

Margaret is rebelling in the best way designed to get at *her* particular parents — choose an area that they have shunned and rejected. Margaret is very upset, and is seeking solace and comfort in the church. Margaret has joined the church because as a spiritual person, it makes the most sense to her. Margaret, like other teens, needs a belief system. I can suggest other possibilities too, as I'm sure, can you. I would have to know more about Margaret before venturing a firm opinion as to which of these or other factors, alone or in combination, are operative.

I have, however, a simpler approach to recommend. If Margaret is doing well with her school or work, with her friends and interests, with family, and above all with herself, why worry at all? It seems that religion is more a problem for *you* than it is for Margaret. Perhaps you should explore that area. That is, have you left the church because it wasn't for you, and you weren't a believer, or did you leave with an angry bitterness?

Understanding your own feelings toward the church will probably help you to better comprehend and deal with Margaret's new piety.

143 **Our 19-year-old son, Ted, was doing well in school and was a devoted son. He went to California on a vacation six months ago, and never came back. He joined the Moonies (the Unification Church) and became a stranger to us. He claims that he is happy, but we know better. We have to get him out because he has obviously been brainwashed. Should we have him kidnapped and deprogrammed?**

This is a highly complex area, which it turns out, I have spent years studying (*Radical Departures*, Harcourt, Brace, Jovanovich, 1984). In a nutshell, my findings have shown that young people, like Ted, join cults at a time in their lives when they have a deep-seated need for a belief system and an intensely supportive group. These groups, whatever we may think of them, help the participant to overcome his or her sense of alienation and feelings of demoralization. The young members become happy, fulfilled, exuberant — and narrow-minded. They give up their studies, their relationships, their former lives. Generally from relatively affluent backgrounds, they choose to live at a subsistence level, and they love it, feeling virtuous, anti-materialistic, and spiritual.

The term "brainwashed" is a loaded one; I prefer to see it as a kind of collusion between an intense, seductive group and a needy, self-hypnotized individual. Some of the groups are dangerous (the worst scenario: Jonestown); others are gentle and loving.

I have found that the vast majority of members return to their homes and families in under two years. After a rough six months or so of re-adaptation, they resume their (usually) middle-class lives.

I am not a sympathizer with the kidnapping and deprogramming route. Not only is it an infringement on their civil liverties, it often doesn't work, sometimes ending in harm to the individual, or an ugly lawsuit against the parents. However, I can well understand the anguish of parents, and their consideration of drastic measures to retrieve their adolescents.

First, ask questions. Learn all you can, not only of the Moonies, but in particular of the specific group he is in. Keep your lines of communication to Ted open: invitations, letters, news and phone calls are all important. Perpetual confrontation is deleterious, as is appeasement. Don't allow yourself to be browbeaten, converted, proselytized to. Visit him, and meet his peers and their leader. Do maintain openness, love and affection. Usually, he'll come back. There are non-coercive techniques used to get young people out of these groups, but frequently, those members who are ready to listen are well on their way to leaving on their own. If he stays within the group (a rare occurrence), he is likely getting something he needs from it.

144 Our 16-year-old daughter, Ruth, who is a terrific kid, is going out with an 18-year-old boy, who seems very nice. For some reason, we don't like him. He's a good student, doesn't do drugs and

comes from a stable working class family. We are Jewish and this boy is Italian, but that's not an issue with us.

What is this "for some reason" business? There are three reasons implicit in your letter that account for your being turned off. One is that you feel that your daughter is too young to get involved. Secondly, you feel that she can do "better," and lastly, you would prefer a Jewish boy. This is not written to you by way of criticism, but rather by calling the facts as they are.

We all want the best for our kids. We all would like them to date and marry beautiful, brilliant, warm, loving (and yes, even rich) young people of the opposite sex. But making premature demands on our adolescents often ends up backfiring. Threats from you often lead to your teens being backed into a corner, from which they can't extricate themselves without resentment or pain.

I can assure you that Ruth is already quite aware of your feelings. We are entitled, certainly (obligated is more accurate), to convey over the course of years our values and priorities to our children. But berating and badgering our adolescents smacks of too little, too late. Let her be; she will respect your opinions and retain her love for you and her own self-respect. If she *does* end up marrying him, or somebody like him, it is simply because it was meant to be.

145 **My husband Kirk and I have been married for 16 years, and I must say that they have been relatively good — until recently, that is. Kirk is from an Anglican background, and I am Jewish. Neither of us is a worshipper and we saw no need for either of us to convert to the other's religion. When our children were born, we decided to offer them a smattering of both religious traditions, and this was what we did. This year, now that Stuart and Gail are 16 and 14 respectively, we've had rip-roaring arguments about them going to church at Christmas with Kirk's**

parents. My family think that they should not go the church if they don't go to synagogue and also that they should be steeped in Chanukah lore and ritual. Kirk and I are finding ourselves caught up in the argument and now we are fighting constantly over this issue.

Mixed marriages are common, especially between Christians and Jews (more than 10,000 a year in the United States alone). "Mixed" often refers to religious beliefs, but race and ethnicity can also qualify in this category. The fact is that any two people from extremely diverse backgrounds of any kind, often with attitudes and values which are contradictory or mutually exclusive, can be tagged with that label. There are inherent difficulties which can be dealt with depending on the planning, tolerance, mutual respect and flexibility of the partners. Some mixed spouses manage very well indeed. For others it is a constant struggle for recognition, and even power. And of course in the latter families it is with the advent of children that these battles begin to rage in earnest. For reasons which often transcend the best planning, the passing on of our traditions and beliefs — or perhaps more properly, our own parents' teachings — become of paramount importance when our children's minds are the issue. Over time, however, most of these conflicts can be resolved, or at least, a stable equilibrium can be achieved.

Your situation is considerably different. Kirk and you had essentially no conflicts in this area until Stuart and Gail reached their adolescent years. I can only hazard guesses as to why it is happening now. It is possible that either or both of you have "finally" realized that if you didn't act soon, the passing on of your heritage would be lost; a kind of delayed response to the impulse I described earlier. But somehow I think that something else is going on. For example, both your sets of parents and other extended family members have gotten into the act. Are they running the show? Are you each trying to appease your own parents, and losing sight of your original agreements and shared ideas? Of course, it is the kids who will bear the brunt of these arguments; they are being pulled in antagonistic directions simultaneously, trying to be fair and co-operative with both of their parents.

Another possibility is that you and Kirk are not getting along for reasons that have nothing whatsoever to do with different religious backgrounds. But religion has been chosen as the battlefield, and the weapons unfortunately, are Stuart and Gail. Of course, I do not know what the real issues between you are; they may have been covered over well for many years, or they may be new. But if those arguments don't abate after the holiday season, or if there is no mutually satisfactory resolution, you should seek the help of a marriage counsellor. These constant conflicts have a nasty habit of spreading to other parts of your relationship.

146 **We are from the old country — Portugal. We have been here for 25 years and we like it very much. But we cannot enjoy your customs between boys and girls. Our daughter Sonia is 21, a nice quiet girl. She told us that she loves a man who is divorced and has a child. She says he is a nice, respectable man; that may be, but I have forbidden her to see him anymore. I don't hit her anymore, but this gets me so angry! She cries a lot, but on this, I cannot change my mind. (My son helped me write this letter).**

It is seldom that I second-guess parental values and traditions regarding rules, codes of behavior and the like, for their own kids. We all come from different backgrounds, religions and societies, and we bring our own personalities and family heritage to bear on the decisions in our own homes. Obviously if there is flagrant sexual or/and violent abuse, there has to be some outside intervention. But as for such areas as curfews, cleanliness and chores, people have a right to set up their own social systems.

In your situation we see a clash of ages and cultures. Who is to say what is right and what is wrong? I might as well tell you that I would not be at all offended if my daughter was in love with a divorced man; that is, if he were a respectable, solvent, loving individual. The fact that he is divorced and a father seems to infuriate you, and I suppose that this is partly based on your religious beliefs, and on your (related) concerns regarding morality. I am relieved that you no longer "hit her" (another traditional custom?), but your forbidding her to see this man strikes me as somewhat cruel. She is obviously extremely upset at the moment. I would guess that she is either going to see him in secret, defy you openly or leave your home.

What does your son say (the one who drafted the letter)? Your wife? Are they scared of you? You sound so angry and adamant that I doubt that you are open to alternative suggestions. It might be a good idea for you to sit down with your daughter and at least hear her out. She is very hurt, but her loyalty to you is quite clear from her tears. Many daughters would have defied their father immediately in such a predicament. Failing that, a social worker or counsellor working with the Portugese community, or one of the Immigration Counselling offices in your city might be able to help you bridge the gap between generations and value systems. A local branch of the Family Service Agency would also be a possible source of help for you — they frequently work with problems between immigrants and their children. This problem can be solved in such a way that both you and your daughter save face and also get some satisfaction. But it will take motivation and compromise on both your parts. Finally, please remember that, at 21, Sonia is legally an adult, free to make her own choices in life.

147 **I am in a religious quandary. My husband has been a born-again Christian for the past seven years. He believes in the absolute truth of the Old and New Testaments, and God help anyone who disagrees with him! Our three teenaged children are really nice and well behaved; they believe in God and go to Church on most Sundays. But that isn't good enough for him. Not only does he rant and rave at them about their "sins" and threaten them with his own as well as the Lord's punishment, but he has hit them rather severely**

**with a belt, without any provocation, in my opin-
ion. If I object he threatens to beat me. What
should I do?**

Forgive my disagreement, but I don't think that you are in a
religious quandary at all. However, you certainly *do* have a major
problem. In this situation, religion is being misused and subverted
in the cause of ignorance, brutality and emotional disturbance.
(As it often has in the past.) A spiritual and benevolent system of
values has perversely become a rationale for rank violence. No
true Christian (or any sincere devotee of any other accepted
religion) would condone your husband's acts of violence.

You are obviously too fearful or powerless to intervene, and
even though your children are now teenagers, they are at risk.
They are being psychologically and physically abused. If any of
the kids are underage, you could call the Children's Aid Society
or any Child Protection Branch of your government. You could
also contact the Public Health department in your city. You could
— and you may have to, as objectionable as it sounds — call the
police for protection, and lay charges.

Ordinarily I would opt for calm discussions, the intervention of a church elder or a close family friend, leading to treatment for your husband (he is obviously a disturbed man) and
perhaps family therapy for all of you. But to be honest, I am
not at all optimistic that this approach has any real possibility
of succeeding. Your husband sounds as if he is closed-minded,
narrowly fixated, and violence-prone. He is a dangerous man
who must be controlled. Religion is truly irrelevant in this
situation.

148 **How do we inculcate our kids with our values? I
don't pretend that my wife and I are paragons of
virtue, but we do try to uphold certain moral
principles — responsibility, hard work, caring
for others, honesty, belief in God, loyalty to our
country. Don't get me wrong; we're not prudes or
Victorians. We like fun as much as anyone. Jake**

(16) and Roz (15) are sweet kids, but they and all their friends seem to live by the credo, "How much can I get away with? How little can I do?" Is this what kids are coming to?

I don't think that kids today are any less value-oriented than those of any bygone era. To adults they have always seemed less responsible and more frivolous than previous generations. In truth, younger adolescents have always tended to be more preoccupied with the biological upheaval in their bodies — growth, genitals, acne, sex drive, strength and other changes — than with issues of ideology and belief. Think back to when you were 15 or 16 — were you into "hard work, loyalty to country" and so on? And if you were, how about the rest of your friends? And just listen to you now!

While Roz and Jake are seemingly unaware of the standards of behavior and morality of their parents, your morality is definitely not escaping them. Being raised by caring parents, who demonstrate by their very actions these higher principles, will have an effect. Values will seep in by osmosis. My prediction is that you will see your teenagers begin to fulfill your aspirations within a very few years.

Even at their relatively youthful ages, you could possibly mobilize your teenagers and their friends to participate in projects which will benefit others. Done as a family activity, that is one idea which has worked wonders for some families. Actually, even young teenagers with time on their hands feel terrific when they have participated in helping others — children, the elderly, the poor or any other underprivileged persons.

I know nothing about Roz and Jake, but I am optimistic. The most extreme possibility (although it is somewhat farfetched) is that their personalities are such that they really embody a selfish and superficial approach to life. For all I know, they could be psychopathic, through no fault of yours. I guess anything is possible, since we do see some terrible individuals coming out of wonderful families. Or they may be influenced by a strong group of terrible friends. Each of these situations is possible and we have to consider all eventualities, even those that are barely likely. As far as your kids are considered, somehow I can find

178 Tell Me It's Only A Phase

little reason to worry about their futures. You *are* inculcating them with your values.

149 **During the late sixties, my wife and I marched with thousands of others in mass anti-war demonstrations, protesting the Vietnam tragedy. We now have two teenagers who not only don't involve themselves in political action (against nuclear war, for example) but seem to have no awareness or interests outside of their immediate comforts. We are disappointed that our kids are so narcissistic and self-indulgent.**

Well, you are now members of a big club. Frankly, most teenagers go through a period of intense navel-gazing, unaware of and uninterested in the broader world around them. It explains why musician Bob Geldof was able to strike such a chord with his rock concerts to raise money to fight starvation in draught-torn Africa. Had he simply mounted a podium and beseeched young people to give generously, you know as well as I that he would have been given barely anything. The largesse he did receive was due to the aggregation of stars and their music.

This is not to say that young people can't be interested in or excited by an ideology or belief system. Older adolescents in particular can and do become intensely involved in political, social and religious movements, especially if the leadership strikes a responsive chord in their hearts, minds and souls. The attraction can be music, style, charisma, group pressure, magic answers (as in cults) or promises of a millenium or better world. Such involvement also offers the chance to fulfill their own personal needs and to fill voids in their lives. (It is interesting to note that the revolutionary movements of the world have largely been populated by zealous adolescents.)

So they aren't all navel-gazers, and even if they are, it tends to be a transient phenomenon. You will also find that kids either emulate or react against their parents. If you have set an example by your preoccupations, discussions and acts of social commitment, at some point your teenagers will probably adopt a similar stance. If you have been brutal with your ideology, lording it over them, then there is a good chance that they will abandon that belief system at some point.

Your kids may also be in a social group in which their behavior is the norm and is socially recognized and rewarded. Again, if you've done your homework, at some point they will begin opening their eyes, and get bored and impatient with trite superficiality as a steady diet (I guess we all indulge in that from time to time).

Finally, with all due respect, what are you doing now about your values and beliefs? So many sixties demonstrators have put down their placards and have picked up the morning stock reports, the fashion magazines and other yuppie paraphernalia. Are you in that category? If not, you have less to fear.

Substance Abuse, Drugs and Alcohol

If there is such a thing as a drug-free society, I'd like to know about it. Even countries where the use of chemicals and alcohol is specifically prohibited by law and religious fiat have problems with drug users and abusers. The desire to escape from a painful reality or to introduce some much-needed pleasure into our lives is an extraordinary temptation. In our own culture, of course, not only is drug use widely recognized (if not accepted), but media attention has at times fueled our fears with alarmist, hysterical reports of doomsayers' prophecies of a newly drug-crazed generation.

The fact is that our youth are merely following our adult lead. With the help of our friendly doctors and pharmacists, tranquilizers and sedatives are extraordinarily widely used and abused. Encouraged by liquor-regulatory agencies, advertising, retail outlets and bars, we consume alcohol in enormous quantities. Our adolescents' use of street drugs pales in comparison to their parents' substance abuse, so that one should not be surprised by their experiments with mind-altering substances. But the use of such chemicals has actually diminished and plateaued in recent years. It is in part due to good education programs (not scare tactics) and the failure of the promise of personal salvation which was the hope and expectation of the drug scene in the late sixties. It has also become clear that *all* drugs have undesirable and at times dangerous side effects;

that *all* drugs can be used or abused destructively; that *all* mind-altering chemicals can cause dependence and many can lead to serious addictive disorders; and that these drugs *never* solved anyone's problems.

We must bear in mind, however, that most adolescents and young adults will experiment with alcohol and drugs at least a few times during those years of change. But the vast majority of young people who are strung out on drugs, or stoned constantly, or who drink too much, have psychological problems which obviously must be addressed. Yet this drug problem itself usually can be eradicated fairly easily at that stage of life through understanding, communication and a firm set of rules. The psychological problems, however, may be more difficult to eradicate. Parents *do* have to be aware of danger signs which may be tell-tale evidence of drug abuse, but these clues invariably come hand-in-hand with other desultory, deteriorating or destructive behavior that should have been noticed anyway.

We should not expect more from our teenagers than we are prepared to expect from ourselves. If we are using chemicals to modify our own moods, it becomes very difficult to avoid hypocrisy when decrying those same actions in our kids. Moralizing and preaching have their (limited) place, but modelling, educating, communicating, loving and limit-setting are even more important in bringing up kids who abuse neither chemicals nor alcohol.

150 **How can I tell if my son is on drugs? Dick is 17, and tells us very little about his comings and goings. The drug scene in his high school is so rampant that I am scared that he's included, although I don't have any facts or clues. He's doing okay in school, and has nice friends.**

Even if he has experimented with some drugs, from what you say, I would doubt that Dick is heavily involved. However, you may want to watch for some of the signs of drug abuse. For example, if his performance at school deteriorates or his personal hygiene shows evidence of neglect; if he has trouble sleeping or his day-night sleep cycle is largely reversed; if he is increasingly moody or withdrawn, or shows rapid changes in his apparent feelings; if he has trouble focussing his mind on issues, tasks or conversations (difficulty in concentrating) or if his relationships with his family or friends have suffered recently you might have cause to worry. However, what is interesting about these symptoms is they could easily be indicative of significant emotional distress in a young person without any relationship whatsoever to drugs. Yet Dick seemingly gives no hint of any of these symptoms.

Of course, there can be some significant findings which are not so much clues as tell-tale evidence of drug involvement. The discovery of syringes, pills, or a stash of marijuana; smoky smells emanating from his room; dilated pupils or needle marks on his arms; reddened nostrils. None of this seems to apply to Dick. The fact that he shares very little with you regarding his personal life might be disconcerting. but it is not that unusual. One last thing: don't be afraid to ask him questions about the drug scene in school, and about himself. It shows interest and caring, and it also provides some "consciousness-raising", showing him that you are aware of some potential problems among kids his age. At the moment, though, I think that your specific fears are groundless.

151 **We are the parents of a 16-year-old girl, Jo-Jo, who goes to a good neighborhood high school. We know that there is fairly widespread drug use**

**in the school. While we are confident that Jo-Jo
is not (yet) involved, we are of mixed mind about
what we should do even if she were. Isn't *some*
experimentation with alcohol and drugs normal?**

If by "normal" you mean that all kids experiment, the answer is a resounding NO. If you mean that a high proportion of kids, by the time they graduate from high school, have tried alcohol and marijuana at least once, the answer is a resounding YES.

Actually, drug use among many high school students seems to have plateaued in recent years. Although they are still widely used, drugs are no longer glorified by journals, clinicians and pop sociologists, as in the sixties. Drugs are utilized for a variety of possible reasons, including group pressure, rebelliousness, assertion of one's autonomy, escape and psychological disorder. Just because someone occasionally indulges does not render him or her a drug abuser, and it certainly does not mean habituation or addiction.(See Question 153). Rather than focussing on global stereotypes, and generalizations, pay attention to what *is* important: the characteristics of the drug in question, the utilization patterns and the personality of the user.

Grass (marijuana) is not innocuous, but it is not as dangerous as cocaine or heroin. Using such a substance once a month in small quantities in a social situation is light years removed from a pattern of use which includes high doses taken very often (daily), and usually alone. A strong individual who is doing well at school, with family and other social relationships, is clearly less at risk than someone who is a loner, isolated, emotionally dependent, low in self-esteem or unstable. *Any* substance can be abused, given the circumstances of a vulnerable individual overusing a chemical for purposes of escape from a painful reality. The sad aspect of this pattern, of course, is that it seldom, if ever, "works".

As far as Jo-Jo is concerned, you really don't provide me with any information about her, except your assumption that she hasn't used drugs, which bespeaks trust and respect on your part, and my assumption that she has two loving parents. If she merits your trust, she is probably doing well, academically, socially and personally, and if this is the case, you really have very little to be worried about.

152   **How can we tell if our 17-year-old son, Jonathan, is on drugs? Last year we found a pouch of grass in his room, and now we think that he's stoned all the time, although he does maintain good grades and habits.**

Don't jump to conclusions. If Jonathan is giving you no other cause for concern, your fears might well be groundless. A young person who is stoned all the time will, over a period of weeks and months, usually show a general deterioration in his or her behavior and functioning. School work, personal hygiene, relationship with parents and general mood all begin to suffer to varying extents. There are often attempts to cover up and compensate (by overdoing neatness, for example) but the truth will come out eventually.

There are exceptions, of course. Why don't you speak to your son? If you have a good relationship, and you gently question rather than confront him, your interest will do no harm. He will most likely deny any drug use vociferously and be angry, but he will also learn that you are concerned about his welfare. In this current climate of substance abuse, it is legitimate to be careful.

We know now that grass is not innocuous. There are serious physical as well as psychological effects of long-term use. In my experience, however, a kid who is stoned all the time (not your son) has some serious problems to work on, but marijuana is not as much the issue as is *why* he is abusing it, and what he's running from. At the moment, however, Jonathan is not in that category.

153   **What is an addiction? I have been reading so much about drug use and abuse lately that I am concerned that it is only a matter of time before my own kids are involved and hooked. Are all street drugs addictive? Are any prescribed medications addictive? What is a habit-forming drug?**

According the World Health Organization, an addictive substance is one:

1) which causes a physiological dependency; that is, the drug becomes part and parcel of the metabolism of the body. It literally becomes needed;

2) to which tolerance is developed; that is, more of the substance is needed to accomplish the same effect, or mood alteration, or "high";

3) which, upon sudden discontinuation (the so-called "cold turkey" approach) can cause withdrawal symptoms (the "abstinence syndrome") which vary from mild discomfort all the way to lethal proportions.

Yet this definition does not apply to all the drugs on the market and their effects. Some drugs don't fit this description exactly but are extremely dangerous (cocaine, amphetamines). Others also don't meet the criteria, but can cause an intense psychological dependency (marijuana, hashish). Still other non-addictive substances can precipitate psychotic reactions (LSD, PCP, cocaine). Many commonly prescribed medications (sleeping pills, tranquilizers, some anti-depressants) are definitely addictive. Drugs vary in their degree of addictive potential; some are mildly addictive (caffeine, nicotine), others are extraordinarily so (heroin, morphine). One of the most commonly used and abused substances in the world — alcohol — is also one of the most dangerous and certainly is very addictive.

Any substance, addictive or not, can be abused by a susceptible individual. I have seen all kinds of abuse — addiction, overdosage, wrong scheduling, wrong reasons, and on and on. It is in fact the *combination* of substance and user which can lead to disaster. There is no doubt that certain individuals are more habit-prone than others. This has to do with genetic, constitutional and psychological (personality) factors, but those susceptible people are, in fact, much more difficult to treat.

There is no reason that your kids should be inevitably involved in the drug scene and "hooked", as you call it. The recent media hype has certainly brought the dangers of drug use to our attention, and made our governments take various kinds of action. But sometimes this effort has smacked of overkill. Indeed, many kids do not experiment at all. Many try out cigarettes, alcohol, and marijuana, but never return to any of these substances. Others still are careful, and drink alcohol (for example) only on social occasions and in moderation. Only a small minority get into real trouble; why should your kids be in that particular group?

154 **My daughter Jenny is 15, and she and her friends smoke cigarettes. I can't stand the idea that a child of mine is engaged in smelly, foul, unhealthy, polluting, self-destructive behavior. How do I get her to stop?**

I happen to agree with you about the negative aspects of smoking, but I haven't taken it on as a cause célèbre, as some of the Non-Smokers Rights Associations have. Actually, I find it interesting that habitual or addictive deviant behavior brings out a kind of zealotry or moralizing in others which can be quite offensive (the cure being almost as bad as the disease). I doubt that your daughter is physiologically addicted (yet) to nicotine and its derivatives, at her young age. No, her reasons for smoking have more to do with social and psychological factors. Most habitual smokers will tell you about the relaxation it provides, the puffing-holding-flicking rituals having "healing" benefits of their own. There is also the teenagers' illusions of looking "with it" and "cool" with cigarettes in their hands. There is the comfort in knowing that they are acceptable to the group by conforming to its norms, as well as the power of group pressure.

You are not dealing with a simple problem. As detrimental as smoking is (and it is, it is), you are well aware of how difficult it is for any confirmed smoker to stop. Certainly, make your daughter aware of the hazards involved. Don't support the habit by giving her spending money for cigarettes. Don't allow smoking in your home. All these are useful and effective strategies, but as long as her group of friends continue indulging in the same vice, it's going to be hard to get her to give smoking up. What is in your favor is the current prevailing public attitude, which is definitely against cigarettes. Even governments are getting into the act, legislating against smoking in all different kinds of public and private locales.

You don't mention any other kind of problems Jenny and her friends are into. I am relieved, because smoking often can be a forerunner of other "misbehaviors". If this is all you are concerned about, you can afford to be optimistic.

155 **My 17-year-old son, Cory, returned from a summer program bemoaning the fact that we don't "smoke up" with him as "many" of his friends' parents do. I couldn't believe it, but I've since found out that this practice isn't uncommon. What do you think of it?**

I think it's ill-conceived, asinine and destructive. These parents are presumably products of the sixties, when marijuana (Mary Jane, Ganga, Grass, heaven, golden harvest) was glorified. Those were the years of flower children, when Timothy Leary stood up in Golden Gate Park in San Francisco and told 20,000 kids (now parents) to "Tune in, turn on, drop out". I was there. It was an era of idealism admixed with naïveté, of fury against the Vietnam War, fun and fantasy. The true believers saw Woodstock, New York as their statement — music, peace, love, sex, tolerance, and grass, while the cynics saw Altamont, California, (a few months later) as more to the point — music, violence, booze, racism, hate and grass.

Since then we have learned that marijuana is not the harmless substance whose virtues we extolled a generation ago, that it can be abused, and that it can cause physical as well as psychological damage. Aside from the negative effects of prolonged or heavy abuse, however, there is the stupidity involved on the part of these "free-thinking" parents. If they want to be destructive to themselves, I suppose that it is their right, but to involve their children is to me the height of irresponsibility. In the guise of honesty, openness and intimacy with their kids, they are giving them a clear message of permission and encouragement to indulge in all mind-altering substances. We have enough problems with drugs in our society without parents turning into pushers!

<u>156</u> **My son Andrew is in his final year in high school, an important one if he is to get into a good university. He's always been a good kid and a good student, but lately he's taken up with a group of guys who feel that it's cool to smoke up and get drunk every Friday and Saturday night. They are loud, raucous and crude, and occasionally get into some scraps and scrapes with the law. The next day he sleeps in to the early afternoon and doesn't do his homework or anything else. He becomes a blob in front of the TV. Yet he tells us to stop picking on him.**

Here it is, the latter half of the eighties, and we are still preoccupied with booze as a potential evil. And you are right. Even in the late sixties and seventies when psychedelic drugs were the rage, and even now when cocaine and crack are the subject of media attention, alcohol was, is and I daresay will be, the drug most used and abused by contemporary adolescents. For decades the Friday night drunk has been a kind of ill-conceived transaction and ritual. Not only have thousands of young people indulged themselves this way, but a high proportion of them are underage (especially with the recent trend towards increasing the legal drinking age in most jurisdictions). In addition, the drinking does often lead to the "scraps and scrapes" you mention. The most dangerous and potentially lethal one is, of course, driving under the influence of alcohol, which is the number-one cause of serious injury and death among young people.

So I can understand your concerns about Andrew. But his drinking in this situation is a clue. It is even worse in his case because he is seemingly letting other things slide. It sounds like he has moved away from old friends, and that his school work may be deteriorating or on the verge of doing so. Your "picking on him" is the least you can do. But it is difficult because he has a supportive peer group that encourages and even rewards his behavior. At the moment it sounds like you are not reaching him; he is closed to admonition from his parents. But that doesn't mean that he will not listen to others. From my perspective, Friday night is not the major issue, although it could become one. I am concerned about Andrew allowing himself to go down the tube completely. I would approach him with these concerns, and concentrate on discovering his feelings, his sense of satisfaction in life, his mood. It is his sense of self that is really at issue here. If he can admit that, especially to himself, he might well recognize the potential fire he's playing with.

I doubt that Andrew has reached the stage of seeing a psychotherapist — not yet, at least. But I find that vice-principals can be of exceptional help at times. The entrée into the problem would be his deteriorating school work; it is tactical, but entirely legitimate. What you are looking for is a handle, a way to reach Andrew and help him get back on track.

157 **My son and daughter (Arthur, 18 and Andrea, 17) know well that my wife and I were so-called "Flower Children" during the Sixties. the pictures of us with long hair and beads, marching with "God on our side" are in quite a few of our albums, and friends and family tease us about our days in the San Francisco Haight-Ashbury district. Like so many other kids in those days, we were into psychedelic drugs like grass, LSD, mescaline and MDA. And also like those others, we outgrew that scene when we got into the antiwar movement. After that heady period, we returned to school and got on with our lives. I am now a successful executive, and lo and behold, what are both my kids into? LSD, and I am appalled and angry but who am I to talk? (I can just hear them thinking that).**

What do you mean, who are you to talk? You are their father, that's who, and you shouldn't forget it, even if your kids do. You were once young and immature, full of idealism and naïveté, believing at that time that "All you need is love". You made mistakes, you learned through experience, and you've gained wisdom. You grew up and now you obviously have a responsibility to educate and control your children. Street drugs in the Sixties are no different from any other trouble we might have gotten into when we were kids, and from which we might now wish to protect our own children. I am not so naive as to believe that there is no connection whatsoever between your kids' choice of drugs and your own experiences, especially if they were somewhat glorified. But there are many other reasons for kids of the Eighties to choose these drugs, such as current usage patterns, group pressure, availability, price, mythology, and so forth. The Sixties are still looked upon by many teenagers as an exalted era, and Arthur and Andrea may take a kind of private pride in the fact that their parents "lived the sixties" in the hub of it all, the Bay Area. You have to convey to them that you made your own mistakes, for which you are sorry. They don't have to repeat them.

LSD (Lysergic acid diethylamide) is not an innocuous substance, and nowadays one doesn't know if it is even pure on the streets. It can still precipitate unpleasant psychological reactions. But before you become overly alarmed, try to ascertain whether this is an isolated incident, or reflects chronic usage; whether there is deterioration in other aspects of their lives (school, friends, social activities); whether their relationships with you have suffered. I am not minimizing the fact that they are using detrimental stuff. But since you don't allude to any other problem, I tend to conclude that this is a transient, although risky, event.

158 **Can drug use make anyone crazy? If so, which ones? My daughter Melanie (15) says that she heard in class that they can't.**

By "crazy" I take it you mean a psychotic reaction, a state in which the individual is largely out of contact with reality. I am going to give you another "it depends" kind of answer, but first I want you to tell Melanie that she is totally wrong! Many drugs have been implicated in precipitating an acute psychosis, especially in vulnerable, stressed or disturbed individuals. Some drugs, however, are more potent in this regard than others. For example, PCP (angel dust) regularly and predictably causes acute psychological distress in users, often leading into more severe reactions. There is a specific kind of paranoid psychosis associated with cocaine abuse and amphetamine abuse. But there have also been well-documented reports of psychotic episodes associated with alcohol, LSD, specific popular mushrooms and even marijuana.

The "it depends" refers to the variable combination of the specific drug, the amount used (dosage), the degree of ongoing distress in the user's life at the time, and of course, the specific personality of the individual (strong, weak, stable, unstable) which may actually predispose that person to a psychotic reaction, given the "right" combination of factors.

Tell Melanie that she should get her facts straight, but also to pass on to her friends and teachers this corrected information.

159 **Our 14-year-old son, Colin, was recently hospitalized because he started acting extremely bizarrely. It turns out that he and a group of boys spent an afternoon sniffing from a canister of leaded gasoline. He had sniffed airplane glue a year earlier, and was punished for it, although he felt so sick afterwards that it was almost punishment enough. Luckily, he improved rapidly and there don't seem to be any lingering ill effects. The doctors have recommended that he now see a psychiatrist, of all ridiculous things! Why?**

First of all, it has long been known that some younger adolescents have achieved a high from inhaling certain aromatic compounds. In addition to airplane glue and gasoline, some kids have sniffed nail polish remover, solvents, even liquid paper and other compounds. This is an extremely dangerous activity. Heavy inhalation over a period of time and personal susceptibility can readily combine to cause disorientation, visual hallucinations, convulsions and even brain damage. It is for this reason that legislation has attempted to ensure that the offending substances have largely (but obviously not thoroughly enough) been removed from readily available over-the-counter products in most jurisdictions.

Frankly, many of those kids who indulge repeatedly in glue or other kinds of sniffing have a variety of problems. It is for this reason that Colin has been referred to a psychiatrist; that is, not because of statistical evidence, but rather because he obviously communicated by word or behavior that he is in distress. Perhaps he is having problems at home, in school or with friends. Clearly there is evidence of trouble. This problem goes deeper than — and is very separate from — the gasoline sniffing, which in all likelihood is an isolated incident, as dangerous as it is. As with so many other habit-forming substances, clinicians can often get the susceptible individuals off them, but then the "real" therapeutic work begins. Colin is not out of the woods even if he never inhales any substance again. I would recommend that for Colin's sake you follow up on the recommendations.

161   **I'm afraid that Jeff, my young teenage son, will be an alcoholic like his father and grandfather. He doesn't drink — yet. I warn him about this danger constantly. Do you think that he'll get the message?**

He'll more than get the message. He'll learn that you are obsessed with this fear that he'll become an alcoholic. He'll learn that his father and grandfather were smitten by the "demon rum", and that it's apparently in the cards that he'll be similarly struck down. He'll learn about his inherent weakness and susceptibility, and inevitability of succumbing to this problem.

Your constant badgering has got to stop. Even though you are doing it out of fear and love for your son, you are actually building up expectations so strong that they can actually shape his behavior. Your expectations are clear — you use the word yet — don't set Jeff's. While it is true that alcoholism is a common and dangerous disorder, and that there are familial trends, it is by no means genetically predetermined! There are thousands of sons and daughters of alcoholics who not only are not addicted to alcohol, but have no tendencies whatsoever in that direction. Support your son's successes; encourage and reinforce the many positive things in his life. He has been amply warned and forewarned. Beware of overkill. (It might be well to discuss *your* preoccupation with a counsellor of the family or teen offshoots of Alcoholics Anonymous — Al-Anon or Al-Ateen.)

161 **My husband is an alcoholic, and has been one for 15 years. Our daughter Lara is 16 and obviously has never known anything else. But it has only been in the last couple of years that he has become violent with me. He has always been verbally abusive to us when he's been drunk, but in between those periods he's been contrite, repentant and full of deep regret and promises to stay off booze. And he has been dry for a few extended periods, but he always goes back. He's gotten some professional help, but obviously it hasn't helped. Frankly, I am much more worried about Lara than her father. She lately has seemed withdrawn and sad. Could this be related to his alcohol problem?**

I would bet anything that it is not only related, but caused by his alcoholism and its related behavior. I've been through this with countless young people from homes with an alcoholic parent and it is a predictable and poignant tale of woe that I hear each time. The feelings that are related to me include fear, depression, insecurity and low self-esteem. The kids are embarrassed and humiliated; they won't ever invite anyone home. They keep this terrible story private; a shameful secret. They feel an uncomfortable mixture of love and hate for the alcoholic parent, and the ones who bear the brunt of all these emotions are the kids themselves. Treating the alcoholic without seeing the family involved is verging on clinical irresponsibility. It is for this very reason that alcohol and drug treatment programs, clinics and residential treatment centers and organizations such as Alcoholics Anonymous have extensive family, and especially adolescent, counselling services. The family and adolescent programs now offered as part of Alcoholics Anonymous are called Al-Anon and Al-Ateen. Counsellors, social workers, and other mental health professionals are now regularly attached to many medical clinics or departments that work with alcoholics.

Alcoholism is a common, dangerous, and destructive disorder. It can drain the lifeblood out of the alcoholic and his or her family. Alcoholics are in dire need of corrective intervention; AA works for many, but not all, and the results are the same for the other available services. But even if the alcoholic refuses to get help, you can still seek it for yourselves. I have seen too many families hang in alone for far too long. If your husband won't get proper attention, you and Lara *must* go for appropriate counselling. She deserves nothing less even if it means having to leave your husband, if all else fails.

162   **My 18-year-old son, Greg, is heavily into co-caine and crack. We are admittedly wealthy people, and he does have access to funds at this point, whether we like it or not. He was always into testing authority, but this latest activity is new and scary to us. Should we be concerned?**

You should be scared stiff! I've been through the coke and crack routine with too many patients too often to not be seriously concerned. These are drugs (coke the more intense, expensive, concentrated and dangerous, and crack the more readily available and rapidly habit-forming) which give users the impression of competence, confidence, control and power. All of these feelings are illusory, invalid, and totally misguided. Eventually, the mythology of accomplishment gives way to the reality of a self-destructive course.

Unless he is one of the lucky few who realize the potential results of their downward spiral, and by some inner intuitive force give up these chemicals, Greg is destined to end up badly hurt, if he is lucky enough to live. Those who don't stop on their own, or get appropriate help, leave a trail of destruction in their lives, at work and among their loved ones — all suffer indiscriminately.

Show him your letter, and this answer. I want to tell him that if he can't stop using cocaine and crack on his own, these same drugs (the most craving-inducing chemicals known) will destroy him and everything and everyone associated with him in their wake. I urge *him* (to urge you is like bringing coals to Newcastle) to seek help at a drug treatment center. These centers are available in most urban centers of the world.

At the risk of sounding melodramatic, your son has few choices left. If he misses this opportunity, his life may well end.

163 We are a well-known family in the local area. My 18-year-old son, Tim, was stopped by the police last year for speeding in his sports car, which I had bought for his birthday. He was given a stern warning and let off. He told me about it, laughing, and said that it's a good thing that he wasn't asked to take a breathalyser test, because he'd had half a dozen beers just before that. I was furious, and told him so, but he obviously thought that I was being unfairly critical. Four months later, the same thing happened, and this time a breathalyser test was done. He was charged with reckless drving, but they dropped the drinking charge. Two months later, it happened again, and they suspended his driver's license. I have since discovered that they will give him "special treatment" if I so indicate; that is, they'll let him off. I am sorely tempted to do this, although I am still seething. What do you suggest?

I am certain that you can answer your own question. You surely know that I don't think that you should intervene. If you are really considering helping your son flout the law, then I have some clues as to where Tim gets his anti-social tendencies. I am sorry to sound so antagonistc, but we are dealing here with a deadly serious situation.

You know as well as I that teenage males form the worst-risk group for automobile accidents; that the combination of drinking and driving is too commonly seen and it is destructive and lethal. Thousands of innocent victims are maimed and killed yearly. And still the carnage goes on. It is for this reason that many jurisdictions are legally raising both the driving and drinking ages. Family members of victims have lobbied long and hard for these changes in our liberal laws.

You don't give me any further information about Tim. How does he do in school? How does he react to authority in general? What are his friends like? I expect that his repetitive drinking and driving is representative of other destructive behavior in which he is involved. In any event, he is a walking time bomb; he has to be disarmed. In his hands, both a car and alcohol are lethal weapons. Society has to be protected from his flirting with irresponsible and indiscriminate violence. He may need psychotherapy, group therapy, punishment, incarceration. Let the courts and professionals decide. You can be most helpful by refusing to intervene on Tim's behalf.

164   **Our 19-year-old son, Garett, is a drummer in a rock band that has done very well in this area. We were shocked to learn last week that their lead singer died as a result of a heroin overdose. We've heard a lot recently about alcohol, cocaine, crack, hash and grass but we thought that heroin was passé.**

It is fascinating to me that certain behaviors only get media attention when "our" own families and friends are involved. When a problem is relegated or restricted to skid row, to the have-nots, or to the criminal population, we just don't care all that much.

When drugs were endemic in the lower class streets decades ago, who was aware or even concerned? When the middle and upper-middle classes began to be involved suddenly there were overwhelming and even hysterical responses. Now that heroin has been supplanted by more "popular" street drugs, we have again been lulled into some complacency.

Heroin is a highly addictive substance (see Question 153); it is a narcotic, closely related to morphine, and they both derive from a poppy-like plant (Rauwolfia) grown for a tremendous profit in many parts of the world (not unlike the cocaine from coca plants in South America). It is big underworld business, with "captive customers", in that once addicted, or physiologically hooked, regular users need their "fix" (injection) just as you and I need our regular mealtme nourishment. It is still widely used and abused, and while we do see heroin addicts from all walks of life (physicians and nurses are particularly at risk), it is again, by and large, a lower class phenomenon, and as such, out of our consciousness.

I don't know if Garett's band-mate was an addict or not. This might have been a case of "simple" suicide, with him using the most available substance at the time. I would bet, however, that he'd had some facility with its usage prior to the final self-destructive act. Another possibility — that he miscalculated the dosage and didn't mean to die — is quite plausible too.

The only purpose this kind of tragic death serves is to remind Garett and others that life is difficult and precious. It also opens our eyes to the realities of substance abuse.

165 **We have a reverse parent-child situation for you. Our teenage kids (David, 18 and Judy, 14) have told us that we should empty our medicine cabinet of all our tranquilizers and sleeping pills, which we desperately need. As caring as they are, we feel that it's none of their business!**

Well, let me start by reiterating what you already have stated: your kids obviously do care for you. But I'll go one step further by disagreeing with you strongly: it certainly is their business! We all know that kids can be moralizing monsters at times, bringing home "thou shalt nots" from school or elsewhere and sticking it to their parents — weight, diet, drinking and smoking are some favorite parental activities that kids like to shoot down. Sometimes the criticism is laced with a touch of rebelliousness, or a sense of reciprocation and paying back of lectures and moralizing they received from you. But usually it is done out of love and real concern for their parents' well-being and health.

Now to the substance of their haranguing you: the tranquilizers and sedatives which you say you "desperately" need. I can't tell if you are addicted (yet) to your medications, but you should know that these are extremely dangerous substances. It's true that they are prescribed by doctors, but that doesn't make them any less dangerous. I know too many stories of doctors who have overprescribed, or who have not carefully enough monitored their patients, and who have contributed strongly to the development of a destructive habit. In this context, they become no better than the dealers and pushers whom we so vehemently decry. Of course, doctors can't be blamed entirely for this problem, because patients can and do go to a variety of doctors, "collecting" pills as they go along. There are now thousands upon thousands of people around the world who are habituated or addicted to prescribed medications. Diazepam, especially (one of its most popular trade names is Valium) is one of the most widely abused substances in the history of humanity. Similarly, *all* sleeping pills are potentially lethal. All of these substances have their place as important therapeutic tools that physicians have at their disposal when indicated, but they have to be used cautiously, judiciously, and with rigid criteria for their prescription. Under the best of circumstances, some abuse-prone individuals will take advantage of their availability. But at least the number of those affected can be kept down considerably.

All this still begs the question of your "desperate" need for these pills. If your lives are so oppressive or your sense of inner control so tenuous that you have to have perpetual chemical crutches, then you are a) vulnerable and b) not receiving proper medical and/or psychiatric attention. Your goal should be to get along in life feeling relatively fulfilled and relaxed without artificial help, at least for a good proportion of the time. Of course we all go through rough times and crises, but I am discussing our constant day-to-day existences. Aside from setting a terrible example for your own kids' eventual attempts to cope with life's inevitable problems, you are doing harm to yourselves. Perhaps visits to a new doctor and therapist are now in order.

Psychological and Psychiatric Problems

I spend so much time reassuring parents that most teenagers are not seriously disturbed and that adolescence is not a time of inevitable misery, because these myths have permeated our consciousness to such an extent that they are very hard to dispel or eradicate. One of the problems with buying into that misguided message is that real problems then get relegated to clichés like "it's just a stage", or "he (she)'ll grow out of it" — a kind of ill-advised reassurance. The fact is that some adolescents, just like some adults, can and do have serious problems, and they don't grow out of them. A teenager in deep psychological trouble, one who is at risk, becomes an adult in deep psychological trouble, perhaps even more at risk.

This section will illustrate typical problems that parents of disturbed teenagers might see, and certainly that we clinicians see in our offices quite regularly. General and unique clues and warning signs are highlighted, as is the difference between the normal problems of living we all run into, and the ones tinged with more "pathology" or deviance. Occasionally, problems begin during the adolescent period, but we human beings are so boringly predictable and consistent that many of the problems are mere continuations and embellishments of behavior that was seen at an earlier stage. For example, adolescents into drugs, destructive sexuality or serious fears, depression or psychosis usually showed early warning signs, often unheeded, years earlier. (These include anxiety, aggressive behavior, isolation, school problems and sleep disturbances.)

As difficult as it is now to find an excellent mental health professional who works with adolescents or an appropriate service for a teenager in trouble, this lack of accessible help is only going to get worse. Demographics are against us. That is, because of the decline in the birthrate over the past couple of decades and the increase in life expectancy in that same time frame, the population bulk is shifting towards the elderly. And that is where dollars, resources, and trained professionals are going to go. To be crass, adolescents have had their day!

Another myth is more prevalent among the professionals: that teenagers won't co-operate with a helping professional and won't respond to treatment. It just ain't so. Adolescents can be recalcitrant and difficult, closed and unco-operative, but given the "right" professional, most will be more than forthcoming. The necessary training and talent have to be there, to be sure. But the main ingredient has to be the motivation, the desire to work with that age group, the comfort with them. That comfort is achieved not by ingratiating friendship, but rather by genuine respect, which then enables the professional to be tough and to say "no" when it is appropriate and necessary.

It is worth searching for and finding such a professional. I am frequently surprised and reassured by the degree to which troubled young people respond to various kinds of intervention — psychotherapy, medication, group homes, group therapy, remedial education, vocational assessment and guidance — all these and more, alone and in combination, are often successfully used. When dramatic improvement takes place, and it often does, there is no more rewarding feeling.

$\underline{166}$ **My 16-year-old daughter, Diane, is totally out of control. She skips school, uses drugs, smokes, drinks and is promiscuous, and her friends are no better. She has stolen money from us. My husband won't even talk to her anymore, and she ignores me, except when she snarls.**

I've become kind of hard-nosed in these terrible situations. I've been through this before with many teenagers and their families, and honestly, I've reached the point of protecting the family first and foremost. Whatever the causes of this type of behavior, and they are complex, it seems that many of these kids have to hit a kind of rock bottom before they come to some sort of realization that they are in deep trouble. Their parents put out enormous amounts of energy and receive little effort in return. In trying to understand and reason, compromise and treat, they often fiddle while Rome burns. Rome, in this case, is their own lives, and those of their other children.

It's not that I don't think that psychological and social intervention is useful or necessary; it decidedly is. But certainly one-to-one psychotherapy is usually unsuccessful for these types of kids. They need a multi-dimensional approach, at times involving services as disparate as the police, psychologists, social workers, residential treatment centers, group homes, training schools and psychiatrists.

You will be more able to benefit from counselling right now than your daughter. Diane's frenetic, anti-social, self-destructive activities more than likely blind her to reason, and preclude her listening to anyone with an authority label. Every now and then we reach these kids at this particular stage, but it is unusual. You will need the support to do what may be necessary: confront, officially charge, expel, place in a residence and similar actions.

At some point — I've seen it too often to doubt its (eventual) appearance — something crystalizes for some of these young people. They stop playing with fire, give up their anger at the world and their rejection of their parents. It is *then* that they may be ready for individual and family therapy.

In the meantime, mobilize help, but get on with being good to yourselves. Some cities have branches of the organization called

"Tough Love", which really is a clinical (and entrepreneurial) attempt at instituting firm limit-setting in the context of loving. I am certainly not trying to drum up business for this group, but parents who attend can be of enormous assistance and moral support to each other.

167 My 17-year-old daughter, Clarisse, has always been high-strung and nervous. Her sleep has suffered over the years, but lately it has been terrible. She often lies in bed for hours without falling asleep, and then can't get up in the morning, or is miserable upon waking. Her explanation for her problem recently was, "I'm worried about nuclear war." Is this possible?

Of course, it is possible, but it is decidedly unusual. Anti-nuclear activists in my profession are convinced that the specter of nuclear annihilation is causing all kinds of symptoms of anxiety and depression among adolescents and younger children. I must say that much as I sympathize with those who wish to eradicate nuclear weapons from our planet, I cannot entirely agree with their simplistic pronouncements. Actually, I find that they are proselytizing politically "on the backs" of young people, and their evidence is, in fact, underwhelming. It is not that your daughter is "wrong"; rather, her problem is more complicated than she thinks.

In a climate of constant discussion and debate, any vital issue can become part of the public consciousness, and in so doing, can be incorporated into the worries and concerns of young (or any) people. Clarisse has been suffering from an anxiety-related disorder for years, and it seems to be part and parcel of her personality. It may well be that she needs professional help (medication or psychotherapy) to help her overcome her problems. Your family doctor, or an adolescent clinic, can evaluate her, and make the appropriate recommendations. Paradoxically, the preoccupation with the anti-nuclear struggle can often serve as a rallying cry for youth, getting them involved, ideologically and enthusiastically, and even helping to *diminish* neurotic symptoms.

168 **I am ashamed to even discuss this problem; at times, I don't believe it myself. Here it is: our 14-year-old daughter, Melissa, who is beautiful, well-developed, and looks 19, comes on to *our* male friends in a flirtatious, sexually aggressive, wantonly seductive manner. She is an average student, although her grades have slipped recently, and she has become somewhat intolerant of her friends. We assume that she isn't into booze and drugs, and that she is still a virgin. She doesn't date that much, but seems to toy with teenage boys' affections. She is also irritable and abrasive at home with us. Is this normal?**

No, it is not normal (as in average, common, healthy behavior). It is decidedly unusual, but whether it is pathological (that is, indicative of psychological problems) can only be conjectured from this vantage point. It is interesting (and frightening to you) that she saves her open seductiveness for considerably older, married, and *unavailable* (I assume) men. Although she is manipulative with younger boys, she does not follow through in her behavior with them.

It sounds like her precocious development has made her feel confused and ill at ease. She experiments in safe, "preliminary" behavior, as a sort of challenge to both her attractiveness, and a testing of the limits of her power over men. But she is still a 14-year-old (in an older body) at heart, excited yet fearful. The awkwardness of this stage, however, is supplemented in Melissa's case by a facade of sophistication and sexuality.

The problem is that one of these older men could take advantage of her in her state of vulnerability. It is no wonder that you see signs at home of tension and diminished concentration (her school work has slipped).

I recommend that you talk to her, as only mother and daughter can, in a gentle, loving, enlightening, insightful way. Certainly, convey to her that you disapprove of her behavior with older men. She may be unaware of the inappropriateness of it, as well as its undesirable aspects and possible consequences. Tell her that you recognize the difficulties of this stage for her, that they are tough on anyone, but particularly for someone as exquisite as she. Even if she denies your analysis, she will have been made aware that her mother cares, is sensitive and empathetic, and that *there is some basis for her unhappiness.* Reassure her that this period will quickly disappear, but caution her about being too friendly with older members of the opposite sex. Don't lay the onus entirely on her, because I am sure that these men play a role in welcoming her advances.

169 **Our 17-year-old son, Jim, has recently and suddenly quit school. He is a handsome, well-dressed, talented young man; his marks were good, he had friends there and he was active and known around the school. But he was found out in a series of elaborate lies that left him exposed and humiliated. He had told concocted stories of great wealth, glamour, travel, and relationships with powerful and famous people. It turns out that everybody believed him because of his sincerity, and many were clearly envious of this "golden boy" with everything going for him. While we are not failures by any means (I am an actuary, my wife a librarian), his stories were so far from the truth that we were dumbfounded. For the past two summers he had worked as a houseboy at an estate in the country, and obviously envied their lifestyle. He has also been somewhat disdainful of ours. Does he need help?**

Jim has experienced in reality the utter core of fear that plagues most people who are in the throes of self-doubt — that they will be "found out" and exposed for the frauds that they think they are. That he brought it on himself makes it even more painful. Appearances are obviously very important to him, as they are to most adolescents, and he felt at once denuded and bereft of a cover. The utter humiliation forced him to quit school in shame.

While one can question the propriety of what he did, and can criticize the willful manipulativeness of it all, it is important to stress that he hurt no one but himself, and that he is going through great sorrow right now. Punishment should be out of the question (he certainly has been punished enough).

Jim has actually prematurely enacted his fantasies for himself. Partly because of his need to aggrandize himself in order to make him look and hence feel "better", he took to his summer bosses' lifestyle, and decided to adopt and adapt it for his own needs. Fantasies which become lies have a way of becoming more elaborate and convoluted, each no longer merely to impress others, but to serve as a cover and rationale for a previous concoction.

The sad thing is that Jim didn't *need* to impress anyone — he already had people who genuinely liked him. He just had trouble liking himself, and the house he built with no foundation came crashing down on his head.

Yes, Jim needs help and I would expect that in his present state, he would be glad to receive it. A psychiatrist or psychologist who works with adolescents would be ideal for him. They will explore together the inner needs which compelled him to act out these lies, and more importantly, help Jim to develop better ways of feeling good about himself.

Finally, you can offer him a note of reassurance. One of the fears of individuals in this position is that none of the friends, who were told all these stories, will talk to him again. I have found that often, in a few short weeks or months, the same old friends return, bearing no ill feelings. If facing them again proves just too much for him to bear, he can, of course, start fresh at an entirely new school.

170 **Our son Glen steals money from us. He doesn't know that we are onto this activity, but we are absolutely certain. He is 14 years old and I'll bet**

**that he has been doing it for a few years, al-
though on the surface our relationship seems
fine. For a long time now we both have felt that
our missing cash was due to each other's sloppi-
ness and ineptitude, but Glen has always had
enough money to do and buy things, treat friends,
and even offer us "loans" when we were short.
It's only been in the past couple of months that
we put two and two together; we instituted a
bookkeeping system and kept track of the numbers on bills. Sure enough, we found the exact
amounts and bills in his room (which we've
searched). I don't know if he has stolen from
others. What do we do?**

The chances are good that you are not the only victims, although
you are the most hurt. There are many important aspects to this
situation, not the least of which are the feelings involved. Is he
angry at you? Is he so miserable in his own life that he seeks
demeaning and ultimately self-destructive activities to overcome
his low self-esteem? Is he short of money ordinarily? Is the cash
used for constructive purposes only or is it supporting drug
abuse? Is the money his pathetic way of impressing others? Does
he genuinely care for you, or is he devoid of a sense of love and
commitment to others?

In the course of a psychological evaluation, these and similar
questions would have to be explored and answered, and the
answers will largely determine the nature, course and prognosis
of therapy. First, though, Glen has to be confronted. Sometimes
a clear message that the jig is up does, in fact, end the game.
More often, with long-standing behavior, the individual will have
to spend some time learning about himself, his reasons for stealing and alternative ways of handling his inner problems and/or
cash shortage (such as earning money). Restitution is in order,
but I leave amounts and method up to you. Sometimes this
therapeutic approach fails, and a more correctional (or punitive)
approach — involving the police and the courts — is in order.

Speak to Glen now. You can show him your letter and this
answer as a good starter.

171 **Our son Kenny is a good kid, but he has been stealing for about two years (he is 15). He has stolen money from us, from neighbors and from relatives. He was picked up for shoplifting recently and at his court date, the judge admonished him, but there was no penalty. We are a comfortable middle-class family, and he gets an adequate allowance.**

This letter raises more questions than answers. Before I could pass any kind of informed judgment, I'd need more information. Is all else going well for Kenny? Is he doing well in school? Has he got friends? Does he dislike himself (his size, stature, face)? Does he get along with his parents or other authority figures? Is he generally unhappy? Is he involved in drugs, or any other anti-social activities? What does he do with the money or merchandise? Is he in with a tough group of kids or even a gang? How has he been dealt with for his series of misdemeanors?

These are all important questions to be answered. If the picture that develops is more broadly negative than is suggested by your letter, Kenny may need intensive institutional care (see Questions 178, 182). But if, as I suspect, Kenny's stealing is a more isolated behavior, it is a less ominous picture. I hope that he has been confronted, criticized, and even threatened in response to these recurrent episodes. But has he been made to apologize to those from whom he stole? Has he had to make restitution? If he wants extra money (for legitimate purposes), let him get a part-time job. Make him account for his time, and ensure that he is engaged in fulfilling activities outside of school.

Most importantly, take him to see a mental health professional who works with adolescents. The stealing can be eradicated fairly readily, but you should make sure that it is not an outlet for covering up more hidden feelings of unhappiness.

172 **Our 18-year-old daughter, Karen, was unceremoniously "released" from the National Gymnastics team three months ago, for the first time**

in over four years. She was let go because, in truth, there were better competitors that they had to make room for. For the past decade she has walked, talked, eaten and drank nothing else but this; it was her entire life. She practiced six hours a day, and frequently had to forego other pleasures and social activities in order to keep up in both her gymnastics and her school work. Since she left the team she has been crying, withdrawn, and has gained 20 pounds! Is this just a temporary phase?

I've seen this syndrome often: for the gymnastics team, you could easily have substituted dance, skiing, skating, riding, tennis, swimming or any other competitive performance skill which reaches the lofty levels of national and international meetings, competitions, finals, standings and medals. All of these activities demand an enormous output of energy and emotional commitment on a daily basis over a long period of time. Many other adolescents have the necessary natural talents, but don't have the particular psychological make-up to give them that almost obsessional drive they require to stay at it day after day, week after week, month after month, year after year. I know that I don't have it.

But once smitten, there is a performance high, a set of goals to aspire to, and a terrific sense of belonging, of team spirit, of communality. Usually there are coaches involved who spur the young people on to higher levels of accomplishment but also can temper their zeal within the limits of the abilities of the particular individuals. Good coaches are also sensitive and psychologically aware, and often "prepare" (or should) members of the team for the *inevitability* of being dropped. Even superstars burn out, and few reach those stratospheric levels.

Karen sounds as if she was ill-prepared for being dropped. Either she was not advised (over a period of months), or she used the mechanism of denial to convince herself that she couldn't be released. Gymnastics not only entails an enormous energy output, but major changes are often instituted in diet in order to keep weight down and agility up — with resulting bodily effects not unlike anorexia nervosa. Everything changed overnight for Karen, and she has reacted to this major stress and shock to her system by her present behavior. She is sad, and probably angry at the coaches and herself. She has suffered a grievous loss; of self-esteem, of friends and of a way of life. I would have to know much more before making a diagnosis, but her unhappy mood, lethargy, withdrawal and eating certainly point toward some kind of depressive reaction. I don't know if this sadness is (yet) affecting her school work and/or relationships, but if it keeps up much longer, these aspects of her life will be affected detrimentally.

I assume that you have spoken to her about her disappointment and unhappiness. If her mood does not show signs of improving soon, perhaps she can speak to her family doctor or get a referral to a mental health professional. Better yet, I am certain that the national gymnastics organization has run into this problem before, and works with specific professionals to help ex-members as well as active members of the team who are having problems. Karen's problems are temporary, but they can be alleviated much more quickly with the proper intervention.

173 **Our 14-year-old son, Rod, is hooked on arcades. You know those places with flashing lights, electronic sounds and kids hunched over each monitor or machine trying to win something. I can't fathom the fascination this pasttime holds for youngsters. Rod will do nothing else if the opportunity presents itself to play video games of any kind. And the money he spends is unbelievable! He gets a small allowance, and he had a newspaper route for a while, but gave it up. He begs, borrows, and I know that he has taken small amounts of loose change around the house. Do we have a problem?**

It depends. Now how's that for an answer? But the fact is that I've seen teenagers (usually boys) with this preoccupation before, and for some it is more of a problem than others. Obviously, if the youth's involvement in this behavior is so overwhelming as to cause a deterioration in school work and relationships with friends and family, then he does have a problem. Does this accurately describe Rod? Sometimes a minimal involvement is so offensive to the parent(s), that the reaction is all out of proportion to the act. They see these games as expensive, useless, mindless, corrupting and destructive, and often located in a less than salutory atmosphere. And they blow their stack at the slightest suggestions of their child indulging that urge. There is a rare variant of preoccupation with repetitive mechanical or electronic games which boys with some forms of brain damage manifest; Rod does not seem to fit into this unusual category.

The young people who have escalated their playing of these games to an obsessional level often use them as an escape from their realities. For a while the player becomes an outer space warrior, automaton or superhuman hero; it can be thrilling. There is also the challenge to hand-eye coordination skills, speed and reflexes. There is a competitive aspect involved, against themselves or against each other. Finally, it may get some kids out of the doldrums, make them feel better about themselves, and give them a social milieu.

There is an element of addiction or high involved for that small minority who cannot seem to stop their indulgence. But not all kids who indulge this passion for a while are video "addicts". It all boils down to the "how much" of Rod's involvement, the extent of its detrimental effect on him and his life, and the degree to which it upsets you. If any or all of these are in the high range of the scale, then some kind of intervention may be necessary. If Rod will not comply with your "orders" to stop playing the games; if he thinks that your point of view is ludicrous and refuses to co-operate, of if the needs that are being fulfilled are overwhelmingly great in comparison to his desire to stop, another approach, or even professional help may be in order. A counsellor at a Family Service Agency may be a good start, but it may come to a psychiatric evaluation of your son, once the reasons for his overwhelming preoccupation become clear.

174 My 15-year-old son, Ricky, has always had active nighttime experiences. As a child he had night terrors, sleep-walking and nightmares, and always ground his teeth. Now, as a young adolescent, he has wet dreams. He has always talked in his sleep, but it sounds like gibberish. Does all this night activity mean that he has problems?

Sleep is becoming a rich area for scientific study. We know that no living being can function without sleep, but that the amounts perceived as needed by individuals vary tremendously. A core of five to six hours is basic to the vast majority of people, but some claim to function well and regularly on as few as four hours, and others say they need nine or ten hours a night. We also know that there are different levels and stages of sleep, and that dreaming in human beings occurs during stage four, or rapid eye movement (REM) sleep. The fact that all vertebrates seem to have REM periods has not put into question the validity of the use of dreams in psychotherapy. There is no doubt that our minds continue to function, albeit differently, while we are getting our beauty rest.

The kinds of sleep behavior you describe for Ricky as a young boy, and which have since disappeared, are sometimes a reflection of inner tension and turmoil — but not always. Before making that determination, a clinician would have to know considerably more about Ricky's waking behavior at that time, his feelings, relationships, and performance. Certainly, nightmares, or at least unpleasant dreams, are experienced by most people from time to time, but they tend to flare up when we are in periods of heavy stress. Similarly, grinding teeth may mean nothing, or it could be an expression of inner tension.

But your only concerns with Ricky are "wet dreams". He doesn't have insomnia (difficulty falling asleep, early wakening), fitful sleep or day-night sleep reversal patterns, all of which would make us think about inner turmoil. He wakes up refreshed, so he is not afflicted with intermittent sleeping or bad dreams. The stains you see on his sheets are either a result of masturbation or what you call "wet dreams", normal and natural ejaculations of semen as a result of erotic fantasies and dreams. There is nothing whatsoever to worry about. I hope that he at least enjoys his dreams.

175   **Our 19-year-old daughter, Vanessa, was travelling with a friend through Europe this summer when she suddenly fell apart and had to be hospitalized in Athens. She remained in hospital for a week, and then returned home. She seems a bit quiet to us, but otherwise okay, and won't say much except that she had some problems and is feeling much better. She is taking no medication. My sister says that Vanessa had a nervous breakdown. What exactly is that?**

This letter could be entitled "Variations on a Theme". I have heard countless stories of emotional problems in adolescents when travelling long distances from home, usually for the first time. The causes are many and varied. There may have been severe conflicts with the travelling partner; there may been sexual exploitation by a Lothario; there could have been a rip-off of all her belongings; the possibility of her having taken drugs which were adulterated, especially hashish, LSD, or angel dust, is a real one; she could have been homesick, missing you or feeling pressured by the return to school and decisions to be made. For Vanessa to have become ill over one of these possible problems, however, necessitated a predisposed and vulnerable personality or psychological state. Vanessa might have experienced a couple or more of these possibilities simultaneously.

What exactly was the diagnosis to get her hospitalized? It is usually one of four possible things. A severe depression (or depressive episode); a major anxiety attack, including panic; a psychotic break (especially schizophrenia); or a drug-induced syndrome. I would opt for the latter because of the relatively short stay in hospital, the lack of continuing medication, and the fact that she seems in pretty good shape right now (a mite chagrined, perhaps). I suggest, however, that Vanessa be evaluated by a psychiatrist in the very near future. A "nervous breakdown" is a common colloquialism that really refers to any massive emotional reaction of an individual which prevents their functioning academically, vocationally or socially. It is an exact analogue of a complex machine breaking down when it is overloaded. So, too, is it with us humans: overload us and we break down in a number of possible ways. A good "mechanic" (psychiatrist, psychologist, counsellor) can help get our energy and parts working smoothly again.

176 **Our daughter, Pat (18) is down on the world. It isn't that she is sad or weepy, it's just that nothing is quite good enough for her — she's a snob! She's critical, cynical and sarcastic about everything and everyone. According to Pat, nobody has a good idea, motive, accomplishment or possession. When we disagree she thinks we're naive. She accuses us of being unfair, even rejecting of her, when we question her totally negative attitude.**

In my experience, people who are so critical of everyone else are particularly critical of themselves. They are insecure and full of self-doubts, but they hide those feelings, sometimes even from themselves. These "real" feelings are cloaked in an outer garment of misanthropy. Pat represents the epitome of the word "misanthropist", essentially one who hates humanity. Unfortunately, people, including those closest to her, will respond only to her criticism and carping, and not even try to look past this facade.

Insecurity is a common human condition, not just among adolescents. We all harbor it to varying extents and it rises and falls within us depending on our circumstances. We handle it by learning about ourselves, by concentrating on our strengths, and compensating for our weaknesses. Open discussion with close friends and self-deprecatory humor are common coping ploys. But dealing with insecurity entails a certain amount of honesty with ourselves plus some insight and sensitivity, which Pat is not displaying. She may be using her cynicism as a defense against facing her innermost fears. I doubt that she'd consider seeing a psychotherapist at this point. What she needs is some gentle confrontation, probing, and empathetic remarks regarding her true feelings from people she trusts. Her parents are a good start.

You could avoid agreeing with her about her latest peeves, and instead comment on her inner unrest and unhappiness. She may not want to hear this message at first, but it will certainly sink in. It could well be that she will at some point enter into individual or group psychotherapy, ostensibly because of lack of friends (social isolation). But the real reasons will rapidly make themselves apparent. She's not there yet, but at the age of 18, she is getting set in her ways; better let her know soon what you see. Your empathy and positive attitude will go a long way towards making her aware of her self-defeating approach to life.

177 **My 18-year-old daughter, Danielle, is always moody, brooding and down. She stays in her room for hours, often crying. Nothing we do seems to help. Will she outgrow this stage once she gets older?**

Danielle needs help. Those who mistakenly believe that emotional upheaval is commonplace during adolescence don't take real upheaval seriously enough when they see it. Your daughter is not just enduring a stage; she is suffering pure, unadulterated pain. It is not due to her period, her age, her stage or her rage. It sounds reminiscent of a clinical depression, which is decidedly treatable, but she could be experiencing other problems as well.

While we all sometimes feel down, clinical depression is marked by intense emotional pain and sadness over a prolonged period of time. It is usually highlighted or accompanied by withdrawal, sleep and appetite disturbances, self-deprecation and guilt. I wouldn't want to "diagnose" from this vantage point; she could also be manifesting signs of another psychiatric disorder.

Danielle deserves to be evaluated and treated — now. Your family doctor can refer her to a psychiatrist. It may be that other therapists could work with her successfully, but with depression, or other disorders, medication may well be in order, and it could expedite her recovery.

178 **My 16-year-old daughter, Ashley, has a gorgeous body, one that I would have died for when I was her age. I was chubby and I have told her about how unhappy it made me. But she is into forcing herself to vomit whatever she eats. She also takes laxatives and diuretics in order to keep her weight normal. She doesn't starve herself, but she is always preoccupied with her weight and appearance.**

Your daughter's condition is known as bulimia, or self-induced vomiting, to enable eating without gaining weight. Sometimes it is associated with anorexia nervosa (see Question 179) but more commonly it is a condition unto itself. Occasionally it is related to a depression, and at other times to anti-social behavior. Most commonly, however, bulimia is found in apparently normal people, usually young women, and occasionally it is a life-long condition.

Contrary to popular belief, bulimia can kill, as easily or moreso than anorexia. The use of medications and the constant vomiting can throw the body into a severe chemical imbalance, and can induce a serious and even fatal illness. I can hit you with all kinds of theories as to *why* your daughter is bulimic, but they would all be conjectural. Suffice to say that upwards of ten percent of college-age women have an eating disorder to some extent. The bottom line is that your daughter needs professional attention fast. Your family practitioner can refer her to an appropriate individual or resource. If your Ashley is reluctant to get appropriate help, show her your letter and this answer. To her I say, "You can and should be helped!"

179 My 15-year-old daughter, Millie, seems to be starving herself to death. Since being slightly overweight six months ago, she has lost 38 pounds and is not about to stop, no matter what anybody says. Is this dangerous?

Yes, it *is* dangerous. I must admit to being surprised that you even asked. You obviously haven't been reading popular magazines over the past few years. If there is one medical subject that has received enormous coverage recently, it is anorexia nervosa, an eating disorder that affects young girls much more often than boys. Anorexics lose 25 percent or more of their body weight, they perceive themselves as fat even when they're not, they cease menstruation, and they starve themselves. Sometimes anorexia is associated with self-induced vomiting (bulimia), which is obviously done to accomplish eating without caloric gain. The causes are many and varied and related to different personality types and disturbances, but the fact that our culture is obsessed with thinness as an ideal is a significant contributor to the incidence of this disease.

Treatment is as complicated as the causes, but it is certainly necessary. Left to their own devices, a number of these young patients would (and do) die. Millie needs help, whether she realizes it or not. She must certainly have a complete physical checkup from her doctor to monitor her health, bodily functions, and safety. A psychiatric and social evaluation is also absolutely necessary. It will entail exploring your daughter's inner — and outer — life, her relationships, her family, her feelings and her attitudes. Therapy will be directed at both the root causes (for example, depression), and the manifest expression (anorexia). You might very likely be involved in some family sessions. Be prepared for a difficult period, but with the proper help, she (and you) should win this battle.

180 Our 18-year-old daughter, Linda, is literally house-bound. Believe it or not, she is afraid to go *anywhere*. If we take her somewhere, or send

her on an errand, she develops these ridiculous panic attacks. It started out as a mild fear, but now she's paralyzed. We have tried everything from advice to threats, but nothing seems to work.

I'm sure that you don't appreciate armchair diagnoses, but I have no doubt Linda is suffering from agoraphobia (literally, fear of open spaces). This condition appears to be relatively common, *especially* among young and middle-aged women. It may simply be that many agoraphobics are making themselves known, since the media have been paying increasing attention to it. We do not know the cause of this psychological disorder. It may be related to depression (psychiatry's point of view) or to faulty conditioned learning (psychology's approach). But the basic issue is that not only is it a common, debilitating condition, but more importantly, it *is amenable to treatment.*

The bind is that to get help your daughter has to go out, and to do that she has to engender a severe anxiety attack. Usually the first visit to a mental health professional is made in the company of somebody close to the patient (possibly yourself, in this case). Treatment consists of a combination of a specific kind of anti-depressant medication, behavior therapy ("desensitizing" the individual), and traditional psychotherapy, usually individually or in a group situation.

You can be optimistic that she *can* be helped. Your threats and advice, all made with her best interests at heart, only serve to increase you and her frustration. Take her to a therapist instead.

181   **It's a good thing we have health insurance because Samantha, our 18-year-old daughter, would have run us into bankruptcy over the past two-and-a-half years. I know it sounds unbelievable, but she has seen over 25 different doctors, had five separate operations, ten hospitalizations, more than 15 discrete diagnoses, and I would say hundreds of symptoms, for which she**

has received hundreds of tests and been treated with hundreds of medicines and pills. For example, she has had appendicitis, ovarian cysts, dislocated knees, infectious monoucleosis, pneumonia twice, asthma, bronchitis, massive diarrhoea, severe food allergies, impacted wisdom teeth, hypothyroidism and even a therapeutic abortion, all in the space of thirty months! Her relationships with doctors usually start off very positively (she can be delightfully charming), but invariably end up soured because they won't proceed with further investigations, medications, or surgery, or they raise doubts as to her veracity, which sends her into a fury. Is she a fake?

First of all, I would have to know more about Samantha's personality and behavior prior to these last two years. I would also like to know what else has been going on recently (on the other hand, who had time?) Where have you and your husband been during all of this upheaval? Do *you* think she's a fake, or a flake?

While many readers might consider this story to be incredible, as in beyond belief, I don't at all. I'll bet that she has been investigated from stem to stern without concrete findings and that a complete immunological workup (to see if she has an innate vulnerability) turned up nothing. Doctors are only too willing to oblige a patient with symptoms; they'll investigate, treat, explore, scope, scan and refer to get to the bottom of the problem. And the patient has the choice; if one physician won't oblige, you can be sure that many others will. So we end up with a story like this one, with many specialists involved, all taking charge of a potential diagnosis and nobody taking charge of Samantha.

She sounds as if she might have Munchausen's Syndrome, or Chronic Factitious Illness Disorder. That mouthful means that she truly believes that she has the illnesses, that she is most likely not willfully or consciously lying, that she is experiencing the symptoms she complains about and that no amount of doctors or surgery will satisfy her. Samantha has some deep-seated needs and conflicts, which she can only (misguidedly) satisfy in this futile and self-destructive manner. It is possible that she is willfully lying, making everything up in a manipulative manner, in order to receive attention or nurturance or whatever she feels that she is missing and can get in no other way. Yet I doubt this explanation very much. She is likely not a hypochondriac, someone who is so preoccupied with her body that she translates every real or imagined creak and sensation into serious illness. I would still bet on the Munchausen's Syndrome.

Whatever the cause, however, the approach and treatment are identical: take her to the one specialist she seems to have avoided — a psychiatrist. In this case, I would strongly prefer the medical specialist as opposed to a psychologist, social worker or counsellor, because of the constant presentation of new somatic symptoms.

One last and most important point. Doctors love to classify and stereotype. If Samantha is widely perceived as untrustworthy, and no single physician is taking the central role in her case, then they might well all be missing something. I have seen some cases like Samantha's finally diagnosed because of an esoteric disease like an obscure virus, or so-called "collagen disease" such as Lupus (Disseminated Lupus Erythematosus). Is there one physician whom you like who could bring it all together?

182   **Our 16-year old son, Nicholas, was involved in a fight in school with another student yesterday. They were both suspended, but we know the other boy, and we know that it wasn't his fault. It hurts me to say this, but I'll bet anything that Nick started it. This has been his pattern since nursery school; we have often been told that he is aggressive, bullyish, short-tempered and even violent. We have seen some terrible outbursts at home — and our house is generally very peaceful — so much so that Nick's 14-year-old sister refuses to speak to him. What can we do?**

You haven't mentioned whether in all these years you have once sought professional help, for both evaluation and treatment for Nicholas. I would find it suspicious if you hadn't, but I have seen parents time and again deny to themselves the gravity of a problem confronting them or their children. If Nicholas has had lifelong troubles with aggression, it is clear that he has a serious problem (to himself and to others), which must be diagnosed, and some form of intervention must be applied.

Diagnosis is obviously a term which implies illness. I am not suggesting that Nick is necessarily suffering from a defined psychiatric disorder, although this explanation is possible. But it is important to ascertain whether his destructive behavior stems from a distorted personality, a psychotic disturbance, resentment at real or imagined slights, anger at authorities and/or his parents, rebellion or even an organic lesion (as in certain types of epilepsy, or a neuroendocrine disorder). The approaches of society will be to label Nicholas as either sick or bad, thus relegating him to the clutches of either treatment or correctional facilities and personnel.

Whatever the ultimate approach, your son needs help, and your family and society need protection. Your family doctor or school vice-principal can suggest to you where Nicholas can receive a comprehensive assessment. It sounds as if it would be worthwhile for all four of you to have some family sessions. These can be arranged at any time with a counsellor from the Family Service Agency or with a private family therapist, but I can assure you that if Nicholas is properly evaluated, you will all be involved in the remediation. Do not delay.

183 **We happen to like a clean, organized way of life. We keep our home impeccably neat, but I'm afraid that our 16-year-old son, Kelly, has carried things to ridiculous extremes. For the past three months, he must have been washing his hands 25 times a day, and each time he does something funny with his head when he finishes. He is quiet and a loner, but manages to keep up in school. He adores his computer and anything to do with**

electronics. But this hand-washing is driving me bananas. He says that his hands are dirty, and he has to wash them.

Kelly has an Obsessional-Compulsive Disorder. Your son is engaging in repetitive behavior over which he has little choice. He has developed a compulsion to wash his hands; it is controlled by a powerful inner-directed need to perform the act. If he doesn't do it, he feels worse; his anxiety goes way up and he feels even more driven. Indeed, he uses the droning repetition of the hand-washing to reduce his inner tension. Evidently, some stress has occurred over the past few weeks or months to cause Kelly to do this, even though it ends up as a fruitless, never-ending endeavor.

He has an obsessional personality; he is more interested in objects than in people. He prefers numbers and electronics to feelings and social interaction. In part he comes by this predilection honestly, since you are all preoccupied with orderliness, tidiness and neatness. This sense of order enables you to feel comfortable, and to exert some control over your lives. When the routines and rituals get upset, I'd expect that you feel quite uncomfortable. All of this behavior is within normal limits. That is, we have all kinds of personality types and styles, some orderly, some sloppy, some exact, some loose, some controlled, some uncontrolled, and every kind of variation in between.

But Kelly has imposed on this family style of fastidiousness an added dollop of obsessionality, so that stress or change are very real threats to him. He needs to control his environment and his life, otherwise he feels terrible. Kelly needs help. A comprehensive psychiatric evaluation is in order, after which you'll know whether he needs medication, psychotherapy or behavior therapy. It is quite possible that if he is left to his own devices, Kelly's immediate problem will clear up, but it will be only a temporary relief, until the next bout of stress.

There is a variant on this disorder, which "only" involves recurrent obsessional thoughts. These are frequent or constant intrusions into the thinking of the affected individual, to such an extent at times that it interferes with the performance of common tasks. Recently it has been shown (and published in *Rolling Stone* magazine) that a particular medication, (Desipramine) is quite effective in alleviating this problem. It is an anti-depressant, and we have learned that other medications in this group (tricyclics) are equally effective. We don't know whether the effectiveness is due to the presence of an underlying depression, or whether it is working on an entirely different neurochemical basis or area.

184 **Our 18-year-old son, Carl, has been acting unusual lately. He has always been shy and a loner, but recently (during the last six months), he has developed unusual mannerisms and has almost withdrawn from our family. We tend to be affectionate and demonstrative as well as very talkative, but Carl usually goes to his room or watches TV when the rest of us are together. Every now and then he'll say something that makes little sense to us, or he'll act as if he's listening to somebody that we can't hear or laugh at something he's thinking about, but he won't share it with us. He is also going to bed later and later, so that we hear him rummaging around at three or four in the morning; then of course he can't get up, and sleeps in until the afternoon. He is on the verge of being kicked out of school, because his attendance is so poor. We've threatened to kick him out unless he goes to school or gets a job. Is that a good approach?**

Ordinarily, that approach would have considerable merit with a young man who refused to go to school, work, or pull his weight around the house, and readers by now should know that I feel that accountability and responsibility are to be expected and even demanded from our youth. But Carl is certainly not a typical youth, and your concern is warranted. Again, at the risk of diagnosing with insufficient data, and even unfairly labelling him, I would guess that he is experiencing a form of psychiatric disorder, possibly schizophrenia. This is a very common disease, afflicting one out of every thousand in the population, and hitting especially the young adult population. When we see someone in that age group acting bizarrely, whose contact with reality seems to be getting more tenuous, whose feelings and actions are seemingly inappropriate, we tend to think of a serious process. It sounds as if Carl may be hearing voices (auditory hallucinations). He cannot get his act together and do anything right now except think very private thoughts, and more and more of his private deliberations and behavior are occurring in the still of the night.

There are further questions that we'd need answered in order to diagnose Carl. For example, is he delusional (harboring false beliefs about himself or others?); is he oriented (does he know where, who, when it is?); are his thoughts illogical or unconnected? I'd want to know about his past history, his underlying personality, stresses he's been under, the atmosphere at home, any family history of psychiatric problems, his drug history and so on. What I am saying in essence is that Carl should be evaluated *soon* by a psychiatrist, to ascertain what, if any, serious disorder is present. Whatever is discovered, one can say even at this stage that he needs psychiatric attention, most likely a combination of medication and individual psychotherapy, as well as the possibility of family therapy and a variety of social therapies or hospitalization. One cannot make predictions as to his prognosis (future chances) at this stage, but even if it is schizophrenia, the sooner he embarks on a treatment and rehabilitation program, the better off he'll be.

185 My 13-year-old daughter, Sheila, has lately voiced concerns about going out at night. She has been reading about the thousands of girls who are abducted each year, and she is afraid that she, too, will become a victim. I tend to agree with her.

It only takes one publicized tragedy or heinous crime to raise hysteria and alarm in parents. We tend to see danger everywhere, and become wary of our freedom and of strangers. "Streetproofing" courses are offered and filled. Milk cartons are festooned with pictures of missing youngsters. Mothers line up in shopping centers to have their children fingerprinted and photographed. Even expensive videotapes are made — all of this frenzied activity is in the service of protecting (and tracing) their offspring in case of attack by the psychopaths and killers lurking in the shadows on the streets.

What are the facts? We have no evidence that more young people (per capita) are abducted today than in any other era. All of us can recall vividly stories of horrible crimes against youth from our own childhoods. The radio and newspaper accounts were full of terror, and occasionally we were even kept indoors. Follow-up studies of thousands of missing kids have shown that fully more than 98 percent can be accounted for by runaways (95 percent), and by those running with a parent in custody disputes (3 percent). Most return home safe and sound. A miniscule proportion are abducted.

I don't want to minimize the tragedies which befall these latter families. Each lost, hurt, or killed young person represents agony of tragic proportions. But if we compare the number of genuinely abducted young people per year with the figures of those killed as passengers in motor vehicle accidents because they didn't buckle up, we find a ratio of 1:50. Why is there not a public outcry about this loss of life?

Certainly caution and care must be taught to our kids (don't go alone into dark alleys, streets, parks or unknown areas). But I fear that by creating an hysterical climate based on misinformation, we are going to turn into a closed, mutually suspicious, paranoid culture.

If this perceived danger is used as an excuse for not going out at all, as in agoraphobia (see Question 180), then she needs professional help. Or if Sheila's fears are based on generalized anxiety, or some other condition, she might need to speak to a professional for an assessment. I doubt that this is the issue here, however. Your daughter should be cautioned, and reassured. There are no guarantees of safety, unfortunately, but the chances of her enjoyment of a long life are enormous.

186   **Why all this fuss about rape and sexual assult? My daughter Stacey is 16 and gorgeous, but if she comes onto a guy, she'll only get what she deserves, right? I'm a normal red-blooded father, and you know as well as I do that if girls make our juices flow, we do what comes naturally. And, hey, they like it when we're aggressive, right?**

I wasn't sure that I should include this letter from an obvious neanderthal. I guess I not only take exception to his goon-like and ignorant attitudes towards females, but I'm also offended by his gratuitous attempt to align himself with me in this brutal approach to sexuality.

It is because of attitudes like those expressed in this letter that we have to warn and protect the Staceys of the world. Rape is a horrible, violent assault, perpetrated by an insecure, macho-type ignoramus, in order to give himself the bizarre and misguided, not to say dangerous, message that he is worthwhile and powerful.

I sometimes wonder if we haven't developed a mutually suspicious and antagnostic attitude between the sexes over the last couple of decades, when we've seen men portrayed as sexist and exploitative and women as hysterical and manipulative. Maybe, I have wondered to myself on occasion, women are overblowing a problem. But I am quickly brought to my senses by regular reports of sexual assault, violence and rape inflicted on innocent women, often resulting in permanent emotional scarring. In my clinical work, I have seen the terrible after-effects of these destructive attacks.

Rape is a heinous crime, and it is guys like you that perpetuate the generalized suspiciousness of many women towards all men. You would do well to visit a center or hostel in your city for battered and sexually assaulted women. You will learn that it is a widespread problem, that women abhor the kind of mentality which breeds it, and that there are no redeeming features to the act.

I hope that Stacey meets guys with attitudes very different from her father's!

187 **What do you do when your daughter is physically abused by the man she loves? Our daughter, Sara, is engaged to be married. We think that she is too young to mary anyone, but especially her fiancé, Peter. Last week he struck her a few times because they had a disagreement about dinner plans. He has hit her before, on a couple of occasions, but never this badly. We can't tolerate any kind of domestic violence, and have told her so. Sara says that we shouldn't butt in, that she can handle Peter and that she still loves him. She says that he's going through a rough personal period and he'll be a terrific husband.**

I think that Sara is wrong. I was going to write "dead wrong" but then I felt that you would say that I was being melodramatic. In fact, serious injury and even death have often resulted from these violent disagreements. If a quarrel over dinner plans is enough to warrant a beating (why pussy-foot by calling it physical abuse?) how will Peter handle a real gut-wrenching dispute? How long will this phase of his last, or is his recurrent personal unhappiness going to be the excuse for further violence?

As you know, violence at home often begets violence in children. It may be that Peter grew up in a home where physical punishment to him, to siblings, or to his mother, was acceptable. So what? To excuse that behavior because we understand it, is to close our eyes (and Peter's) to accountability and to the very real danger to Sara. The reasons why Sara takes it, given that she comes from a family where violent behavior was totally unacceptable, are of concern. I'm sure that some feminists and psychologists would see it in terms of the traditionally subservient role adopted by women; it could also be related to Sara's fragile self-esteem, which can only be shattered by Peter. Whatever the cause, she is in obvious jeopardy.

In a way Sara is "lucky", because most abusive husbands wait at least until after the honeymoon period before they show their true colors. But she certainly has seen his faults. Peter's behavior will not change; his abuse is merely a portent of things to come. The problem is, of course, that she rejects your concerns and would resent your intervention. She is over the age of majority, (18 in most jurisdictions) and so you have somewhat less legal responsibility as protective parents. If you have to, make adamant demands that they go for immediate pre-marital counselling and that Peter straighten himself out before the wedding or "there ain't gonna be no wedding!", at least insofar as your financial (and emotional) support is concerned. Perhaps you can get Sara to speak to a counsellor at one of the shelters or hostels for abused women, located in most urban centers. Failing this solution (and there is every likelihood that it will fail, given Sara's demonstration that "love is blind") you should consider calling the police and pressing charges. The last I heard, beating up on someone is still illegal.

Show Sara your letter, and this answer. Perhaps it will jar her out of her dangerous complacency. "Sara, by your reluctance to do anything, you are merely perpetuating and even encouraging his violent outbursts. Surely you deserve better."

188 **I'm embarrassed to write this letter, but I think that my husband is doing something he shouldn't with my 14-year-old daughter. Patsy is a lovely girl, but lately she can't look me in the eye, and she looks sad. My husband left the bed one night last year and I followed him to her room. The noises I heard were not discussions. It has happened quite a few times since.**

I wish that I could tell you that there is nothing to worry about, but there is a very real and frightening problem here. I suspect sexual abuse, pure and simple — and terrible. Terrible, aside from the morality problem, because your daughter is being ruthlessly exploited, and she is involved in acts for which she will suffer terribly for many years to come. And she is obviously very upset now.

You have no choice but to act to protect your daughter. Frankly, I have met more than a few mothers who have closed ranks with their husbands in order to protect them, thereby isolating their daughters. I doubt that this description will apply to you. Patsy is at a very tender age, whether she is sexually mature or not. She is either being coerced, going along with the abuse out of fear, compassion, or love for her father; or she is largely confused by her own new sexual feelings and her father's demands. Your husband, on the other hand, is abusing your daughter because of his own perverse conflicts, a sense of sexual inadequacy and an arrogance that tells him he can take whatever he wants. It may reflect problems the two of you have been having, but not necessarily. You certainly will have problems to work on now.

First of all, tell your husband that you not only know what he is doing, but it has to stop immediately. Second, contact the section of your Provincial or State Government responsible for child sexual abuse, or a branch of the Children's Aid Society, or the city or hospital department of social welfare, and make an appointment with a counsellor. He or she will guide you to find help for all three of you, and prevent any further damage. I won't mislead you by telling you that all will be straightforward from now on; these are always complex, convoluted cases. You may know that your husband could well face charges brought by the police or others. But you have no choice but to act *immediately*, before Patsy is damaged any further.

189 We don't know our neighbors very well, but we think that their 15-year-old, Laurie, is out of control. She has attempted suicide twice, overdosing on her mother's pills once and aspirin another time. She has cut herself with a razor blade and burned herself with lighted cigarettes. She smokes, drinks, and everybody knows that she has used marijuana. We hear her screaming fits over the hedge, or we see her running out in tears. What bothers us most is that her parents seem to be doing nothing. What can we do?

Well, I would venture to say that you don't know what her parents are doing or not doing. It is very difficult for any of us to objectively and correctly evaluate what is going on in the families and homes of others, even those who are close friends of ours. Unless we are told directly (and even then we usually hear only one side), we can only surmise, and often incorrectly.

The little you've told me, however, is enough to convince anyone that your neighbors have a very disturbed girl on their hands, and one who is a major management problem. With this minimal information I will even make a stab at a diagnosis; she sounds like she has a "borderline personality disorder" a label which refers to individuals who are impulsive, destructive and unstable, very much along the lines of the behavior you've described.

Even with the best of intentions, young people like Laurie are extremely difficult to control and to treat. For all you know, this girl has already seen a psychiatrist. I would be surprised if this move hasn't at least been contemplated. If parents cannot manage it, for what ever reason, the referral will more often come from school authorities (when she is truant, fails, or steals, for example), the police (when she is caught with drugs), or from the hospital (when she is self-destructive). It sounds as if this girl will be in a treatment setting in the near future, most likely in spite of herself. Her parents are to be supported, but given that you barely know them, I don't think there is really anything you can do.

190 **A neighbor's 15-year-old daughter killed herself last year. She had tried twice before, but this time she did it for keeps. Are we in the midst of an epidemic of teenage suicide?**

One can seldom read an article on teenage suicide in a newspaper nowadays without a screaming headline about, as you say, an "epidemic." Let us look at the facts. There is no doubt that the suicide rate among young people between 16 and 24 years of age *has* increased over the past few decades. It now stands at ten out of 100,000 for that age cohort (the suicide rate for those 15 and under is, and always has been, negligible). While some of the increase can be attributed to better, more reliable and more honest reporting by parents and by doctors (on death certificates, for example), it is clear that there has also been an increase. Just how much, however, is open to serious question. When one examines the statistics more carefully, it appears that among many groups, the suicide rate for adolescents has actually plateaued over the last few years, while increasing in other groups (North American Indians, for example).

The news of an adolescent suicide always raises alarmist concerns, and also serves as a symbol of the possibility of others. The study of suicide (suicidology) has, paradoxically, created a climate of tolerance and possibility for some equivocating individuals.

Another commonly heard statement is that the suicide rate among youth is the number two or number three cause of death in that age group. This is a valid statistic, but it is important to remember that young people belong to an exceptionally healthy age group. They don't die of cardiovascular disease, carcinoma, or other degenerative diseases, at least, not in relatively large numbers. In absolute terms, the suicide rate is still higher among the elderly and the middle-aged. The loss of a young person by suicide is particularly tragic, but a proper perspective is important before we cry "epidemic." We end up trivializing the topic, and preventing maximal services reaching those *truly* at need. (See Question 191).

191 **Last fall (eight months ago) our 18-year-old son, Carson, committed suicide. He was always a serious youngster, a bit of a loner, but he was doing well at school. Nobody who knew him would have predicted such a terrible fate. Somehow, we can't help blaming ourselves for allowing this to happen. His younger brother and sister have gradually resumed normal lives, but we are still grief-stricken.**

Suicide in any age group is terrible, but it is particularly tragic when a young person snuffs out his life. Such hopes and promise unfulfilled; such pain and misery inflicted. I have yet to see parents who survive the self-inflicted death of their teenager who don't blame themselves. Did we do something wrong? Could (should) we have prevented it? These and other questions are common and "natural".

Your son ended his life because he felt that his inner resources were used up, that nobody would understand, that nobody could help him out of his tortured, tormented state. It wasn't your fault. We are all brilliant retrospectively; that is, we can see things that we missed on the first go round. I don't know anything about your family, but given the tone of your letter, it sounds like you were (and are) loving and caring parents. In spite of everything you could have known and done, it is delusionary to feel that you could have put all Carson's problems in order. An individual who is hellbent on self-destruction will accomplish that goal.

Perhaps psychotherapy would have reached him, but there is no guarantee, I assure you. If you and your husband cannot reduce your sadness, and it is interfering with your work, loving, and even playing, you might do well to speak to a counsellor. Adapting to this loss is a difficult, long-term process, and the wounds remain as perpetual scars. But you have lives to lead, relationships, responsibilities and loving; you owe it to yourselves, and your late son, to resume living.

192 **We adopted a native Canadian infant 17 years ago with the best of intentions. We have two naturally born children, excellent health, and ample money. We wanted to "rescue" a less fortunate child whose parents could not keep him, and offer him a new life. Unfortunately, there have been nothing but problems since he came into our home. Starting with hyperactivity and aggressiveness as a toddler and young child, moving up to truancy, school failure and thefts, all the way to drugs, breaking and entering, violence, and exploitation of others, especially females. What have we done wrong, and what can we do?**

What I am about to say is both controversial and fraught with difficulties. I have to be careful, because I don't want anyone to interpret my attitude as rascist. But I have seen many similar cases over the years. The fact that he is of a different ethnic racial background is irrelevant to me. Some clinicians see the ethnic or racial background as the most important determinant of conflict in an adopted home, based on the child's feelings of being different, exploited, singled out, and so on. While these factors may play a part, my own feelings about your son are quite different.

When I hear histories like this one, I really think of biology: of genetics, constitution, and prenatal care. There are just too many youngsters who start off on the wrong foot practically from day one, and have an almost inborn, inexorable momentum towards behaviors which as often as not are anti-social. At the least these kids determinedly come up against authority, time and again (parents, teachers, police). As they grow older, the behavior becomes more complex, tinged with illegalities and manipulation of others; there is a consistent propensity to take advantage of situations and people. If these kids are bright and charming, they get away with more, but eventually life catches up with them.

The old term "psychopath" is probably most appropriate here, although it has been shunned by clinicians who feel it is an unfair stereotype of many, and a condemnatory label. It refers to exploitative, manipulative, anti-social, self-indulgent individuals who are conscience-less and do not learn from experience or punishment.

In response to your questions, I don't think that you did anything wrong. You do, however, feel guilt-ridden and concerned about his future and yours. Our (psychiatry's, psychology's, social work's) track record with this kind of kid is abysmal. If he gets in sufficient trouble with the law, he'll end up in jail. If he begins to fall apart, he might be hospitalized in a psychiatric institution. The best place for him, as far as I am concerned, is away from home, in a fairly rigid communal living environment, where he is accountable and responsible to others for his behavior. There are intense residential schools and rural treatment programs which most closely approximate the ideal treatment environment for kids such as your son. Speak to an adolescent psychiatrist in your area.

Postscript: I want to make clear that adopting any children, the same or racially different, can be a very rewarding and loving experience; that not all adolescents who engage in anti-social acts are like your son; and that his racial background is irrelevant to the diagnosis.

<u>193</u>   **Our 16-year-old son, Terry, is in what they call a "therapeutic group home". He lives with eight other kids in a large home in the city, together with childcare workers. There is also a supervisor, a social worker, and even a psychiatrist, who is there weekly. Our problem is that they won't let us visit or allow him to come home on weekends, nor can he phone us. They say that he has been there for too short a time (six weeks) to permit those things, which they feel would be destructive to him. We are very annoyed, and we have called a lawyer about getting him out of there.**

I have to tread a fine line because I, too, have worked with group homes and have seen excesses and abuses from both sides (staff and parents), and it is the child in the middle who ends up getting shafted. Rules of group homes vary, and while they may be somewhat strict, they are certainly not Draconian. Their programs have to take into account their experience with kids in the past, their present array of teenagers (all with problems), and Terry's own needs.

You don't mention just why Terry has been placed there, rather than being allowed to remain at home. Usually it is because the chemistry between parents and son or daughter proves to be flammable at that period. There may be no doubt that Terry harbors problems of his own, but it is the difficulty of living in the community and specifically with you which has necessitated putting him there in the first place. Even if you are successful in extricating him by legal means, then what happens? Is Terry going to come home, and enable the spiral of problems between you to begin again?

You also haven't added what is inevitable in these treatment programs. I am sure that there is a social worker already assigned to work with you and Terry. Why can't you call him or her to express your concern? You could also call the supervisor or the House Head, who will explain (again) the program and the rationale for those early restrictions. And I'm sure that you know that phone calls and visits will start when both Terry and you are ready.

I am also sure that you know all of this information anyway. So why are you so angry? Couldn't it be related to a sense of failure and frustration, anger at Terry or at yourself, for being in this muddle? It can happen to any of us, and we take the best kind of advice and help which we can get, which in this case is a therapeutic group home.

Terry has only been in the program a few short weeks; as you know, stays of a year or two are not uncommon. Why don't you give it a chance?

194 I'm writing on behalf of myself and my two teen-aged children. My wife has been diagnosed as having a manic-depressive illness or, as it is now called, a bipolar affective disorder. She is on medication all the time, but every now and then she becomes either very depressed and barely movable, or disorganized and euphoric, experiencing a kind of agitated high. She is receiving regular medical and psychiatric help; she's been hospitalized about eight times in the last few years. But the problem isn't the highs and lows; we can handle them. It's the in-between times, when she is impossible to live with. She is critical, nasty and verbally cruel and rejecting. She brings the kids to tears or makes them leave the house. I would have left her years ago if not for them!

This is unfortunately not an uncommon problem. Sometimes the behavior of a (verbally) abusive parent is excused for a while because of mental illness, such as a bipolar affective disorder, schizophrenia or alcoholism. Sometimes the personality of that parent is intrinsically abusive and offensive. But depending on the degree of tolerance and vulnerability of the other family members, patience does wear thin. Spouses and children can rally round each other, supporting, protecting and defending. In so doing, they can also as a unit be helpful to the tormented (and tormenting) mother or father. But eventually, if there is no respite, or no alternative outlets, the offending parent is shunned.

Your family is obviously in a state of chronic crisis. You already have an entrée into the mental health profession. You must convey to your wife's psychiatrist exactly what your concerns are, and ask him or her to recommend a course of action. He might see you all as a family himself, increase his involvement with your wife, or refer you to a family therapist who can work with the four of you. If somebody's hold on civil behavior is so tenuous that they can't function in a family situation, then they shouldn't be in that family. I say the same thing about adolescents who are out of control. If your wife does not take more control of herself, and if the family does not get help soon, then it will cease to exist as a unit. It will either fall apart, or there will be permanent emotional scarring of your kids. You may well have to leave with them and live without her.

This may sound callous, and without compassion for your wife's suffering, but I feel that it is more irresponsible to let her destroy everyone in sight. She certainly is not being helped by this passivity and tolerance. The time to act is *now*.

Index